Microsoft® SQL Server™ 2005:

Applied Techniques
Step by Step

Solid Quality Learning

PUBLISHED BY
Microsoft Press
A Division of Microsoft Corporation
One Microsoft Way
Redmond, Washington 98052-6399

Library of Congress Control Number 2006924455
978-0-7356-2316-3
0-7356-2316-3

Printed and bound in the United States of America.

2 3 4 5 6 7 8 9   QWE   1 0 9 8 7 6

Distributed in Canada by H.B. Fenn and Company Ltd.

A CIP catalogue record for this book is available from the British Library.

Microsoft Press books are available through booksellers and distributors worldwide. For further information about international editions, contact your local Microsoft Corporation office or contact Microsoft Press International directly at fax (425) 936-7329. Visit our Web site at www.microsoft.com/mspress. Send comments to mspinput@microsoft.com.

Microsoft, Active Directory, BizTalk, Excel, IntelliSense, Internet Explorer, Microsoft Press, MSDN, SharePoint, Visual Basic, Visual Studio, Windows, and Windows Server are either registered trademarks or trademarks of Microsoft Corporation in the United States and/or other countries. Other product and company names mentioned herein may be the trademarks of their respective owners.

The example companies, organizations, products, domain names, e-mail addresses, logos, people, places, and events depicted herein are fictitious. No association with any real company, organization, product, domain name, e-mail address, logo, person, place, or event is intended or should be inferred.

This book expresses the author's views and opinions. The information contained in this book is provided without any express, statutory, or implied warranties. Neither the authors, Microsoft Corporation, nor its resellers, or distributors will be held liable for any damages caused or alleged to be caused either directly or indirectly by this book.

Acquisitions Editor: Ben Ryan
Project Editors: Valerie Woolley, Kristine Haugseth
Technical Editor: Kurt Meyer
Editorial and Production: Custom Editorial Productions, Inc.

Body Part No. X12-21124

Table of Contents

Introduction

Database solutions are integral to every organization that needs to store, analyze, and report on data. Microsoft SQL Server 2005 provides a robust platform for implementing your database solution. SQL Server 2005 is packed with easy-to-use features that make it an ideal environment. In particular, this latest version of SQL Server is more secure, more scalable, and easier to use and manage than ever.

This book is for developers and database administrators who are already familiar with SQL Server and want to explore the latest features in SQL Server 2005. Developers and administrators with experience on other platforms will be able to use this book even if they are new to the topic of SQL Server. By following the step-by-step procedures in each chapter, you'll get a comprehensive hands-on introduction to the most important options for implementing your database solution using SQL Server 2005.

This book will cover the basics, including design, security, backups, and distribution. Along the way it will touch on related issues, such as migration from earlier versions of SQL Server. It gives extensive coverage to the question of retrieving and analyzing data, including data from remote sources, with an entire chapter devoted to accessing SQL Server through the Internet. You'll also find a thorough introduction to some of the features that make SQL Server such a comprehensive solution. These features provide for transactions, snapshots, auditing, reporting, and notification, as well as new features, such as enhanced support for XML.

Organization of This Book

Part 1 of this book describes the essentials for creating a database solution through SQL Server 2005: what to consider when designing your database, how to secure your data against unauthorized access, how to protect your data from unexpected loss, and how to distribute your data to other servers.

Part 2 explains how to retrieve the data in your database: using aggregates to turn data into information through summary and analysis, designing your database for the fastest possible retrieval of data, providing your users with flexibility in how they view the data, linking data from other sources, and connecting to SQL Server via the Internet.

Part 3 gives you a taste of the power of SQL Server 2005 with a discussion of additional features: using transactions to ensure the integrity of your data, keeping historical information for your environment, designing reports using Reporting Services, and updating applications when data changes through Notification Services.

After reading this book, you will have mastered all you need to know to implement your own database solution. You'll be armed with an overview of the capabilities of SQL Server 2005 and enough information to explore its full depth on your own.

Finding Your Best Starting Point in This Book

If you are:	Follow these steps:
New to SQL Server	1. Install the code samples as described in the "Code Samples" section of this Introduction.
	2. Work through Chapters 1 through 7.
	3. Complete Chapters 8 through 13 as your level of experience and interest dictates.
New to Database Administration	1. Install the code samples as described in the "Code Samples" section of this Introduction.
	2. Work through Chapters 1 through 4. Skim Chapters 5 through 13 for an overview of SQL Server 2005 features.
Migrating from Other Database Platforms	1. Install the code samples as described in the "Code Samples" section of this Introduction.
	2. Skim the first two chapters, then concentrate on Chapters 3 through 13.
Migrating from An Earlier Version of SQL Server	1. Install the code samples as described in the "Code Samples" section of this Introduction.
	2. Skim the first seven chapters, then concentrate on Chapters 8 through 13, which cover features that are new or have been updated in SQL Server 2005.
Referencing the Book after Working Through the Exercises	1. Use the index or the table of contents to find information about particular subjects.
	2. Read the Quick Reference sections at the end of each chapter to find a brief review of the syntax and techniques presented in the chapter.

Conventions and Features in This Book

This book presents information using conventions designed to make the information readable and easy to follow. Before you start the book, read the following list, which explains conventions you'll see throughout the book and points out helpful features in the book that you might want to use.

Conventions

■ Each exercise is a series of tasks. Each task is presented as a series of numbered steps (1, 2, and so on).

■ Notes labeled "tip" provide additional information or alternative methods for completing a step successfully.

■ Notes labeled "important" alert you to information you need to check before continuing.

- Text that you type appears in italics.

- SQL keywords appear in uppercase.

- Visual Basic programming elements appear in italics.

- A series of menu commands are shown separated by the pipe character (|).

- A plus sign (+) between two key names means that you must press those keys at the same time. For example, "Press Alt+Tab" means that you hold down the Alt key while you press the Tab key.

Other Features

- Sidebars throughout the book provide more in-depth information about the topic. The sidebars might contain background information, design tips, or features related to the information being discussed.

- Each chapter ends with a Quick Reference section. The Quick Reference section contains quick reminders of how to perform the tasks you learned in the chapter.

System Requirements

You'll need the following hardware and software to complete the practice exercises in this book:

> **Note**   The SQL Server 2005 software is **not** included with this book! The CD-ROM packaged in the back of this book contains the code samples need to complete the exercises. The SQL Server 2005 software must be purchased separately.

- Microsoft Windows XP with Service Pack 2, Microsoft Windows Server 2003 with Service Pack 1, or Microsoft Windows 2000 with Service Pack 4

- Microsoft Visual Studio 2005 Professional Edition

- Microsoft SQL Server 2005 Developer Edition

- 600 MHz Pentium or compatible processor (1 GHz Pentium recommended)

- 256 MB RAM (512 MB or more recommended)

- Video monitor (800 x 600 or higher resolution) with at least 256 colors (1024 x 768 high-color 16-bit recommended)

- CD-ROM or DVD-ROM drive

- Microsoft Mouse or compatible pointing device

Code Samples

The companion CD inside this book contains the code samples that you can use as you perform the exercises in the book. You can use the samples as they are to experiment on your own, or you can copy and paste code from the sample files as you build your own files while following the exercises. The files and the step-by-step instructions in the lessons let you learn by doing, which is an easy and effective way to acquire and remember new skills.

Installing the Code Samples

Follow these steps to install the code samples on your computer so that you can use them with the exercises in this book.

1. Remove the companion CD from the package inside this book and insert it into your CD-ROM drive.

> **Note** An end user license agreement should open automatically. If this agreement does not appear, open My Computer on the desktop or Start menu, double-click the icon for your CD-ROM drive, and then double-click StartCD.exe.

2. Review the end user license agreement. If you accept the terms, select the accept option and then click Next.

   A menu will appear with options related to the book.

3. Click Install Code Samples.

4. Follow the instructions that appear.

   The code samples are installed by default to the following location on your computer:

   My Documents\Microsoft Press\SQLAppliedTechSBS

Using the Code Samples

Each chapter in this book explains when and how to use any code samples for that chapter. When it's time to use a code sample, the book will point you to the appropriate file or folder. The chapters are built around scenarios that simulate real programming projects, so you can easily apply the skills you learn to your own work. For SQL Script samples, you will typically open the file in SQL Server Management Studio, highlight the relevant portion of the script, and execute only that portion before proceeding. For Visual Studio projects, you will double-click the .sln file to open the project and navigate within Visual Studio to the relevant code.

Uninstalling the Code Samples

Follow these steps to remove the code samples from your computer.

1. In Control Panel, open Add Or Remove Programs.

2. From the list of Currently Installed Programs, select Microsoft SQL Server 2005 Applied Techniques Step by Step.

3. Click Remove.

4. Follow the instructions that appear to remove the code samples.

Configuring SQL Server 2005 Express Edition

This book makes frequent use of the AdventureWorks sample database that ships with SQL Server 2005. Make sure you have installed the sample database, following the instructions in the SQL Server installation program. Then follow these steps to grant access for this database to the user account that you will be using when performing the exercises in this book:

1. Log onto Microsoft Windows on your computer using an account with administrator privileges.

2. On the Windows Start menu, click All Programs, click Accessories, and then click Command Prompt to open a command prompt window.

3. In the command prompt window, type the following case-sensitive command:

   ```
   sqlcmd –S YourServer\InstanceName –E
   ```

   Replace *YourServer* with the name of your computer, and replace *InstanceName* with the name of the SQL Server instance you will be using.

   You can find the name of your computer by running the *hostname* command in the command prompt window, before running the *sqlcmd* command.

4. At the 1> prompt, type the following command, including the square brackets, and then press Enter:

   ```
   sp_grantlogin [YourServer\UserName]
   ```

   Replace *YourServer* with the name of your computer, and replace *UserName* with the name of the user account you will be using.

5. At the 2> prompt, type the following command and then press Enter:

   ```
   GO
   ```

   If you see an error message, make sure you have typed the **sp_grantlogin** command correctly, including the square brackets.

6. At the 1> prompt, type the following command, including the square brackets, and then press Enter:

   ```
   sp_addsrvrolemember [YourServer\UserName], dbcreator
   ```

7. At the 2> prompt, type the following command and then press Enter:

   ```
   GO
   ```

   If you see an error message, make sure you have typed the **sp_addsrvrolemember** command correctly, including the square brackets.

8. At the 1> prompt, type the following command and then press Enter:

   ```
   exit
   ```

9. Close the command prompt window.

10. Log out of the administrator account.

Support for This Book

Every effort has been made to ensure the accuracy of this book and the contents of the companion CD.

Microsoft Learning provides support for books and companion CDs at the following address:

   http://www.microsoft.com/learning/support/search.asp

If you have comments, questions, or ideas regarding the book or the companion CD, or questions that are not answered by visiting the sites above, please send them to Microsoft Press via e-mail to:

   mspinput@microsoft.com

Or via postal mail to:

   Microsoft Press
   Attn: Microsoft SQL Server 2005 Step by Step Editor
   One Microsoft Way
   Redmond, WA 98052-6399

Please note that Microsoft software product support is not offered through the above addresses.

Acknowledgments

Authors

Herbert Albert

Steve Hughes

Daniel Seara

Antonio Soto

Jordi Rambla

Adolfo Wiernik

Technical Editors

Ben Ewing

Kurt Meyer

Part I
How to Create a SQL Server Database to Store Your Application Data

In this part:

Chapter 1
Choosing Which Application Data to Store in Your Database

After completing this chapter, you will be able to:

- Make sense of where to store application settings
- Determine the best place to store various types of user settings
- Decide where to store XML data
- Choose where to store external application files, such as Microsoft Word documents and Microsoft Excel spreadsheets

With the advent of better performing and more flexible database engines like the one in Microsoft SQL Server 2005, the line is blurring between what should be stored in a database and what should not. In the past, databases were good at storing only highly structured data. However, with recent advances in database engine technology, it is becoming easier and more feasible to store non-structured data, such as documents and images, in a database as well. How you use the data will affect whether you should store all or only some of your application's data in a database.

In this chapter, we'll examine why you should store application settings in a database. We'll also look at how to handle user settings stored in a database. Because XML is a natural counterpart to storing hierarchical data, we'll discuss XML data in depth. Lastly, we'll look at how to store large items in your database that typically require their own file for storage.

Where to Store Application Settings

In .NET programming, it's standard practice to store application settings in XML documents (usually with a .config extension). The difficulty arises when you need or want to have your application behave differently in different situations. You must either support this in the configuration file or look to a data-driven settings architecture in which you use data to configure your application. If you choose the latter solution, a database is the natural place to store the data that drives your application's settings.

Before you adopt the data-driven settings model, you should first understand some of the reasons to use configuration files for your application. If your application does not require a database for any other function, you may not want to include database functionality for the application settings only. Likewise, if your application requires settings during startup, a database is typically not available at that point in the process, so a configuration file is a more natural solution. (In the past, application settings in these situations were often stored in the Windows Registry, but currently they are more often stored with the application in configuration files.). One of the chief advantages of storing your application's configuration settings in a file is that the file can easily be manipulated by the user. An XML file can be edited in Notepad, so any user can modify the settings. If you need to prevent users from viewing or manipulating sensitive settings, configuration files can be encrypted.

Although not readily available during application startup, application settings stored in a database can be advantageous. In a database, you can control access to the settings using database security, including encryption in SQL Server 2005. This helps keep users who might not understand the impact of their changes from easily modifying settings. If you are using some form of role-based security (see Chapter 2, "Basic Database Security Principles"), you can manage who has the ability to change individual application settings. Application settings stored in the database are also helpful in distributed applications. Thus, you will be able to store settings, such as timezone or office policies, in one place—the database. These settings can be managed by the appropriate personnel and can be set up so that the application has different versions of settings for different users or groups of users. Table 1-1 shows the advantages offered by both of the two options.

> **Tip**   If you want to take advantage of settings stored in a database, but you don't want to burden your client with a full-service database, consider implementing database-stored application settings using Microsoft SQL Server 2005 Express Edition, which is free, or using Microsoft SQL Server 2005 Workgroup Edition, which has a compelling price point for smaller implementations.

Table 2-1   Application Settings Storage Comparison

Feature	Database Storage	Configuration File Storage
User can easily modify settings		✓
Application does not require a database engine		✓
Settings are readily available during application startup		✓
Application can implement role-based security	✓	
Application can implement centralized control of settings	✓	
Application can easily restrict access to settings	✓	
Application can provide for granular control of settings	✓	

As you can see from the comparison in Table 1-1, you will need to choose the option that best suits your application. There is no absolute right answer concerning whether the application settings should be stored in a database or a configuration file. Carefully evaluate your needs and environment and use the the information presented here to make the appropriate decision for your application.

Where to Store User Settings

Often an application needs to store data about the user's experience. In Web applications, this is typically accomplished using cookies (small text files that store user information), but with increased security on the Web, this can be troublesome. If you use some type of user identification, you can store user settings in a database. This will allow you to manage those settings without relying on client computers. There are a variety of user settings that can be stored. You can store settings as XML data, which gives you maximum flexibility. We'll discuss storing XML data later in this chapter. You can also use standard data methods of tracking user settings. When you use SQL Server to store the user's settings, the user is able to "take" those settings from client to client.

Implementing a User Settings Table

1. Determine the settings you want to store. While it is possible to store all of the user settings in your application's database, it is important to decide which settings are necessary to make your application function in a particular way and which settings must be available whenever and wherever the user logs on.

2. Once you have you determined which settings you will store, design the table necessary to store those settings. Table 1-2 gives an example of a table schema for maintaining user settings in your database.

Table 2-2   Sample Table Design to Store User Settings

Logical Column Name	Purpose
User ID	Stores the unique user ID that will be used to identify and retrieve the user settings. The data type of this column will depend on how you implement user IDs in your application.
Date Created	Records the date when the user was created. The first user-setting record is usually created when the user is created.
Date Updated or Date Refreshed	Helps you manage active users and verify how current the settings are. Refresh date is often more important than the created date.
Last Login	Tracks the last time a user logged in. In some cases, this duplicates the Date Refreshed column. Depending on your implementation of the refresh date, you may decide to eliminate this column and use only the Date Refreshed column.
User Setting column or columns	Tracks the settings that need to be stored for the user.

There are a couple of common implementations of the User Setting columns. The first is relational. In a relational implementation, each setting is stored in a separate column in the table. The problem with this solution is that in order to add additional settings, you need to expand the table by adding columns. The second option is to store the user settings in a single column. With the advent of XML, you can use an XML document to store the settings you need either in a TEXT column or in the new XML datatype column that we'll discuss later in this chapter.

3. Next, design the required data objects to retrieve and maintain the user settings table. You will need the following:

- **An Insert Stored procedure**   Inserts the initial user settings record. Often this is done when the user is created, so you might combine this with the procedure that creates the user.

- **An Update Stored procedure**   Updates the user settings record. This procedure will be called often in order to maintain the user settings in the application.

> **Important**   When tracking highly volatile data in the user settings table, you will need to actively monitor the performance and tune your implementation as necessary. This will be especially true if you are updating user settings for events other than simply logging in and logging out of the application.

- **A Delete Stored procedure**   Deletes the user settings record. Like the insert operation, this can be a part of the user delete procedure. You might want to keep the two procedures separate, however, if you need to support a concept, such as resetting the user's settings to their default values.

Where to Store XML Documents

A few years ago, XML documents were "the wave of the future." Now they are here to stay. Most likely, you have seen and used XML documents for configuration and other uses in applications you have used. SQL Server 2005 and the Microsoft .NET Framework use XML files extensively for setting configuration settings and implementing other features, such as SQL Server Integration Services (for which the XML is stored in .dtsx files) and SQL Server Reporting Services (for which the XML is stored in .rdl files). XML has a number of advantages, not the least of which is flexibility when the configuration requirements of your application change. As mentioned before, XML files also allow the user of the application to easily change configuration settings.

XML also stores hierarchial data very well. Some examples of hierarchical data are store receipts, bills of material, and healthcare service invoices. All of these examples involve parent records with varying levels of child records. Retrieving complete sets of this kind of data from a database engine can be complicated, but XML stores this data in a form that is easy to review. Because XML is so powerful and is becoming so widely used, Microsoft included the XML data type in SQL Server 2000 and SQL Server 2005 and implemented specific optimizations and T-SQL statements for managing XML data.

> **Note**   XML documents are already being used extensively to share data between internal and external consumers in a variety of businesses. In particular, healthcare applications use XML schemas to share data between external partners and internal systems. Microsoft BizTalk Server 2006 is designed for business process management and integration in situations just like this and uses XML documents for this purpose.

SQL Server 2005 XML Support

With SQL Server 2005, Microsoft introduced a number of new XML-specific features in the database engine. These improvements allow developers to access and manipulate XML data more easily. Here are a few of the improvements:

- Native XML datatype
- Support for XML schemas
- Ability to use XQuery against XML data stored in XML datatyped columns and variables
- Ability to index XML data stored in XML columns
- Support for the XML Data Manipulation Language (XML-DML)
- Improvements to existing SQL Server 2000 XML functionality, including the OPENROWSET, FOR XML, and OPENXML keywords.

Using the XML Datatype

SQL Server 2005 introduces a fully functional XML datatype. This datatype makes it possible to use XML-specific SQL to access and search XML data. This datatype is available for both tables and variables. If you store your data using the XML datatype, you can use SQL Server's implementation of the XQuery language to query the data. Prior to the introduction of the XML datatype, database designers had to extract the XML into a relational version of the data in order to query it. Having to extract the XML into tables and columns (called *shredding* the data) so that the data could be queried limited the flexibility of XML documents. Now, with the ability to use the XML datatype, developers can reference the contents of the document without first shredding it. Table 1-3 lists the XML data type methods supported in SQL Server 2005.

Table 2-3   XQuery Methods Supported in SQL Server 2005

Method	Syntax	Purpose
query()	.query(*XQuery expression*)	Selects data in the XML document or fragment, similar to a SELECT statement.

Table 2-3   XQuery Methods Supported in SQL Server 2005

Method	Syntax	Purpose
value()	.value(XQuery expression, SQL datatype)	Combines the functionality of the query() method with the CONVERT function in SQL. It allows you to select a value from the XML document or fragment and convert it to the specified datatype.
exist()	.exist(XQuery expression)	Returns TRUE if the expression being searched for is found in the XML document, similar to the EXISTS statement in T-SQL.
modify()	.modify(XML-DML expression)	Allows you to insert, update, or delete nodes in the XML document. The modify() method must be used in a T-SQL UPDATE statement. (See SQL Server Books Online for more information about XML-DML.)
nodes()	.nodes(XQuery expression) as TableName(ColumnName)	Allows you to shred the document, putting the results into a relational format.

The following example will show you how you can query XML data with *XML* variables.

Using the XQuery Query() Method

1. From the Start Menu, select All Programs | Microsoft SQL Server 2005 | SQL Server Management Studio.

2. In Microsoft SQL Server Management Studio, create a new query by clicking the New Query toolbar button. (The completed query is included in the sample files as XQueryQueryMethod.sql.)

3. Declare a variable using the XML datatype by typing the following code in the query pane:

```
DECLARE @SampleXML XML
```

4. Fill the variable with an XML expression by adding the following code in the query pane:

```
SET @SampleXML = '
<root>
    <L1>
        <L2>This is the First Line</L2>
    </L1>
    <L1>
        <L2>This is the Second Line</L2>
    </L1>
</root>'
```

5. Use the *query()* method to retrieve the values from the L2 node. Enter the following code in the query pane:

```
SELECT @SampleXML.query('/root/L1/L2)')
```

6. Execute the query by clicking the Execute toolbar button or by pressing the F5 function key. The following results will be displayed in the results pane:

```
<L2> This is the First Line<\L2><L2> This is the Second Line<\L2>
```

While this is a simple example, it should give you some insight into what can be done using the new XQuery functionality in SQL Server. You could use the *data()* method to return data from an element without the XML tags, or use the *exist()* method to verify whether or not a specified node exists.

The following code (included in the sample files as XQueryQueryDataMethod.sql) provides an example of using the *data()* method to return a specific piece of XML data without XML tags:

```
DECLARE @SampleXML XML
SET @SampleXML = '
<root>
    <L1>
        <L2>This is the First Line</L2>
    </L1>
    <L1>
        <L2>This is the Second Line</L2>
    </L1>
</root>'
SELECT @SampleXML.query('data(/root/L1[L2 = "This is the Second Line"])')
```

Your result set should be This is the Second Line.

The following code (included in the sample files as XQueryQueryExistMethod.sql) provides an example of using the *exist()* method to determine whether a specific piece of XML data is present in a node:

```
DECLARE @SampleXML XML, @Exists bit
SET @SampleXML = '
<root>
    <L1>
        <L2>This is the First Line</L2>
    </L1>
    <L1>
        <L2>This is the Second Line</L2>
    </L1>
</root>'
SET @Exists = @SampleXML.exist('/root/L1/L2[text() =
    "This is the First Line"]')
SELECT @Exists
```

Your result set should be 1.

One of the advantages of using an *XML* variable is that you can cast a column that has a different datatype, like TEXT or VARCHAR, as XML in order to use XQuery methods on data in that column. If you have an existing environment in SQL Server 2000 where you use XML, you are most likely storing your data in a TEXT or VARCHAR column. In SQL Server Management Studio, you can view the data as XML. This was not possible in Query Analyzer, which returned the data in multiple rows. The following code sample shows how to cast text data as XML.

```
SELECT CAST(textdata AS XML) FROM dbo.SomeTable WHERE SomeColumnID = 1
```

Figure 1-1 shows the results displayed as a row from a query that returns XML data in SQL Server Management Studio.

```
USE AdventureWorks;
go

SELECT TOP 1 Demographics
FROM Sales.Store
```

Results	Messages
Demographics	
1	<StoreSurvey xmlns="http://schemas.microsoft.com/sqlserver/2004/07/adventur...

Figure 2-1   SQL Server Management Studio's result from an XML Query displayed as a row.

If you click the link in the results shown in Figure 1-1, you will see the results displayed as XML, as shown in Figure 1-2.

```
Demographics2.xml   xmlresult1.xml   Demographics1.xml   stevehlaptop.A...SQLQuery1.sql*   Summary
<StoreSurvey xmlns="http://schemas.microsoft.com/sqlserver/2004/07/adventure
    <AnnualSales>300000</AnnualSales>
    <AnnualRevenue>30000</AnnualRevenue>
    <BankName>International Bank</BankName>
    <BusinessType>BM</BusinessType>
    <YearOpened>1970</YearOpened>
    <Specialty>Road</Specialty>
    <SquareFeet>7000</SquareFeet>
    <Brands>AW</Brands>
    <Internet>T1</Internet>
    <NumberEmployees>2</NumberEmployees>
</StoreSurvey>
```

Figure 2-2   XML as viewed in SQL Server Management Studio after clicking the link in the results pane.

XML: Typed or Untyped?

SQL Server 2005 supports XML schemas with the XML datatype. Figure 1-3 shows the location of schema collections in SQL Server Management Studio. If you use schemas, or schema collections as they are called in SQL Server, SQL Server will apply the schema to the XML stored in the table. Applying a schema enforces datatypes and constraints by parsing the XML against the schema that has been loaded into the XML datatype column. By using typed XML columns, you will be able to guarantee the format of the XML data.

Figure 2-3   The location of XML Schemas in SQL Server Management Studio.

If you store XML data as untyped, that is, if you do not apply a schema to the data directly, it does not change the fact that the datatype is XML, and you can still use the XML functions with that data. In either case, a number of T-SQL statements and functions are generally available to both typed and untyped XML columns.

By now you can see the benefits of using the XML datatype. For new applications with XML requirements, you will of course want to use the XML datatype. However, if you are in the process of upgrading the database engine for an existing system, the decision may not be easy. For example, if you have existing code that deals with XML data in a TEXT or NTEXT column, it may be in your best interest to keep your data as is. Unless switching to the XML datatype provides functionality you absolutely need, consider using the XML datatype for future development or down the line in a separate application upgrade.

Caution   If you are upgrading your database engine, it is best to upgrade the engine separately from making major upgrades to your application. While the XML datatype is a great new feature, the amount of redevelopment and testing required to implement significant application changes can be detrimental to your database engine upgrade if you try to upgrade your application at the same time.

Using the File System with XML Data

Even though SQL Server 2005 has made significant improvements to XML stored in the database, it can still access XML documents stored outside of the database. By using the FOR XML and OPENXML statements, you will be able to write to XML files and shred the files for insertion into a database. Both of these statements were available in SQL Server 2000 and function the same way in SQL Server 2005. Furthermore, you can use OPENROWSET to bulk-load XML documents into the database.

Where to Store External Application Files

You might be in a situation where other types of files—such as Microsoft Word documents (.doc files), Microsoft Excel spreadsheets (.xls files), images (.jpg or .bmp files), video (.mpeg files), or even sounds (.wav files)—are required to support your application. Where should you store these files when they are necessary to your business application? There are two common methods of storing these files.

- Store the files in the file system and reference them in the database.
- Store the files in LOB (large object) columns in a database table.

In either case, the goal is to store some of the metadata about these files in the database so that they can be referenced in your application. If you use files instead of LOBs, you will need to store file paths, file names, and file types in the table. You may also find it beneficial to store searchable information along with the file information. Appropriate searchable information might include keywords, creator's name, editor's name, creation date, or modified date. By adding this information to the table, your users will be able to search more meaningfully for a particular file. Your application can also use indexing on this information to make searching for a file with these criteria much more efficient.

Tip   You can also implement versioning on files in a table. Depending on your implemention, you can store previous and current versions in the same table. However, you might find it more useful to keep only the current version in the table, which will also make querying faster. If you do not need to use the previous versions often, but you do need to keep them for reference, create a second table that contains previous versions with the necessary versioning information. This will allow you to get the current version quickly, yet still be able to reference previous versions when necessary.

When you store the files in the file system, you get benefits similar to those discussed earlier for storing application settings in a configuration file. You are able to access the files quickly and easily using tried and true techniques, such as Windows Explorer in Microsoft Windows. Your users will be able to access these files outside the context of your application (which may or may not be desirable, depending on how the files are being used). If you are working with files in a document repository situation, referencing the files from a table is probably appropriate—it keeps the table streamlined for quick searches. However, if your application depends on certain characterics of the file, for instance if you expect Column A in Excel to contain account numbers, letting users have access to these files puts the integrity of your application at risk.

Why would you store the files in the database? If you store the files in the database using a LOB datatype such as BINARY or IMAGE, you can control access to the files. You don't have to concern yourself with file paths and other operating system-specific issues that would arise if you stored the files outside the database and its application. However, your application will need to account for the various external applications required to open the files. Regardless of whether you choose to store the files in a database table or store them in the file system, you should consider referencing and tracking information about them in the database.

> **Note**   If you are wondering if SQL Server can handle storing files in database tables, especially if you need to store multiple previous versions, check out Microsoft's collaboration tools—Windows SharePoint Services (included with Microsoft Windows Server 2003) and Microsoft Office SharPoint Portal Services. Both of these applications use SQL Server databases to manage files by storing versions of the files in database tables.

Conclusion

You can see that there is no single right answer to the question of where to store your data. However, Microsoft has made significant improvements in the database engine so that you can store more types of data more efficiently. If you need to store XML data, you should seriously consider using the new built in XML datatype because of the functionality it offers. SQL Server can also handle other types of application files that you may need for tracking application data, incuding settings files. You should be able to use what you have learned in this chapter to make sound decisions on data-storage locations when designing your application.

Chapter 1 Quick Reference

To	Do This
Start SQL Server Management Studio	From the Start Menu, select All Programs	Microsoft SQL Server 2005	SQL Server Management Studio.

To	Do This
Enter and execute a new query in SQL Server Management Studio	Click the New Query button, type your query in the query pane, and click the Execute button.
View XML data for a row returned by a query	Click the link in the Results pane below the query window.
Use the XQuery *query()* method to return data stored in the *SampleXML* variable	Use the T-SQL statement `SELECT @SampleXML.query('/root/L1/L2')`

Chapter 2
Basic Database Security Principles

After completing this chapter, you will be able to:

- Design secure access to Microsoft SQL Server

- Manage access to SQL Server instances

- Manage access to SQL Server databases

- Manage access to schemas

- Manage access to tables and columns

- Manage access to programmable objects

In Chapter 1, you learned what to store and what not to store in your database. In this chapter, you will learn the basic security concepts that all database developers should know in order to develop secure databases.

Security is a crucial part of most database applications and should not be considered as the last step in the development process. Every element of a database application should be designed with security in mind. You will learn how to grant access to SQL Server instances and databases and how to manage roles at both the database and server levels. Also, you will learn how to use schemas to provide a secure and robust object namespace. Finally, you will learn how to secure access to tables and columns and programmable objects, such as stored procedures and functions.

Designing Network Security to Secure Your Database System

SQL Server 2005 is the first SQL Server version developed under the Microsoft Trustworthy Computing initiative. One of the principles of the Trustworthy Computing initiative is the *Secure by Default* principle. In implementing this principle, SQL Server 2005 disables some network options in order to keep your SQL Server environment as secure as possible.

Granting Remote Access

SQL Server is a database management system designed to run on a server, accepting connections from remote users and applications. It is possible to connect locally to SQL Server from the same computer on which SQL Server is running, but production database systems typically don't use this feature. Therefore, it is important to configure SQL Server appropriately to accept secured connections from remote computers.

To access a SQL Server instance remotely, you need a network protocol to establish the connection. Activate only the protocols you want to use to avoid wasting system resources.

The default installation of SQL Server leaves many features disabled to reduce the attackable surface area of the database system. For example, SQL Server 2005 does not allow remote connections by default (except in the Enterprise version), so you should use the SQL Server Surface Area Configuration tool to enable remote connections, as shown in Figure 2-1.

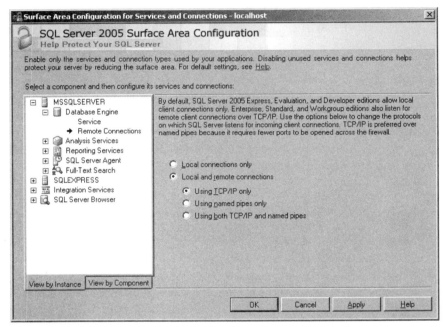

Figure 2-1   SQL Server Surface Area Configuration tool for services and connections.

You can accomplish this task by following the procedure below.

Enabling Remote Connections

1. From the Start Menu, select All Programs | Microsoft SQL Server 2005 | Configuration Tools | SQL Server Surface Area Configuration.

2. Under the heading Configure Surface Area For Localhost at the bottom of the window, click the Surface Area Configuration For Services And Connections item.

3. The left side of the resulting window displays a list of components for configuration. In this list, expand the Database Engine icon and click the Remote Connections item.

4. Select the Local And Remote Connections option, then select a protocol option.

You can enable remote connections using the TCP/IP or Named Pipes network protocols. TCP/IP is the recommended protocol due to security and performance considerations.

Securing External Access

Database servers should be well protected from unauthorized external access due to the critical information they store. SQL Server should never be accessible directly from the Internet. If you need to provide SQL Server access to Internet users or applications, you should ensure that your network environment provides a protection mechanism, such as a firewall or IDS (Intrusion Detection System).

> **More Info**   SQL Server allows connections using different endpoint types. You will learn about endpoints in Chapter 9, "Reading SQL Server Data from the Internet."

Managing Access to SQL Server Instances

When you connect to a SQL Server instance, you must provide valid authentication information. The database engine performs a two-step validation process. First, the engine checks whether you have provided a valid login that has permission to connect to the SQL Server instance. Second, the engine checks whether the login has permission to access the database to which you are trying to connect.

SQL Server 2005 defines *Principals* as the persons, groups, or processes that request access to database resources. Principals are arranged at Operating System, Server, and Database levels and can be *indivisible* or a *collection*. For example, a SQL login is an indivisible principal at the SQL Server instance level, and a Windows group is a collection principal at the Windows level.

Selecting an Authentication Mode

SQL Server 2005 supports two authentication modes for granting access to a SQL Server instance: Windows Authentication Mode and Mixed Authentication Mode. You can configure the authentication mode from SQL Server Management Studio as follows:

Configuring the Authentication Mode

1. From the Start Menu, select All Programs | Microsoft SQL Server 2005 | SQL Server Management Studio.

2. In the Connect To Server dialog box, click the Connect button.

3. In the Object Explorer, right-click the SQL Server instance and choose Properties from the context menu.

4. In the Select A Page pane, choose the Security icon.

5. In the Server Authentication section, select the authentication mode you want, as shown in Figure 2-2.

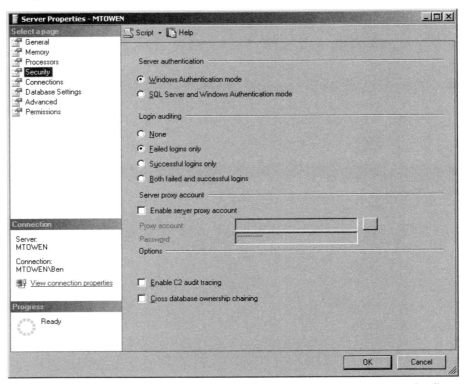

Figure 2-2   Setting the Authentication Mode from SQL Server Management Studio.

Important   Restart the SQL Server instance for the change in authentication mode to take effect.

To decide which authentication mode to use, keep the following guidelines in mind:

■ **Windows Authentication Mode**   In this mode, SQL Server relies on the operating system to authenticate a user requesting access to the SQL Server instance. The user does not need to provide any user credentials in the connection string because the user has already been authenticated by Windows.

■ **Mixed Authenication Mode**   In this mode, users can connect to SQL Server using either Windows Authentication Mode or SQL Server authentication. In the latter case, SQL Server validates the user credentials against existing SQL Server logins. Using SQL Server authentication requires that the user provide a username and password to SQL Server in the connection string.

> **Note**   It is not possible to specify SQL Server Authentication Mode only in SQL Server 2005. However, if necessary, it is possible to set up security in a SQL Server instance to restrict access to most Windows users.

In general, Windows Authentication is the recommended authentication mode. In Windows Authentication, there are no passwords flowing through the wire. Also, you can manage user accounts in a central enterprise store, such as Active Directory, and can take advantage of all the security features already available in the operating system.

However, there are scenarios where Windows Authentication is not the best option. For example, when you need to provide access to users who do not belong to your operating system environment, such as external suppliers, or who use an operating system with an incompatible security system, select Mixed Authentication Mode and use SQL Server logins to connect these users to SQL Server.

Connecting to a SQL Server Instance

When a user needs access to a SQL Server instance, an administrator must provide valid authentication information to the user. This authentication information depends on the authentication mode you have configured. This section will explain how to create logins for operating system users to support Windows Authentication and how to create SQL logins to support SQL Authentication.

Granting Access to Windows Users and Groups

You can allow operating system users to connect to SQL Server by creating a login for a Windows user or a Windows group. Only members of the local Windows Administrators group and the service account that starts SQL services have access to SQL Server by default.

> **Note**   It is possible to remove access rights to SQL Server from the local Administrators group.

You can grant access to a SQL Server instance by creating a login, either through code or through SQL Server Management Studio. The following code grants access to your SQL Server instance for the ADWORKS\jlucas Windows domain user:

```
CREATE LOGIN [ADVWORKS\jlucas] FROM WINDOWS;
```

> **Note**   When you use SQL Server Management Studio to create logins, the tool executes a similar T-SQL statement.

Default Windows Logins

When you install a SQL Server 2005 instance, the installation process creates the Windows logins described in Table 2-1.

Table 2-1   Default Windows Logins

Windows Login	Description
BUILTIN\Administrators	Login for local Administrators group on the computer where this SQL Server instance is installed.
	This login is not essential for SQL Server to run.
<Servername>\ SQLServer2005MSFTEUser$ <Servername>$MSSQLSERVER	Login for the SQLServer2005MSFTEUser$ <Servername>$MSSQLSERVER Windows group. Members of this group have the required privileges to be assigned as the logon account for the associated instance of SQL Server FullText Search.
	This account is essential for SQL Server 2005 Full Text Search to run.
<Servername>\ SQLServer2005MSSQLUser$ <Servername>$MSSQLSERVER	Login for the SQLServer2005MSSQLUser$ <Servername>$MSSQLSERVER Windows group. Members of this group have the required privileges to be assigned as the logon account for the associated instance of SQL Server.
	This account is essential for SQL Server 2005 to run because it is the service account for SQL Server when the instance has been set up to use the local service account as its service account.
<Servername>\ SQLServer2005SQLAgentUser$ <Servername>$MSSQLSERVER	Login for the SQLServer2005SQLAgentUser$ <Servername>$MSSQLSERVER Windows group. Members of this group have the required privileges to be assigned as the logon account for the associated instance of SQL Server Agent.
	This account is essential for SQL Server 2005 Agent to run.

When you connect to SQL Server 2005 using a Windows login, SQL Server relies on operating system validation and only checks whether the Windows user has a mapped login defined in this instance of SQL Server or whether this Windows login belongs to a Windows group with a mapped login in this instance of SQL Server. A connection using a Windows login is known as a *Trusted Connection.*

Caution   It is possible for a Windows user or group mapped to a Windows login to be removed from the operating system without notifying SQL Server. SQL Server 2005 does not check for this situation, so you should examine your SQL Server instance periodically in order to detect orphaned logins. You can do this easily by using the *sp_validatelogins* system stored procedure.

The following Microsoft Visual Basic code (included in the sample files as ConnectUsing WindowsAuth.vb.txt) shows how to connect to SQL Server using Windows Authentication:

```
' Create an instance of a SQLConnection object
Dim oConn as New SQLClient.SQLConnection
' Define the connection string
oConn.ConnectionString="server=localhost; database=AdventureWorks;" + _
    "Integrated Security=SSPI"
' Open the connection
oConn.Open()
' Do some work
...
' Close the connection
oConn.Close()
```

Granting Access to SQL Server Logins

In Mixed Authentication Mode, you can also create and manage SQL Server logins. When you create a SQL Server login, you should assign a password for the login. The users must provide this password when connecting to the SQL Server instance. When you create a SQL login, you can assign the default database and the default language for this login. When an application connects to SQL Server without specifying the database context and the language, SQL Server uses the default properties from this login for the connection.

Note   SQL Server 2005 uses a self-signed certificate to encrypt logon packets to prevent unauthorized access to login information. However, once the login process terminates and the login has been validated, SQL Server sends all subsequent information packets in clear text. If you need to provide security and confidentiality for your communications, you could use two approaches: Secure Sockets Layer (SSL) and Internet Protocol Security (IPSec).

You can grant access to a SQL Server instance by creating a SQL Server login, either through code or through SQL Server Management Studio. The following sample creates a SQL login called "Mary" and assigns AdventureWorks as the default database for Mary:

```
CREATE LOGIN Mary
WITH PASSWORD = '34TY$$543',
DEFAULT_DATABASE =AdventureWorks;
```

The SQL Server 2005 installation process creates a single SQL Server login named sa. The sa login is always created, even when you select Windows Authentication Mode during the installation wizard.

Best Practices   Although you cannot remove the sa login, you should rename and disable it to avoid unauthorized access to SQL Server through this login. See the section titled "Denying User Access" later in this chapter to learn how to disable a login.

You can obtain information about SQL Server logins from the *sql_logins* catalog view using the following code:

```
SELECT *
FROM sys.sql_logins;
```

Enforcing Password Policy

When you use SQL Server logins, you should implement strong password policies for these logins to avoid weakening SQL Server security over time. SQL Server 2005 provides the ability to enforce the operating system password policy on SQL Server logins. If you are running SQL Server on a Windows 2003 server, SQL Server uses the *NetValidatePasswordPolicy* API (application programming interface) to control:

- Password complexity
- Password age
- Account lockout

If you are running SQL Server on a Windows 2000 server, SQL Server uses the SQL Server Native Password Complexity rule, introduced by Microsoft Baseline Security Analyzer (MBSA) to enforce the following password rules:

- Password cannot be blank or NULL
- Password cannot be the login name
- Password cannot be the machine name
- Password is not "Password," "Admin," or "Administrator"

You can turn on the password policy using Transact SQL code:

```
CREATE LOGIN Mary
WITH PASSWORD = '34TY$$543' MUST_CHANGE,
CHECK_EXPIRATION = ON,
CHECK_POLICY = ON;
```

Managing Instance Permissions

You've learned how to give a user access to a SQL Server instance, but we haven't discussed what permissions these logins might have in SQL Server. Typically, a user needs access to some data. However, you might need to create some logins with permissions to perform administrative tasks.

SQL Server provides server roles at the instance level to accomplish this task. (Server roles are fixed, so you cannot create roles at the instance level.) Table 2-2 lists the fixed server roles created by SQL Server 2005.

Table 2-2   Fixed Server Roles

Fixed Server Role	Description
bulkadmin	Can run the BULK INSERT statement
dbcreator	Can create, alter, drop, and restore databases
diskadmin	Can manage disk files
processadmin	Can terminate processes
securityadmin	Can manage logins and assign permissions
serveradmin	Can change server options and shut down the server
setupadmin	Can manage linked servers and execute system stored procedures
sysadmin	Can perform any activity on the server

Getting server role membership information   By querying the *IS_SRVROLEMEMBER* system function, you can find out whether the current user belongs to a server role or not. The following Transact SQL sample returns 1 if the actual login belongs to the sysadmin server role and 0 otherwise.

```
SELECT IS_SRVROLEMEMBER ('sysadmin');
```

Adding a login to a server role   You can add a login to an existing server role using the *sp_addsrvrolemember* system stored procedure. The following sample adds Mary to the sysadmin server role:

```
EXECUTE sp_addsrvrolemember 'Mary', 'sysadmin';
```

Removing a login from a server role   To remove a login a from a server role, you can use the *sp_dropsrvrolemember* stored procedure. The following sample removes Mary from the sysadmin server role:

```
EXECUTE sp_dropsrvrolemember 'Mary', 'sysadmin';
```

Granting individual permissions   SQL Server 2005 provides a more granular permission structure that allows you to have finer control over login operations. You can manipulate permissions with the GRANT, DENY, and REVOKE statements. Information about servers' permissions is accessible from the *sys.server_permissions* catalog view.

The following sample grants Mary rights to create and execute a SQL Server Profiler trace:

```
GRANT ALTER TRACE TO Mary;
```

Users can obtain information about their own permissions by using the *fn_my_permissions* function. The following sample displays the permissions for the user:

```
SELECT * FROM fn_my_permissions (NULL, 'SERVER');
```

> **More Info**   You can see the list of server permissions in SQL Server Books Online in the sec-
> tion titled "GRANT Server Permissions (T-SQL)."

Denying User Access

In some situations, such as when a user leaves the organization, you need to deny access to a
specific login. If this denial is temporary, you can disable the login instead of removing the
login from the instance. By disabling the access, you retain the login properties and mappings
to database users. When you re-enable the login, you can work with the same properties as
before. To disable and enable a login, execute the following ALTER statement.

```
-- Disable the login
ALTER LOGIN Mary DISABLE;
-- Enable the login
ALTER LOGIN Mary ENABLE;
```

You can check for disabled logins by querying the *sql_logins* catalog view, as in the following
sample:

```
-- Disable the login
ALTER LOGIN Mary DISABLE;
GO
-- Query the system catalog view
SELECT * FROM sys.sql_logins
WHERE is_disabled=1;
GO
-- Enable the login
ALTER LOGIN Mary ENABLE;
```

> **Tip**   SQL Server Management Studio marks disabled logins with a red arrow. This arrow
> appears on the login icon, found in the Object Explorer pane under the Security/Logins folder.

On the other hand, if you need to remove a login from the instance, you should use the DROP
LOGIN statement. The following sample removes a login.

```
DROP LOGIN Mary;
```

> **Caution**   When you drop a login, SQL Server 2005 does not remove database users mapped
> to that login.

> **Caution**   Dropping a login mapped to a Windows user or group does not guarantee that
> this user or members of this group cannot get access to SQL Server. Keep in mind that this user
> might still belong to some other Windows group with a valid login.

Connecting to SQL Server Using SQL Server Authentication

The following Visual Basic code (included in the sample files as ConnectUsingSQL Auth.vb.txt) shows how to connect to SQL Server using SQL Server authentication:

```
' Create an instance of a SQLConneciton object
Dim oConn as New SQLClient.SQLConnection
' Declare the connection string,
' with specific username and password
oConn.ConnectionString="server=localhost; database=AdventureWorks; " + _
    "user id= Mary; password=34TY$$543"
' Open the connection
oConn.Open()
' Do some work
...
' Close the connection
oConn.Close()
```

Managing Access to SQL Server Databases

Granting access to a SQL Server instance is not enough for applications that need access to data. After granting access to the SQL Server instance, you need to grant access to specific databases. You grant access to databases by creating database users and mapping logins to database users. Each login is mapped to a database user for each database to which the login needs access. Each database user is mapped to one login only with the exception of the dbo database user.

> **Note** In earlier versions of SQL Server, you could use the system stored procedure *sp_addalias* to map multiple logins to a single database user. You can still do so in SQL Server 2005. However, you should not use this feature because it is considered outmoded, and it might be removed from future versions.

Granting Access to Databases

Database users are the principals at the database level. All logins, except members of the sysadmin server role, need to be mapped to a user mapped for databases to which they need access. Members of the sysadmin role are mapped to the dbo user on all server databases.

Creating Database Users

You can create database users by using the CREATE USER statement. The following Transact SQL sample creates a login called Peter and a mapped user in the AdventureWorks database:

```
-- Create the login Peter
CREATE LOGIN Peter WITH PASSWORD='Tyu87IORO';
-- Change the connection context to the database AdventureWorks.
USE AdventureWorks;
```

```
GO
-- Create the database user Peter,
-- mapped to the login Peter in the database AdventureWorks.
CREATE USER Peter FOR LOGIN Peter;
```

Managing Database Users

You can check whether the current login has access to a database by executing the following statement:

```
SELECT HAS_DBACCESS('AdventureWorks');
```

To obtain information from database users, you can use the *sys.database_principals* catalog view.

If you need to disable database access temporally for a database user, you can revoke the CONNECT permission to that user. The following sample revoke, the CONNECT permission to Peter:

```
-- Change the connection context to the database AdventureWorks.
USE AdventureWorks;
GO
-- Revoke connect permission from Peter
-- on the database AdventureWorks.
REVOKE CONNECT TO Peter;
```

You can drop a database user using the DROP USER statement.

> **Caution**   SQL Server 2005 does not allow you to drop a user that owns a database schema. You will learn about schemas later in this chapter.

Managing Orphaned Users

Orphaned users are database users that are not mapped to a login in the current SQL Server instance. In SQL Server 2005, a user can become orphaned when you drop the mapped login. In order to obtain information about orphaned users, you can execute the following code:

```
-- Change the connection context to the database AdventureWorks.
USE AdventureWorks;
GO
-- Report all orphaned database users
EXECUTE sp_change_users_login @Action='Report';
```

SQL Server 2005 allows you to create a user not mapped to a login by using the WITHOUT LOGIN clause. Users created with the WITHOUT LOGIN clause are not considered to be orphaned users. This feature can be very useful in scenarios where you need to change the execution context of a module. You will learn about execution contexts later in this chapter. The following sample creates a user not mapped to a login:

```
-- Change the connection context to the database AdventureWorks.
USE AdventureWorks;
GO
-- Creates the database user Paul in the AdventureWorks database
-- without mapping it to any login in this SQL Server instance
CREATE USER Paul WITHOUT LOGIN;
```

Enabling Guest Users

When a login that doesn't have a mapped user tries to connect to a database, SQL Server tries to connect using the Guest user. The Guest user is created by default without permissions. You can enable the guest user by granting the CONNECT permission to the Guest user, as shown below.

```
-- Change the connection context to the database AdventureWorks.
USE AdventureWorks;
GO
-- Grant Guest access to the AdventureWorks database.
GRANT CONNECT TO Guest;
```

Use caution when considering whether to enable guest users because they add potential security risks to the database environment.

Granting Database Permissions

Once you have created database users, you need to manage permissions for them. You can manage a user's permissions by adding the user to database roles or by granting granular permissions to the user.

Creating Database Roles

Database roles are database-level principals. You can use database roles to assign database permissions to a group of users. SQL Server 2005 creates a set of default database roles. The default roles are listed in Table 2-3.

Table 2-3   Default Database Roles

Database Role	Description
db_accessadmin	Can manage access to databases
db_backupoperator	Can back up databases
db_datareader	Can read all data from all user tables
db_datawriter	Can add, delete, and update data in all user tables
db_ddladmin	Can execute any DDL command in a database
db_denydatareader	Cannot read any data in user tables
db_denydatawriter	Cannot add, update, or delete any data in user tables

Table 2-3   Default Database Roles

Database Role	Description
db_owner	Can perform all configuration and maintenance activities
db_securityadmin	Can modify database role membership and manage permissions
public	A special database role. All database users belong to the public role. You cannot remove users from the public database role.

You can add database roles in order to group users according to specific permission require-ments. The following sample creates a database role called Auditors and adds the user Peter to the new role.

```
-- Change the connection context to the database AdventureWorks.
USE AdventureWorks;
GO
-- Create the role Auditors in the database AdventureWorks.
CREATE ROLE Auditors;
GO
-- Add the user Peter to the role Auditors
EXECUTE sp_addrolemember 'Auditors', 'Peter';
```

Managing Database Roles

You can check if the current user belongs to a database role by querying the *IS_MEMBER* sys-tem function. In the following sample, you check if the actual user belongs to the db_owner database role.

```
-- Change the connection context to the database AdventureWorks.
USE AdventureWorks;
GO
-- Checking if the current user belogs to the db_owner role
SELECT IS_MEMBER ('db_owner');
```

> **Tip**   You can use the *IS_MEMBER* system function to check whether the current user belongs to a specific Windows group as well, as in the following example:
>
> ```
> -- Change the connection context to the database AdventureWorks.
> USE AdventureWorks;
> GO
> -- Checking if the current user belogs to the Managers group
> -- in the ADVWORKS domain
> SELECT IS_MEMBER ('[ADVWORKS\Managers]');
> ```

Users can be removed from a database role by using the *sp_droprolemember* system stored pro-cedure. If you need to drop a database role, you can use the DROP ROLE statement. The fol-lowing code removes Peter from the Auditors database role and then removes the Auditors role.

```
-- Change the connection context to the database AdventureWorks.
USE AdventureWorks;
GO
```

```
-- Drop the user Peter from the Auditors role
EXECUTE sp_droprolemember 'Auditors', 'Peter';
-- Drop the Auditors role from the current database
DROP ROLE Auditors;
```

> **Warning**   SQL Server 2005 does not allow you to remove a role that contains members. You must remove all users from the database role before dropping the role.

Granting Granular Database Permissions

As an alternative to using fixed database roles, you can grant granular permissions to database roles and users. You can manage permissions by using the GRANT, DENY, and REVOKE statements. In the following sample, you grant the BACKUP DATABASE permission to Peter user:

```
-- Change the connection context to the database AdventureWorks.
USE AdventureWorks;
GO
-- Grant permissions to the database user Peter
-- to backup the database AdventureWorks.
GRANT BACKUP DATABASE TO Peter;
```

When you use the DENY statement to remove a permission from a user, the user cannot inherit the same permission by being a member of a database role that has this permission. However, if you use the REVOKE statement to remove the permission, the user can inherit the same permission by being a member of a database role with this permission already granted. Use the REVOKE statement only to remove a permission that had previously been granted.

> **Best Practices**   To reduce the effort required to maintain a permission structure, you should assign permissions to database roles only instead of assigning permissions to individual database users.

Managing Application Roles

Application roles are special database roles that you can use to allow access to specific data only to users that connect through a specific application. Application roles do not contain members, and you should activate them in the current connection before use. When you activate an application role, the current connection loses its user-specific permissions and gets only the permissions applicable to the application role.

Creating Application Roles

You can create an application role by using the CREATE APPLICATION ROLE statement. This code is included in the sample file ApplicationRoles.sql.

```
-- Change the connection context to the database AdventureWorks.
USE AdventureWorks
GO
```

```
-- Create the Application role FinancialRole
-- in the current database
CREATE APPLICATION ROLE FinancialRole
WITH PASSWORD = 'Pt86Yu$$R3';
```

Using Application Roles

Application roles must be activated before you can use them. You can activate application roles by executing the *sp_setapprole* system stored procedure. Once you activate an application role in the current connection, it remains activated until the connection is closed or you execute the *sp_unsetapprole* system stored procedure. Although application roles are meant to be used from client applications, you can use them from ad-hoc T-SQL batches as well. The following procedure (included in the sample files as ApplicationRolesUse.sql) describes how to activate the FinancialRole application role and how to revert this activation.

```
-- Change the connection context to the database AdventureWorks.
USE AdventureWorks;
GO
-- Declare a variable to hold the connection context.
-- We will use the connection context later
-- so that when the application role is deactivated
-- the connection recovers its original context.
DECLARE @context varbinary (8000);
-- Activate the application role
-- and store the current connection context
EXECUTE sp_setapprole 'FinancialRole',
'Pt86Yu$$R3',
@fCreateCookie = true,
@cookie = @context OUTPUT;
-- Verify that the user's context has been replaced
-- by the application role context.
SELECT CURRENT_USER;
-- Deactivate the application role,
-- recovering the previous connection context.
EXECUTE sp_unsetapprole @context;
GO
-- Verify that the user's original connection context
-- has been recovered.
SELECT CURRENT_USER;
GO
```

Dropping Application Roles

If you need to drop an application role, use the DROP APPLICATION ROLE statement, as shown below (this code is included in the sample file ApplicationRoles.sql):

```
-- Change the connection context to the database AdventureWorks.
USE AdventureWorks;
GO
-- Drop the application role FinancialRole
-- from the current database
DROP APPLICATION ROLE FinancialRole;
```

Managing Access to Schemas

SQL Server 2005 implements the ANSI concept for schemas. Schemas are container objects that allow you to group database objects. Schemas have a large impact on how you reference database objects. In SQL Server 2005, a database object is referenced by a four-part name with the structure

<Server>.<Database>.<Schema>.<Object>.

Introducing Schemas

You can create database schemas using the CREATE SCHEMA statement. When you create a schema, you can create database objects and assign permissions in the same transaction that calls the CREATE SCHEMA statement. The following sample (included in the sample files as ManagingAccessToSchemas01.sql) creates a schema called Accounting, specifies Peter as the schema's owner, and creates a table called Invoices. The sample also grants select permission to the public database role.

```
-- Change the connection context to the database AdventureWorks.
USE AdventureWorks;
GO
-- Create the schema Accounting with Peter as owner.
CREATE SCHEMA Accounting
AUTHORIZATION Peter;
GO
-- Create the table Invoices in the Accounting schema.
CREATE TABLE Accounting.Invoices (
InvoiceID int,
InvoiceDate smalldatetime,
ClientID int);
GO
-- Grant SELECT permission on the new table to the public role.
GRANT SELECT ON Accounting.Invoices
TO public;
GO
-- Insert a row of data into the new table.
-- Note the two-part name that we use to refer
-- to the table in the current database.
INSERT INTO Accounting.Invoices
VALUES (101,getdate(),102);
```

You can drop a schema by using the DROP SCHEMA statement. SQL Server 2005 does not allow you to drop a schema if the schema owns objects. You can obtain information about schemas by querying the *sys.schemas* catalog view. The following sample queries the *sys.schemas* catalog view in order to obtain schema information:

```
SELECT *
FROM sys.schemas;
```

The following code (included in the sample files as ManagingAccessToSchemas02.sql) demonstrates how to drop an existing schema by quering the objects owned by the schema and dropping these objects first:

```
-- Change the connection context to the database AdventureWorks.
USE AdventureWorks
GO
-- Retieve informatiomn about the Accounting schema.
SELECT s.name AS 'Schema',
o.name AS 'Object'
FROM sys.schemas s
INNER JOIN sys.objects o
   ON s.schema_id=o.schema_id
WHERE s.name='Accounting';
GO
-- Drop the table Invoices from the Accounting schema.
DROP TABLE Accounting.Invoices;
GO
-- Drop the Accounting schema.
DROP SCHEMA Accounting;
```

Introducing User-Schema Separation

One of the advantages of schemas is the separation of users from objects. In SQL Server 2005, all objects belong to schemas, so you can modify and remove database users without any impact on database objects or on references to these objects from database applications. This abstraction allows you to have objects owned by multiple users since you can create a schema owned by a database role.

Using the Default Schema

When an application references a database object without the qualified schema, SQL Server tries to find the object in the user's default schema. If the object is not on the default schema, SQL Server tries to find the object in the dbo schema. The following sample (included in the sample files as ManagingAccessToSchemas03.sql) shows how to create a schema and assign it as a default schema for a user.

```
-- Create a SQL Server login in this SQL Server instance.
CREATE LOGIN Sara
WITH PASSWORD='TUT87rr$$';
GO
-- Change the connection context to the database AdventureWorks.
USE AdventureWorks;
GO
-- Create the user Sara in the Adventureworks database
-- and map the user to the login Sara
CREATE USER Sara
FOR LOGIN Sara;
GO
-- Create the schema Marketing, owned by Peter.
```

```
CREATE SCHEMA Marketing
AUTHORIZATION Peter;
GO
-- Create the table Campaigns in the newly created schema.
CREATE TABLE Marketing.Campaigns (
CampaignID int,
CampaignDate smalldatetime,
Description varchar (max));
GO
-- Grant SELECT permission to Sara on the new table.
GRANT SELECT ON Marketing.Campaigns TO Sara;
GO
-- Declare the Marketing schema as the default schema for Sara
ALTER USER Sara
WITH DEFAULT_SCHEMA=Marketing;
```

Managing Access to Tables and Columns

Tables and columns store the data that applications retrieve and create. Access to this data is managed by the SQL Server 2005 permission hierarchy. You can manage this permission hierarchy with the GRANT, DENY, and REVOKE statements.

- **GRANT**   Allows a user or role to perform the operation specified by the granted permission.

- **DENY**   Denies a user or role the specified permission and prevents them from inheriting this permission.from other roles.

- **REVOKE**   Drops a previously denied or granted permission.

Modifying Access to a Table

Access to a table is controlled by the effective permissions that the user has on the table. You can control user access to tables by managing permissions on tables. The permissions that you can manage on tables are specified on Table 2-4. You can assign these permissions to database users and roles.

Table 2-4   Table Permissions

Permission	Description
ALTER	Can modify table properties
CONTROL	Provides ownership-like permissions
DELETE	Can delete rows from the table
INSERT	Can insert rows in the table
REFERENCES	Can reference the table from a foreign key
SELECT	Can select rows from the table
TAKE OWNERSHIP	Can take ownership of the table
UPDATE	Can update rows on the table
VIEW DEFINITION	Can access the the table's metadata

Granting Access to a Table

You can provide access to database users and roles by using the GRANT statement. The following sample grants SELECT, INSERT, and UPDATE permissions to Sara on the Sales.Customer table. (The code in this and subsequent sections for managing access to tables is included in the sample files as ManagingAccessToTables.sql.)

```
-- Change the connection context to the database AdventureWorks.
USE AdventureWorks;
GO
-- Grant some permissions to Sara on the Sales.Customer table.
GRANT SELECT,INSERT,UPDATE
ON Sales.Customer
TO Sara;
```

Limiting Access to a Table

When you need to prevent a user from accessing a table, you might face one of two scenarios. If you have granted permission to the user on the table before, you should use the REVOKE statement to clear the previously granted permissions. For example:

```
-- Change the connection context to the database AdventureWorks.
USE AdventureWorks;
GO
-- Revoke SELECT permissions from Sara on the Sales.Customer table
REVOKE SELECT
ON Sales.Customer
TO Sara;
```

However, the user might maintain the revoked permission by belonging to a role with this permission granted. In that case, you need to use the DENY statement in order to deny access for that user. For example:

```
-- Change the connection context to the database AdventureWorks.
USE AdventureWorks;
GO
-- Deny DELETE permission to Sara on the Sales.Customer table,
-- regardless of what permissions this user might
-- inherit from roles.
DENY DELETE
ON Sales.Customer
TO Sara;
```

Providing Access to Columns Individually

SQL Server 2005 provides you the option to grant or refuse access to columns individually instead of working with tables. This feature gives you the flexibility to refuse access, for example, to confidential data from some columns. The permissions that you can manage on table columns are described in Table 2-5.

Table 2-5 Column Permissions

Permission	Description
SELECT	Can select the column
UPDATE	Can update the column
REFERENCE	Can reference the column from a foreign key

Granting Access to Columns

You can grant access to columns individually by using the GRANT option. The following sample grants SELECT and UPDATE permissions to Sara on the Demographics and Modified-Date columns for the Sales.Individual table. (The code in this and subsequent sections for managing access to columns is included in the sample files as ManagingAccessToColumns. sql.)

```
-- Change the connection context to the database AdventureWorks.
USE AdventureWorks;
GO
-- Grant SELECT and UPDATE permissions to Sara
-- on some specific columns of the Sales.Individual table
GRANT SELECT,UPDATE (
Demographics,
ModifiedDate)
ON Sales.Individual
TO Sara;
```

Revoking Access to Columns

Similarly, you can revoke access to columns individually using the REVOKE statement. Remember that if you want to prevent a user from gaining permission, you need to use the DENY statement.

```
-- Change the connection context to the database AdventureWorks.
USE AdventureWorks;
GO
-- Revoke previosly granted or denied permissions
-- from Sara on the Demographics column.
REVOKE UPDATE (Demographics)
ON Sales.Individual
TO Sara;
```

Managing Access to Programmable Objects

Programmable objects, such as stored procedures and user-defined functions, have their own security context. Database users need permissions in order to execute stored procedures, functions, and assemblies. Once the database engine has checked for permission to execute a programmable object, it then checks permissions for operations performed inside programmable objects. When database objects access each other sequentially, the sequence forms an ownership chain. You will learn about ownership chains later in this chapter.

Managing Security for Stored Procedures

Stored procedures are probably the most frequently used database objects for a database developer. As with other database objects, stored procedures are subject to security. You need permissions to perform operations, such as creating a stored procedure, and users must have appropriate permissions in order to execute a stored procedure. Table 2-6 lists the permissions that you can grant on stored procedures.

Table 2-6   Stored Procedure Permissions

Permission	Description
ALTER	Can modify stored procedure properties
CONTROL	Provides ownership-like permission
EXECUTE	Can execute the stored procedure
TAKE OWNERSHIP	Can take ownership of the stored procedure
VIEW DEFINITION	Can view stored procedure metadata

Executing a Stored Procedure

When an application makes a call to execute a stored procedure, SQL Server checks if the current database user has the EXECUTE permission on the stored procedure. The following sample grants EXECUTE permission to Sara on the *dbo.uspGetBillOfMaterials* stored procedure. (The code in this and subsequent sections is included in the sample files as ManagingAccessToProgrammableObjects.sql.)

```
-- Change the connection context to the database AdventureWorks.
USE AdventureWorks;
GO
-- Grant EXECUTE permission to Sara on a stored procedure.
GRANT EXECUTE On dbo.uspGetBillOfMaterials
TO Sara;
```

In the same way, if you want to prevent a user from executing a stored procedure, you can revoke or deny the EXECUTE permission for the user.

Managing Security for User-Defined Functions

User-defined functions are programmable objects, such as stored procedures. Basically, there are two types of user-defined functions: *scalar functions*, which return a single value, and *table-valued functions*, which return a table. Depending on the type of user-defined function, you need to grant either EXECUTE or SELECT permission (see Table 2-7).

Table 2-7   User-Defined Functions Permissions

Permission	Description
ALTER	Can modify stored procedure properties
CONTROL	Provides ownership-like permission

Table 2-7   User-Defined Functions Permissions

Permission	Description
TAKE OWNERSHIP	Can take ownership of the stored procedure
VIEW DEFINITION	Can view stored procedure metadata
SELECT	Can select data returned from the user-defined function (for table-valued functions only)
EXECUTE	Can execute the user-defined function (for scalar functions only)

Executing Table-Valued Functions

When a user executes a table-valued function, SQL Server checks whether the user has SELECT permission on the table. You can grant this permission on a function in the same way you grant the SELECT permission on tables. The following sample grants SELECT permission to Sara on the *dbo.ufnGetContactInformation* user-defined function.

```
-- Change the connection context to the database AdventureWorks.
USE AdventureWorks;
GO
-- Grant permission to Sara to execute a user defined function.
GRANT SELECT ON dbo.ufnGetContactInformation
TO Sara;
```

> **Note**   There is another type of table-valued function, called an *inline function*. Inline functions are functionally equivalent to views, but support parameters. This type of function is equivalent to a view from a security standpoint.

Executing Scalar Functions

In order to execute a scalar function, a user needs to have EXECUTE permission on the function. You can grant EXECUTE permission on a scalar function in the same way that you grant EXECUTE permission on a stored procedure. The following sample grants Sara EXECUTE permission on the *dbo.ufnGetStock* function.

```
-- Change the connection context to the database AdventureWorks.
USE AdventureWorks;
GO
-- Grant Sara permission to execute a user defined function.
GRANT EXECUTE ON dbo.ufnGetStock
TO Sara;
```

Managing Security for Assemblies

SQL Server 2005 provides you the ability to include .NET assemblies (objects which reference .dll files) inside the database engine and invoke these assemblies in stored procedures and functions. You can assign the same permissions to assemblies as for stored procedures. Refer to Table 2-6 for those permissions.

Defining a Permission Set

When you create an assembly, you need to specify a *permission set*. The permission set specifies a set of code access permissions that are granted to the assembly in SQL Server. There are three different permission sets:

- **SAFE**   The code executed by the assembly cannot access external system resources. SAFE is the most restrictive permission set and the default one.
- **EXTERNAL_ACCESS**   The assembly can access external system resources.
- **UNSAFE**   The assembly can execute unmanaged code.

SAFE is the recommended permission set for assemblies that do not need to access external resources.

> **More Info**   You can find more information about Code Access Security on the following URL: *http://msdn.microsoft.com/library/default.asp?url=/library/en-us/secmod/html/secmod116.asp*.

Executing an Assembly

When an application tries to access an object inside an assembly, the database engine checks whether the current user has EXECUTE permission. The following code is used to grant EXECUTE permission on an assembly to the user Sara:

```
-- Change the connection context to the database AdventureWorks.
USE AdventureWorks;
GO
-- Grant Sara permission to execute an assembly.
GRANT EXECUTE ON <AssemblyName>
TO Sara;
```

By providing EXECUTE permission for one assembly, you are granting EXECUTE permission on all assembly objects to the user.

Managing Ownership Chains

An *ownership chain* is the sequence of database objects accessing each other. For example, when you insert rows in a table from a stored procedure, the stored procedure is the *calling object* and the table is the *called object*. When SQL Server traverses a chain, the database engine evaluates permissions in a different way than it would if you were accessing objects individually.

When you access an object within a chain, SQL Server first compares the owner of the object with the owner of the calling object. If it is the same owner, permissions on the called object are not evaluated. This feature is very useful for managing object permissions. For example, suppose Sara creates a table called Person.SupplierContacts and a stored procedure called *Person.InsertSupplierContacts* through which Sara inserts rows into the PersonSupplierContacts table. Since these two objects have the same owner, Sara, you only need to grant EXECUTE permission to other users on the *Person.InsertSupplierContacts* stored procedure in order to allow them EXECUTE permission on the PersonSupplierContacts table. You do not need to grant permissions on the table to other users.

> **Important**   Ownership chains provide a powerful encapsulation mechanism. A database can be designed to expose access to data only through well documented public interfaces, such as stored procedures and user-defined functions, which hide the complexity of the database's actual implementation. Using ownership chains to maximum advantage, a database developer can deny access to all tables in a database to all users, yet still give them access to the data they need.

Managing the Execution Context

The login and user connected to a session or executing a procedure determines the execution context. Login and user tokens provide SQL Server 2005 the information for evaluating object permissions. SQL Server 2005 provides you the ability to change the execution context using the EXECUTE AS statement. This operation is called Context Switching.

Running EXECUTE AS

The EXECUTE AS statement allows you to explicitly define the execution context for the current connection. You can use EXECUTE AS to change the login or the user for the current connection. The execution context change is valid until another context change is made, until the connection is closed, or until a REVERT statement is executed. The following sample uses EXECUTE AS to change the execution context to user Sara.

```
-- Change the connection context to the database AdventureWorks.
USE AdventureWorks;
GO
-- Change the execution context to the user Sara.
EXECUTE AS USER='Sara';
-- The following statement will be executed under Sara's credentials.
TRUNCATE TABLE dbo.ErrorLog;
```

The above code will finish with an error because Sara does not have permission to truncate a table. The following code to truncate the table will succeed.

```
-- Change the execution context back to the original state
REVERT;
-- Now the following statement will be executed under
```

```
-- the original execution context.
TRUNCATE TABLE dbo.ErrorLog;
```

Managing Context Switching

Apart from controlling execution context for batches (groups of T-SQL statements sent to the server for execution, as in the TRUNCATE TABLE example above), you can control execution context for stored procedures and user-defined functions. When you switch the context in these modules, you can control which user account will be used to access objects referenced in the stored procedure or function. To accomplish this task, you can use the EXECUTE AS statement with the following modifications:

- **CALLER**   Statements inside the stored procedure or user-defined function are executed in the context of the caller of the module.

- **SELF**   Statements are executed in the context of the user who created or altered the stored procedure or function.

- **OWNER**   Statements are executed in the context of the current owner of the stored procedure or function.

- **<User>or<Login>**   Statements are executed in the context of the specified user or login.

The following sample creates a stored procedure that switches the context to the dbo user. Then it grants EXECUTE permission to Sara on the stored procedure and changes the context to test the execution of the stored procedure.

```
-- Create a stored procedure to execute statements
--' as dbo.
CREATE PROCEDURE dbo.usp_TruncateErrorLog
    WITH EXECUTE AS 'dbo'
    AS
    TRUNCATE TABLE dbo.ErrorLog;
GO
-- Grant permissions to execute this procedure to Sara.
GRANT EXECUTE ON dbo.usp_TruncateErrorLog TO Sara
-- Change the execution context of this batch to Sara.
EXECUTE AS [USER=]'Sara'
-- Execute the stored procedure.
EXECUTE dbo.usp_TruncateErrorLog
```

As you can see in the sample above, context switching can be a good approach to allow some operations to users that you cannot grant through permissions.

Conclusion

In this chapter, we discussed how to secure access to a SQL Server instance, its databases, and objects inside a database. It is important to understand the role of each security element in the security hierarchy in a SQL Server system. The first step is to enable SQL Server to accept network connections, without which there would be no access to the system.

Once the physical network is possible, you must enable users to connect to a SQL Server instance. You can perform this task by creating logins for Windows users and groups and SQL Server logins. Before doing so, decide what authentication method the system should use.

Getting access to a SQL Server instance only gives access to perform specific server-wide operations, for which you can apply specific permissions through the use of fixed server roles or through assigning specific permissions to the logins.

In order to get access to a specific database, it is necessary to create users on that database. These users are typically mapped to a specific login in SQL Server. Once a user exists in a database, you can apply specific permissions for database-wide operations.

You control a user's access to database objects in different ways, depending on the type of object. These permissions can be applied to individual users or to database roles, which can either be fixed or be created on demand to satisfy business needs.

It is better to assign permissions to programmable objects, instead of tables and columns, to provide for easier maintenance and encapsulation.

Controlling the execution context also provides a way of letting users perform operations that can't be controlled through permissions.

Chapter 2 Quick Reference

To	Do This
Enable remote connections	In the SQL Server Surface Area Configuration tool, click on the Surface Area Configuration For Services And Connections item, expand the Database Engine icon, click the Remote Connections item, select the Local And Remote Connections option, then select a protocol option.
Configure the authentication mode	In SQL Server Management Studio, right-click the SQL Server instance and choose Properties. Choose the Security icon in the Select A Page pane. In the Server Authentication section, select the authentication mode.
Grant SQL Server access to a Windows domain user	Execute the SQL statement `CREATE LOGIN [<domain>\<user>] FROM WINDOWS;`

Create a SQL Server login for a particular database	Execute the SQL statement
	
	`CREATE LOGIN <user>`
	`WITH PASSWORD = '<password>',`
	`DEFAULT_DATABASE =<database>;`

List SQL Server logins	Execute the SQL statement `SELECT * FROM sys.sql_logins;`

To	Do This
Turn on strict password policy	Execute the SQL statement ``` CREATE LOGIN <user> WITH PASSWORD = '<password>' MUST_CHANGE, CHECK_EXPIRATION = ON, CHECK_POLICY = ON; ```
Grant individual permissions to a user	Execute the SQL statement ``` GRANT ALTER <permission> TO <user>; ```
Remove a SQL Server user	Execute the SQL statement ``` DROP LOGIN <user>; ```
Report all orphaned database users	Execute the SQL statement ``` EXECUTE sp_change_users_login @Action='Report'; ```
Enable the Guest user	Execute the SQL statement ``` GRANT CONNECT TO Guest; ```

Chapter 3

Disaster Recovery Techniques to Protect Your Database

After completing this chapter, you will be able to:

- Decide which database backup strategy you need
- Configure the right recovery model
- Perform full database, differential, and transaction log backups
- Restore user and system databases
- Schedule backups

The previous chapter considered security—protecting your data from unauthorized users. This chapter will look at protecting your data from unanticipated loss. Preventing data loss is one of the most critical issues involved in managing database systems. Data can be lost as a result of many different problems:

- Hardware failures
- Viruses
- Incorrect use of UPDATE and DELETE statements
- Software bugs
- Disasters, such as fire or flood

To prevent data loss, you can implement a recovery strategy for your databases. Recovery strategies need to be planned, implemented, and tested according to the possible failures that can occur and the level of protection needed for the data. In a data warehouse where data can be recovered from other systems, it is probably unnecessary to back up every single transaction. To have full backups of the data in regular time intervals might be enough. On the other hand, for a database storing online shop transactions, you might want to back up every single transaction. SQL Server provides rich functionality to implement the type of backups you need. In this chapter, we will discuss the most common strategies used in Microsoft SQL Server to protect data.

Using Full Database Backups

A very common backup strategy is to back up the whole database in a predefined time series (once each night, for instance). With such a backup strategy, it is possible to recover a database to the state it had when the last backup occurred. This strategy is implemented by using full database backups, which are explained below.

A full database backup contains all data and database meta information needed to restore the whole database, including full-text catalogs. When you restore a full database backup, it restores all database files yielding data in a consistent state from the time the backup completed. While the backup is performed, the database is online and users can send transactions, changing data as usual. The term *consistent state* means that all transactions that are committed while the backup is being performed are applied and all transactions that are not finished are rolled back. To handle situations that would lead to inconsistencies due to transactions changing data while SQL Server is performing backups, SQL Server has a special process to guarantee data consistency. This process involves writing both data pages and transaction log records to the backup device.

> **Tip**   Full-text catalogs are added to databases to enable SQL Server's full-text indexing functionality. Full-text indexing allows you to perform quicker, more accurate searches on data in your database. For more information on full-text indexing, see the SQL Server Books Online topic "About Full-Text Indexes."

The speed of the backup is determined by the underlying I/O devices (Input/Output devices, used to gather and store data). To get the best performance, SQL Server reads the file sequentially. If your I/O devices are capable of handling the I/O resulting from backing up data along with the I/O produced by normal system use, then creating a backup has only a minimal effect on the performance of your system. Nevertheless, it is a good practice to perform full database backups in off-peak hours.

In the following section, we will discuss options for implementing such a backup strategy.

The Simple Recovery Model

SQL Server needs to know which kind of backups you plan to perform on a database in advance; you need to configure the database in the manner required for performing the types of backups you will be using. This configuration is done by setting the recovery model database option. The default recovery model a database uses is derived from the recovery model of the model database specified at its creation. To implement a backup strategy that includes only full database backups, the recovery model should be set to SIMPLE.

Setting the Recovery Model to SIMPLE

1. From the Start Menu, select All Programs | Microsoft SQL Server 2005 | SQL Server Management Studio.

2. In the Connect to Server dialog box, click the Connect button.

3. From the Standard toolbar, click the New Query button to open a New Query window.

4. To set the recovery model, you can use an ALTER DATABASE statement. Type the following statement and click the Execute button.

```
USE master;
GO
ALTER DATABASE AdventureWorks
SET RECOVERY SIMPLE;
GO
```

> **More Info** This chapter focuses on accomplishing backups and restores using T-SQL statements. Chapter 4, "Transferring Your Database to Other Systems," will discuss how to perform many of these same procedures using the SQL Server Management Studio user interface instead of T-SQL statements.

Verifying the Recovery Model Setting

1. To view and verify the recovery model of a database, you can use the DATABASEPROPERTYEX function, which retrieves the current database options or properties of the specified database. Execute the statement below to retrieve the recovery model of the AdventureWorks database.

```
SELECT DATABASEPROPERTYEX('AdventureWorks','Recovery')
```

2. Verify that the result of the query shows SIMPLE as the recovery model.

3. Close SQL Server Management Studio.

Backup Devices

Before starting a backup, you need to know where it will be stored. The storage location of a backup is called a backup device. Each backup device can store multiple backups of different types. There are two different types of backup devices.

■ **Tape devices** Can be used to store backup data on tapes. Tape devices must be attached locally. Backups can span several tapes, and SQL Server backups can be mixed with Windows backups.

■ **Disk devices** Files on the local or remote disk or disk storage media. They are referenced using the path to the file where the backups are stored. Remote locations must be referenced using the UNC Path.

> **Note** We will discuss only backups to disk devices in this book. SQL Server backups to tape devices are no longer very common. When SQL Server backups are stored on tapes, they are normally performed using a third-party vendor product that offers additional functionality, like remote tape storage. Alternatively, a tape device might be used as additional insurance to backup data that has already been backed up to a disk device.

Backup devices are identified by a device name. A device name can be a logical or a physical device name. The physical name of a disk device is the path of the backup file, such as '\\BACKUPSERVER\Backups\adv\AdventureWorks.bak'. This path can be used directly in the backup statements. Logical device names are names stored in SQL Server that point to the physical names of the backup devices. When a logical device name is used in the backup statement, SQL Server searches for the corresponding physical location in its system catalog and performs the backup to this location.

To add a logical device to the system catalog, you can use the *sp_addumpdevice* system stored procedure. The example below defines a logical device called Adv_FullDb_Dev.

```
EXEC sp_addumpdevice 'disk', 'Adv_FullDb_Dev',
'T:\BACKUPS\AdvFullDbDev.bak';
```

> **Tip**   Be sure to change the file path to one that is appropriate to your machine. If you don't have a drive mapped to T:\, change this part of the above file path to match the drive mapping on your machine. Also, be sure any folders specified in this file path exist on your machine.

Logical and physical device names can be used interchangeably when backing up and restoring a database. Of course, it is generally a good idea to consistently use one of the two naming conventions so as not to complicate your code. You should decide in advance which naming convention you prefer.

Backups should never be done to a disk device that resides on the same physical storage unit as the database itself. Even when the disk storage has a failure tolerance through some RAID level, it is always possible that the controller might fail and destroy the data on the disks. Also, you should consider archiving the backup device files to tape and storing the tapes at a remote location.

> **Tip**   The acronym RAID stands for "redundant array of independent disks." These arrays are disk systems with multiple drives used to improve reliability and storage capacity.

Performing Full Database Backups

After setting the recovery model to SIMPLE and deciding on which backup devices you want to store your backups, you can start performing backups. Full database backups are performed using the BACKUP DATABASE statement, which is quite easy to use. In the simplest form, you only need to tell the system which database to back up to which device. To back up the database AdventureWorks to the logical device you defined earlier, the statement is as follows:

```
USE master;
GO
BACKUP DATABASE AdventureWorks
TO Adv_FullDb_Dev;
```

If you want to perform a full database backup to a physical device, you have to specify the device type and the location in the BACKUP DATABASE statement. To back up the database to the location t:\adv.bak, use the statement below.

```
USE master;
GO
BACKUP DATABASE AdventureWorks
TO DISK='t:\adv.bak';
```

As mentioned before, every backup device can store more than one backup. You can specify whether you want SQL Server to overwrite or append to existing backups on the device in an argument of the BACKUP DATABASE statement. The options used for this are INIT and NOINIT. If you specify INIT, the backup device is truncated before the backup starts, overwriting any backup existing on the device. NOINIT, which is the default if you specify nothing, lets SQL Server append the backup to the existing backup device, preserving all existing backups. Options are set through a *WITH* block at the end of the BACKUP DATABASE statement.

If you want to do the same backup as the previous example but tell SQL Server to truncate the device first, use the following statement:

```
USE master;
GO
BACKUP DATABASE AdventureWorks
TO DISK='t:\adv.bak'
WITH INIT;
```

As you can see, performing full database backups is quite simple. You will see in the next section that full backups are the backup type that all other backup types rely on. Other backup types depend on full database backups because they need a rebuilt database from which to work. These other types of backups, including differential backups, store changes that have occured in the database since the base full backup was taken. Thus, you will see that full database backups are not only important in a recovery strategy where only full database backups are performed, but also in the backup strategies we will discuss next.

Using Differential Backups

The main advantage of a full database backup is that it contains all the data needed to rebuild the entire database. But this advantage can also be a disadvantage. Consider a database where full database backups are performed each night. If you need to recover the database, you always have to use the backup from the previous night, resulting in the loss of a whole day's .work. One way to reduce the potential period of time that can be lost would be to perform full database backups more often. But this itself can be a problem. Because all data and parts of the transaction log are written to the backup device, it can be very time-intensive to make a backup. Also, you need a lot of storage space to hold these backups, and a full backup can decrease the performance of your database as a result of the large amount of I/O it requires. Wouldn't it be better to perform one full database backup at night and only take backups of data changes made during the day? This sort of functionality is provided by the differential backup.

The differential backup stores only the data changes that have occured since the last full database backup. When the same data has changed many times since the last full database backup, a differential backup stores the most recent version of the changed data. Because it contains all changes since the last full backup, to restore a differential backup, you first need to restore the last full database backup and then apply only the last differential backup, as shown in Figure 3-1. Like the full database backup, the differential backup includes a part of the transaction log in order to recover to a consistent state.

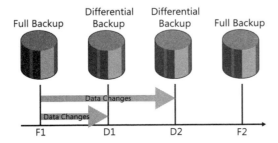

Figure 3-1   Backup strategy with differential backups.

Performing Differential Backups

Performing a differential backup is very similar to performing full database backups. The only difference is that you state in the WITH option of the backup that you want to perform a differential backup. The syntax of the BACKUP DATABASE statement to perform a differential backup of AdventureWorks to a physical device, overwriting other existing backups on the backup device, is as follows:

```
USE master;
GO
BACKUP DATABASE AdventureWorks
TO DISK='t:\adv_diff.bak'
WITH INIT,DIFFERENTIAL;
```

If you want to use logical devices, you must create them first just as with the full database backup.

```
USE master;
GO
EXEC sp_addumpdevice 'disk', 'Adv_Diff_Dev',
'T:\BACKUPS\AdvDiffDev.bak';
GO
BACKUP DATABASE AdventureWorks
TO Adv_Diff_Dev
WITH INIT,DIFFERENTIAL;
```

> **Important** To restore a differential backup, you always also need the most recent full database backup. Be careful not to overwrite or delete the full database backup as long as you require it for differential backups.

Using Transaction Log Backups

With the combination of full database and differential backups, it is possible to take snapshots of the data and recover them. But in some situations, it is also desirable to have backups of all events that have occured in a database, like a record of every single statement executed. With such functionality, it would be possible to recover the database to any state required. Transaction log backups provide this functionality. As its name suggests, the transaction log backup is a backup of transaction log entries and contains all transactions that have happened to the database. The main advantages of transaction log backups are as follows:

- Transaction log backups allow you to recover the database to a specific point in time.

- Because transaction log backups are backups of log entries, it is even possible to perform a backup from a transaction log if the data files are destroyed. With this backup, it is possible to recover the database up to the last transaction that took place before the failure occurred. Thus, in the event of a failure, not a single committed transaction need be lost.

As with differential backups, you need a base full database backup in your strategy to recover a database from transaction log backups. A backup strategy using transaction log backups is represented in Figure 3-2. Full database backups are done during the off-peak hours and transaction log backups are done at predefined times during the day. A transaction log backup contains all transactions that have occurred since the previous transaction log backup. Therefore, to restore a database using transaction log backups, the full database backup and all transaction log backups since the full database backup was taken are needed. As you can see, it is important to have all the backups available. If the full database backup or one of the transaction log backups is missing, it is not possible to perform the restore as desired.

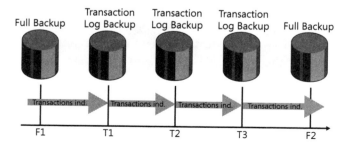

Figure 3-2 A backup strategy with transaction log backups.

Combining Transaction Log and Differential Backups

Another possibile backup strategy is to combine full database, differential, and transaction log backups. This is done when restoring all transaction log backups would take too much time. Because restoring from a transaction log backup means that all transactions have to be executed again, it can take a great deal of time to recover all the data, especially in large databases. Differential backups only apply data changes, which can be done faster than re-executing all transactions.

To recover a database when you have a combined backup strategy, as shown in Figure 3-3, you need to restore the last full database backup, the last differential backup, and then all subsequent transaction log backups.

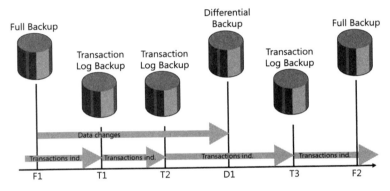

Figure 3-3   A combined backup strategy.

For example, to recover to transaction log backup point T3, you must restore the full database backup F1, the differential backup D1, and the transaction log backup T3.

The time period you should allow between transaction log backups depends on:

- The quantity and size of the transactions occuring in the database. For this backup strategy, SQL Server has to store all transactions until they are saved by a transaction log backup. Therefore, the transaction log file must be capable of holding all transactions that happen in the time period between two consecutive transaction log backups. If the log file fills up too fast, you can decrease the time between transaction log backups or increase the size of the log file.

- The acceptable amount of work loss. As mentioned above, it is possible to recover up to the last transaction if the data files are lost. But if a transaction log becomes lost or damaged, it is only possible to recover up to the last transaction log backup. Decreasing the amount of time between transaction log backups will reduce the amount of work lost if this situation occurs.

The Full Recovery Model

As mentioned before, you need to tell SQL Server in advance which backup strategy you plan to implement. If only full database and differential backups are used, the database has to be set to the simple recovery model. If you also want to use transaction log backups, the recovery model must be set to FULL (or BULK_LOGGED). The full recovery model tells SQL Server that you want to perform transaction log backups. To make this possible, SQL Server keeps all transactions in a transaction log until a transaction log backup occurs. When the transaction log backup happens, SQL Server truncates the transaction log after the backup is written to the backup device. In simple mode, the transaction log is truncated after every checkpoint, which means that committed transactions (which are already written to the data files) are deleted from the transaction log. Thus, in simple mode, transaction log backups cannot be created.

> **Important**   It is important to perform transaction log backups when your database is in full recovery mode. If no transaction log backups are done, the log file will increase to its maximum size. When it is full and cannot increase anymore, it will no longer be possible to perform trans-actions. The code for performing transaction log backups can be found in the section titled "Performing Transaction Log Backups."

To set the recovery model to FULL, use the ALTER DATABASE statement again. The following code sets the recovery mode of AdventureWorks database to FULL:

```
USE master;
GO
ALTER DATABASE AdventureWorks
SET RECOVERY FULL;
GO
```

The Bulk-Logged Recovery Model

In the full recovery model, all bulk operations (single operations that alter large amounts of data) are fully logged to make the restore of a transaction log backup possible. In some databases, this recovery model cannot be used all of the time because of limitations on transaction log size and the performance issues arising from fully logged bulk operations. Therefore, the bulk-logged recovery model exists. It allows a transaction log backup to capture both the log and the results of any bulk operations, but it does have drawbacks. Under the bulk-logged recovery model, it is not possible to restore a database to a specific point in time. It is also no longer possible to perform a transaction log backup when the data file is damaged and a bulk operation has occurred since the last transaction log backup. This was one of the main benefits of transaction log backups. Therefore, the bulk-logged recovery model should be turned on only in the time periods when bulk operations are performed and should be used for as short a time as possible. The rest of the time the full recovery model should be used. Don't use the bulk-logged recovery model if you don't have any problems using only full logged operations. For further information, see the SQL Server Books Online topic "Backup Under the Bulk-Logged Recovery Model."

Performing Transaction Log Backups

To perform a transaction log backup, your recovery model should be set to full and you must have performed at least one full database backup since changing to the full recovery model. Transaction log backups are done with the BACKUP LOG statement. As always, the name of the database and the backup device must be provided. Backup device types are the same as those used for full database and differential backups.

To back up the transaction log of AdventureWorks to a physical device, perform the following steps:

Backing Up the Transaction Log File

1. Set the recovery model to FULL.

2. Perform at least one full database backup.

3. Backup the transaction log of AdventureWorks to a physical device using the following SQL statements:

```
USE master;
GO
BACKUP LOG AdventureWorks
TO DISK='t:\adv_log.bak'
```

As with the other backup statements, the backup process appends to the backup device when no option is specified in the BACKUP statement. To overwrite the device, the WITH INIT statement is used.

```
USE master;
GO
BACKUP LOG AdventureWorks
TO DISK='t:\adv_log.bak'
WITH INIT
```

Recovering a Database

In the previous section, you performed different kinds of backups but considered the recovery process only in theory. Now you will see how to restore a database in different recovery scenarios.

Retrieving Backup Information

Before you can start restoring databases, you need to know which backups you need to restore. SQL Server stores backup history about every single backup performed on databases in the msdb database. The msdb database can be queried to find the backups to restore.

Creating Simple Backup Information

1. From the Start Menu, select All Programs | Microsoft SQL Server 2005 | SQL Server Management Studio.

2. In the Connect to Server dialog box, click the Connect button.

3. From the Standard toolbar, click the New Query button to open a New Query window.

4. Write and execute the following BACKUP statements to perform a full and a differential backup of AdventureWorks database.

```
ALTER DATABASE AdventureWorks
SET RECOVERY SIMPLE;
--Perform Full Database Backup
BACKUP DATABASE AdventureWorks
TO DISK = 'T:\BACKUPS\ADVFULL.BAK'
WITH INIT;

--Perform a differential Backup
BACKUP DATABASE AdventureWorks
TO DISK = 'T:\BACKUPS\ADVDIFF.BAK'
WITH INIT,Differential;
```

Retrieving Simple Backup Information

1. To get information about which backups have occurred on the AdventureWorks database, execute the following SELECT statement:

```
USE msdb
GO
SELECT backup_start_date,type, physical_device_name,backup_set_id
FROM backupset bs inner join backupmediafamily bm
ON bs.media_set_id = bm.media_set_id
WHERE database_name ='AdventureWorks'
ORDER BY backup_start_date desc
```

The results pane shown below indicates that the most recent backup was of backup type I, a differential backup. As you know, to restore a differential backup, you first need to restore the most recent full database backup. This backup can be found on line 2, with type D indicating a full database backup.

2. Every backup gets a unique id called a backup set id that can be seen in the results window, as shown below:

	backup_start_date	type	physical_device_name	backup_set_id
1	2005-11-06 17:17:10.000	I	C:\Backup\ADVDIFF.BAK	63
2	2005-11-06 17:17:02.000	D	C:\Backup\ADVFULL.BAK	62
3	2005-11-06 17:16:25.000	I	C:\Backup\ADVDIFF.BAK	61
4	2005-11-06 17:16:17.000	D	C:\Backup\ADVFULL.BAK	60
5	2005-11-06 17:15:57.000	D	C:\Backup\ADVFULL.BAK	59
6	2005-11-06 16:45:08.000	I	C:\Backup\ADVDIFF.BAK	58
7	2005-11-06 16:44:57.000	D	C:\Backup\ADVFULL.BAK	57

Using the above information, you can find out which data and log files were affected by the backup and what their original locations were. The following query gets this information for backup set id 62. When running this query, be sure to change the backup_set_id from 62 to the backup set id of the full database backup found in the previous step.

```
SELECT filegroup_name,logical_name,physical_name
FROM msdb..backupfile
WHERE backup_set_id = 62 --change to your backup_set_id
```

3. In some situations, the msdb database doesn't have the backup history information you need. This can happen if the msdb database was destroyed by a disaster or if the backup was taken on another system. In these cases, it is only possible to get the information directly from the backup device. To get information about backups that reside on 'T:\BACKUPS\ADVFULL.BAK', type and execute the following statement.

```
RESTORE HEADERONLY FROM DISK='T:\BACKUPS\ADVFULL.BAK'
```

4. To get information about the data and log files affected by the backups stored on the device, execute the RESTORE FILELISTONLY statement.

```
RESTORE FILELISTONLY FROM DISK ='T:\BACKUPS\ADVFULL.BAK'
```

Restoring a Database Using SQL Server Management Studio

In many cases, the easiest way to restore a database is to use SQL Server Management Studio. SQL Server Management Studio uses the backup history stored in the msdb database to show us the best way to restore a database.

Performing a Restore Using SQL Server Management Studio

1. Execute the following statements in the query window of SQL Server Management Studio to simulate a scenario in which you have the AdventureWorks database in a simple recovery strategy using full database and differential backups. Change the paths of the backup devices as needed.

```
ALTER DATABASE AdventureWorks
SET RECOVERY SIMPLE;
--Perform Full Database Backup
BACKUP DATABASE AdventureWorks
TO DISK = 'T:\BACKUPS\ADVFULL.BAK'
WITH INIT;
--Simulate a transaction
UPDATE AdventureWorks.Person.Contact
SET EmailAddress = 'kim@testbackup.com'
WHERE ContactID=3;
--Perform a differential Backup
BACKUP DATABASE AdventureWorks
TO DISK = 'T:\BACKUPS\ADVDIFF.BAK'
WITH INIT,Differential;
```

2. To restore the database, open Object Explorer by selecting Object Explorer in the View menu or by pressing the F8 key.

3. In the tree view shown, expand your SQL Server instance, open the Databases folder and right-click the AdventureWorks database. In the context menu, select Tasks | Restore | Database.

4. The Restore Database dialog box opens and you will see that the most recent backup sets are already selected for restoration, as shown in Figure 3-4. To complete the restore, simply click the OK button.

> **Note**   Make sure no connections are open to AdventureWorks because no connections to the database are allowed while a restore is in progress.

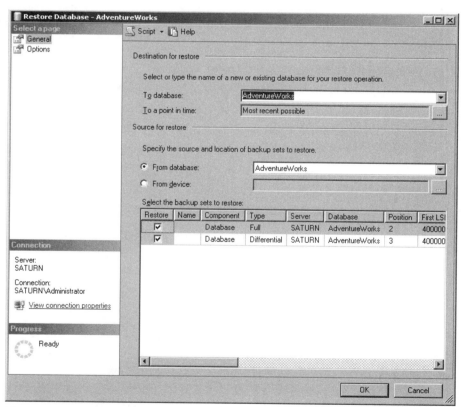

Figure 3-4   The Restore Database dialog box.

5. A message box should appear to inform you that the restore was successful.

6. Open a New Query window and check that both backups are restored successfully by typing and executing the following code.

```
USE AdventureWorks
GO
SELECT EmailAddress
FROM Person.Contact
WHERE ContactID =3;
```

The results should show kim@testbackup.com.

> **Note** As you can see, it is not nessecary to drop the database you want to restore first. The restore process automatically drops the database as a first step.

Restoring a Database from a Simple Backup Strategy Using T-SQL

Imagine you have performed the same backups as in the previous example. To restore the database using T-SQL, you use the RESTORE DATABASE statement. This statement has a similar syntax to the BACKUP statement. You will need to provide the database name and the location of the backup device.

Restoring a Full Database Backup Using T-SQL

1. Within SQL Server Management Studio, open a New Query window.

2. Type and execute the following RESTORE DATABASE statement to restore the AdventureWorks database. Again, be sure you have no other connections open to the database when executing this query.

```
USE MASTER
GO
RESTORE DATABASE AdventureWorks
FROM DISK='T:\BACKUPS\ADVFULL.BAK'
```

3. Execute the following query. The result should now show kim2@adventure-works.com because the update occurred after the full database backup.

```
SELECT EmailAddress
FROM AdventureWorks.Person.Contact
WHERE ContactID = 3
```

In this procedure, you only restored the full database backup. After the restore, the database was brought online automatically by performing a recovery. If you want to apply the differential backup as well, you need to tell SQL Server not to bring the database online after the full database restore because that would make it impossible to restore the differential backup. This is done by using the NORECOVERY option. The NORECOVERY option must be used with every RESTORE statement except the last to be performed. In the following example, you will make use of the NORECOVERY option to restore the full and the differential backups you have previously performed.

Restoring Differential Backups Using T-SQL

1. In SQL Server Management Studio, open a New Query window.

2. Type and execute the following RESTORE DATABASE statement to restore the AdventureWorks database with the NORECOVERY option.

```
USE MASTER
GO
RESTORE DATABASE AdventureWorks
FROM DISK='T:\BACKUPS\ADVFULL.BAK'
WITH NORECOVERY
```

3. Type and execute the following RESTORE DATABASE statement to restore the differential backup.

```
USE MASTER
GO
RESTORE DATABASE AdventureWorks
FROM DISK='T:\BACKUPS\ADVDIFF.BAK'
```

4. Execute the following query. The result should be kim@testbackup.com. Because this update occurred between full and differential backups, you can be sure that the differential backup was applied succesfully.

```
SELECT EmailAddress
FROM AdventureWorks.Person.Contact
WHERE ContactID = 3
```

Restoring a Database from a Full Backup Strategy Using T-SQL

In a full backup strategy, you have a combination of full and transaction log backups. Now you will see how to restore them using T-SQL queries.

Restoring a Combination of Full and Transaction Log Backups

1. Execute the following code to create backups of the AdventureWorks database. This code will also update some data, which you can use to check that your restore was effective:

```
ALTER DATABASE AdventureWorks
SET RECOVERY FULL;
--Perform Full Database Backup
BACKUP DATABASE AdventureWorks
TO DISK = 'T:\BACKUPS\ADVFULL.BAK'
WITH INIT;
--Simulate a transaction
UPDATE AdventureWorks.Person.Contact
SET EmailAddress = 'AfterFull@test.com'
WHERE ContactID=3;
--Perform a Transaction Log Backup
BACKUP LOG AdventureWorks
TO DISK = 'T:\BACKUPS\ADVLOG1.BAK'
```

```
WITH INIT;
--Simulate a transaction
UPDATE AdventureWorks.Person.Contact
SET EmailAddress = 'AfterLog@test.com'
WHERE ContactID=3;
```

2. Now imagine that the data file of the AdventureWorks database gets corrupted. As discussed before, it is still possible to perform a transaction log backup to capture the tail of the log that contains the transactions completed after our most recent transaction log backup. This must be done using a special option called NO_TRUNCATE.

```
--Perform a Transaction Log Backup of the tail of the log
BACKUP LOG AdventureWorks
TO DISK = 'T:\BACKUPS\ADVLOG2.BAK'
WITH INIT, NO_TRUNCATE;
```

> **Note**   When the transaction log gets corrupted, it is no longer possible to perform this sort of backup. In this case, only the backups already performed can be restored.

3. After the backup of the log has been performed, the RESTORE statement can be used to start restoring first the full database backup and then the two transaction log backups. As with differential backups, the NORECOVERY option has to be used for all restores except the last. The transaction logs are restored using the RESTORE LOG statement.

```
-- Switch to the master db
USE master
GO
-- Restore the full database backup
RESTORE DATABASE AdventureWorks
FROM DISK = 'T:\BACKUPS\ADVFULL.BAK'
WITH REPLACE, NORECOVERY;
--Restore the first Transaction Log Backup
RESTORE LOG AdventureWorks
FROM DISK = 'T:\BACKUPS\ADVLOG1.BAK'
WITH NORECOVERY;
--Restore the second Transaction Log Backup
RESTORE LOG AdventureWorks
FROM DISK = 'T:\BACKUPS\ADVLOG2.BAK';
```

The REPLACE option in the RESTORE DATABASE statement directs SQL Server to skip its safety checks and replace the database without any questions.

4. Execute the following query. The result should be AfterLog@test.com, which shows that all transactions were successfully applied.

```
SELECT EmailAddress
FROM AdventureWorks.Person.Contact
WHERE ContactID = 3
```

Restoring System Databases

The system databases master, msdb, and model are the heart of a SQL Server installation. Without the system databases, SQL Server will not function properly or at all if the master database is corrupt. Therefore, it is extremely important to have backups of these databases in order to be prepared for a system failure. System databases are normally backed up using a simple model with full database backups performed on a regular schedule. This is an effective strategy because the informations inside these tables doesn't change often. Nevertheless, after making major changes to your system, including creating databases, logins, or changing configuration options, additional backups of the system databases should be made.

Database backups and restores in SQL Server are performed online. Therefore, SQL Server has to be in a running state before the system databases can be restored. There are two possibles ways of getting SQL Server up and running:

- If the databases are corrupt but the binaries (compiled computer programs, or executables) are not affected, the system databases can be rebuilt using the SQL Server Setup program. Instructions for this task can be found in the SQL Server Books Online topic "How to: Install SQL Server 2005 from Command Prompt."

- If the whole system is corrupt, install the system from scratch with the Setup program. Also, all Service Packs and Patches that were on the system prior to its failure need to be reapplied.

Now SQL Server should be up and running, but it still lacks information about the user databases, logins, jobs, alerts, and configurations that the system had before. To rectify this situation, the system databases must be restored. The process of restoring the system databases always starts with restoring the master database. To restore the master database, use the special procedure detailed below.

> **Important**   Practice this procedure only on a test system. If anything goes wrong, your data can be lost! This example assumes that SQL Server is installed as the default instance.

Restoring the Master Database

1. Perform backups of master, msdb, and model databases.

```
--MASTER DATABASE
BACKUP DATABASE MASTER
TO DISK = 'T:\BACKUPS\master.bak'
WITH INIT
--MSDB DATABASE
BACKUP DATABASE MSDB
TO DISK = 'T:\BACKUPS\msdb.bak'
WITH INIT
--MODEL DATABASE
BACKUP DATABASE MODEL
```

```
TO DISK = 'T:\BACKUPS\model.bak'
WITH INIT
```

2. Close SQL Server Management Studio and any other programs that have a connection to your SQL Server.

3. From the Start menu, select All Programs | Microsoft SQL Server 2005 | Configuration Tools | SQL Server Configuration Manager.

4. Within SQL Server Configuration Manager, click on SQL Server 2005 Services in the lefthand pane. This will display all current services in the righthand pane. Stop any services that are running by right-clicking on them individually and clicking the Stop item on the context menu. Note which services you have stopped; you will want to start them again later. Once all services are stopped, your screen should look like this:

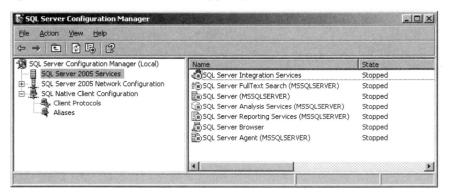

5. Start a Command Prompt by clicking Start | Run, typing *cmd,* and clicking the OK button.

6. Change the directory to the binn folder of your SQL Server installation by using the following statement. This statement provides the default path used by SQL Server setup. Type the statement on a single line (it is shown broken here to fit on the printed page) and press the Enter key.

```
C:\Documents and Settings\Administrator>cd "\Program Files\
Microsoft SQL Server\MSSQL.1\MSSQL\binn"
```

7. Start SQL Server in single user admin mode by providing the <;$MI>m option as demonstrated by the following statement. Enter the statement and press the Enter key.

```
C:\Program Files\Microsoft SQL Server\MSSQL.1\MSSQL\Binn>sqlservr -m
```

8. Leave this Command Prompt open and start a second one in the same manner as step 5 above.

9. Type *sqlcmd −E* into this Command prompt to connect to SQL Server.

10. Perform the restore of the master database with sqlcmd by typing the following T-SQL statement. When entering the statement, press the Enter key to add each new line. Once you type in the line GO and press the Enter key, the full statement will be executed.

```
RESTORE DATABASE master
FROM DISK ='T:\BACKUPS\master.bak';
GO
```

The results will look like this:

11. Switch to the first Command Prompt. SQL Server issued a shutdown automatically. Both command prompts can now be closed.

12. Switch to the SQL Server Configuration Manager and start the *SQL Server (MSSQLSERVER)* service only.

Restoring the Msdb and Model Databases

1. Open SQL Server Management Studio. The msdb and model databases can be restored like any other database. Because no connection to the databases is allowed while restoring, you did not start the other services in the previous procedure.

2. Open a New Query window and execute the following RESTORE DATABASE statements to recover the msdb and model databases.

```
--MSDB DATABASE
RESTORE DATABASE MSDB
FROM DISK = 'T:\BACKUPS\msdb.bak'
--MODEL DATABASE
RESTORE DATABASE MODEL
FROM DISK = 'T:\BACKUPS\model.bak'
WITH REPLACE
```

3. Switch to the SQL Server Configuration Manager and start all the other services that you shut down in step 4 of the previous section. These probably include SQL Server Intergration Services, SQL Server FullText Search (MSSQLSERVER), and SQL Server (SQLEXPRESS).

Scheduling Backups Using the SQL Maintenance Plan Wizard

Until now you have performed our backups through a Query Window in SQL Server Management Studio. Of course, in production systems, backups need to be scheduled to run automatically, without any user input. This can be done using any scheduling software. SQL Server has a built-in scheduler as part of the SQL Server Agent Service. With SQL Server Agent Jobs, it is possible to define T-SQL batches to run on given schedules. This feature provides the functionality you need to automate your recovery strategy.

Have a look at another easy way to schedule backups by using a wizard. The SQL Maintenance Plan Wizard is a tool that helps perform standard tasks, like Backup, Index Defragmentation, and Check Database Integrity. It relies on the SQL Server Agent Services because it schedules jobs that are started by SQL Server Agent at requested times. Therefore, the SQL Server Agent Service has to be running at all times. You can configure the SQL Agent Service using SQL Server Configuration Manager. Configure it to start up automatically and start it if necessary by using the following steps:

Starting SQL Server Agent Automatically

1. Open SQL Server Configuration Manager using the steps provided in the previous section.

2. In the lefthand pane, select SQL Server 2005 Services. In the righthand pane, right-click the SQL Server Agent icon and select Properties from the context menu.

3. On the Service tab, find the Start Mode item and change its setting to Automatic. Click the Apply button, then click the OK button.

4. You can now start the Agent by right-clicking the SQL Server Agent icon and selecting Start from the context menu.

Using the SQL Maintenance Plan Wizard

1. Open Object Explorer in SQL Server Management Studio by selecting Object Explorer in the View menu or by pressing the F8 key.

2. In the tree view shown, expand your SQL Server instance, open the Management folder, and right-click the Maintenance Plans folder. Select Maintenance Plan Wizard.

3. A welcome page apears. Click the Next button.

4. Type a name for your Maintenance Plan. Use Daily AdventureWorks Backup for this example and click the Next button.

5. Select Back Up Database (Full) and click the Next button twice.

6. Select AdventureWorks at the Databases dropdown list, and click the OK button.

7. Select the Create A Backup File For Every Database option, check the Create A Sub-Directory For Each Database checkbox, and specify a file path for the folder where your backups will be stored. Click the Next button.

8. Click the Change button to create your schedule. When you have finished, click the OK button, and then click the Next button.

9. On this page you can define whether a report should be written to a directory and whether an e-mail notification should be sent. Make your selections and click the Next button.

10. Click the Finish button.

Database Maintenance Plans can be changed through SQL Server Management Studio. Simply navigate in Object Explorer to Maintenance Plans, which is a subfolder of Management, and right-click the maintenance plan you want to change. The history log can also be opened through this menu.

Conclusion

In this chapter, you have seen the different backup types SQL Server provides. The combination and scheduling of these different types should form a backup strategy that meets your system performance and data integrity needs. These strategies range from simple models using only full database backups to full models using transaction log backups to provide the functionality to recover data right up to the time of data corruption.

Remember that a backup strategy should be planned, implemented, and tested for every database you have. Don't wait to test your strategy until after data corruption has already occurred!

Chapter 3 Quick Reference

To	Do This
Set the recovery model	Execute the SQL statement ``` USE master; GO ALTER DATABASE AdventureWorks SET RECOVERY SIMPLE; GO ```
Verify the recovery model	Execute the SQL statement ``` SELECT DATABASEPROPERTYEX ('AdventureWorks','Recovery') ```

To	Do This

Retrieve simple backup information	Execute the SQL statement
	
	``
	USE msdb
	GO
	SELECT backup_start_date, type,
	    physical_device_name, backup_set_id
	FROM backupset bs
	inner join backupmediafamily bm
	    ON bs.media_set_id = bm.media_set_id
	WHERE database_name ='AdventureWorks'
	ORDER BY backup_start_date desc
	``

Find out which data and log files were affected by a backup id	Execute the SQL statement ``` SELECT filegroup_name,logical_name, physical_name FROM msdb..backupfile WHERE backup_set_id = <backup id> ```

Retrive information directly from a backup device	Execute the SQL statements
	
	``
	RESTORE HEADERONLY FROM DISK=
	    'T:\BACKUPS\ADVFULL.BAK'
	RESTORE FILELISTONLY FROM DISK=
	    'T:\BACKUPS\ADVFULL.BAK'
	``

Restore a database using SQL Server Management Studio	Right-click the database in the Object Explorer window and select Tasks	Restore	Database.
Start the SQL Server Agent Service	Open SQL Server Configuration Manager. Open the SQL Server Agent properties window. Change the Start Mode item on the Service tab to Automatic, right-click the SQL Server Agen icon, and select Start.
Schedule a backup	In SQL Server Management Studio, open the Management folder in the Object Exlorer window. Select Maintenance Plan Wizard and follow the prompts.

Chapter 4
Transferring Your Database to Other Systems

After completing this chapter, you will be able to:

- Use backup and restore techniques to move your data
- Detach, copy, and re-attach your database to move the data
- Understand when replication may be the best option
- Use SQL Server Integration Services (SSIS) to move tables and databases
- Schedule jobs to automate data movement between servers

So, you need to have your data in more than one place. You might distribute your data for performance or to provide for disaster recovery. Maybe you have a corporate center that needs to distribute data to regional or local offices. There can be many reasons to move your data.

When determining the scope of your data distribution needs, you should consider factors including:

- **Latency**   How often does the data change? How often do changes need to be uploaded to the recipients?
- **Editing**   Who needs to be able to modify the data? Do the modifications need to be merged together?
- **Sharing**   Do you need to send only a segment of the data or the entire database?
- **Security**   Is the data sensitive?

In the previous chapter, you learned how to use T-SQL to back up and restore databases. In this chapter, you will learn about four methods within SQL Server 2005, including backing up and restoring, for transferring your data. Each method has its strengths and weaknesses, and each is suited to a particular type of data transfer. The four methods are:

- Backup and Restore
- Detach and Attach
- Replication
- SQL Server Integration Services (SSIS)

Some of these methods require running wizards, which we will cover as well. SSIS and SQL Server Agent can be used to schedule and automate the method that you choose; this technique is covered in the last section of this chapter.

As we go through these methods, the term "target" will be used in reference to the system to which you are moving data. The term "source" will be used to refer to the system that is the source of the data you are transferring. All of the examples in this chapter will use the AdventureWorks database as the source running on the default instance of SQL Server 2005. The target server will be a named instance, "target," on the same server. We will be using various targets to illustrate the options for transferring data based on different requirements.

Converting Your Database to SQL Server 2005 from SQL Server 2000

The following methods for transferring data can be used to upgrade a database by copying it to a server running SQL Server 2005:

- Backup and Restore
- Detach and Attach
- Copy Database Wizard

Before you venture down the upgrade path, run the Microsoft SQL Server 2005 Upgrade Advisor and review the SQL Server 2005 Upgrade Handbook. Both of these resources are available as free downloads on *www.microsoft.com/sql*.

Using Backup and Restore to Transfer Your Data

What? Use backup and restore as a transfer method? Sure! One of the key advantages of using backups is that they have minimal impact on the operation of your system. A backup is a live operation that allows you to continue conducting business while it is running. There are three types of backups that can be used, each of which is appropriate in different situations. The three types are full database backups, differential backups, and transaction log backups. Detailed information about these backup types and their appropriate uses is given in Chapter 3.

All of the backup strategies use a full backup as the starting point, so you will need to plan for it first. The backup strategy you employ for transferring data will depend on the volatility of your data and the requirements for the target system. If you need the same data in both locations but the data changes frequently, simply using a full database backup will not be adequate. However, if you need to move data that is less volatile and does not change on the target system, then a full database backup may be a great option for you.

When you restore a database, there are a few options you should be aware of. First, you need to know what kind of recovery you are trying to perform. If you are using differential and transaction log backups, you will need to restore the pieces in order. You will use the NO RECOVERY option to let SQL Server know there are more pieces to be restored. Use the

RECOVERY option to let SQL Server 2005 know that you have finished restoring the data to the desired point.

Let's look at two of the available backup/restore transfer options. The first option uses only a full database backup. The second option uses a full database backup together with both differential and transaction log backups.

> **Tip**   Keep in mind that using a full database backup with both differential and transaction log backups is similar to using only full backups and transaction log backups with no differential backups. To perform a transfer that uses only full and transaction log backups, follow the steps found in the section titled "Full Backup with Differential and Transaction Log Backups," omitting all parts pertaining to differential backups.

Full Backup Only

There are a couple of ways to set up backups. You can script them yourself or use SQL Server Management Studio. We will show you both techniques.

> **Note**   Keep in mind that if you use SQL Server Management Studio, you can use the Script button to generate the script for later use.

Creating a Backup with SQL Server Management Studio

1. From the Start Menu, select All Programs | Microsoft SQL Server 2005 | SQL Server Management Studio.

2. In the Object Explorer pane, right-click the database you want to back up. In the context menu, select Tasks | Back Up. This will open the following dialog box:

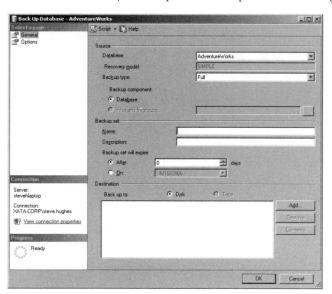

3. In this dialog box, select the Backup Type of Full. You can also set the Backup Set details here. Refer to SQL Server Books Online for more information on these settings and their use.

4. Set the Destination properties by clicking the Add...button. This will open the next dialog box:

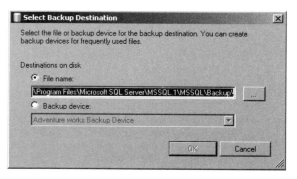

For transferring data, you typically use a file name destination. You do have the option to set up a Backup Device, but this is most commonly used for tape devices, which aren't typically used when transferring data.

> **Warning**   Be cautious if you choose a UNC path for the backup. This can hurt the performance of the backup and, in SQL Server 2000, it will reduce the overall performance of the server. Be sure to test the performance impact of backing up to the network before implementing it in your production environment.

> **Note**   At this point, you can click the Script button in the Back Up Database dialog box and get the generated backup results in a New Query window. The following script was created in our example and is included in the sample files as FullBackupScript.sql:
>
> ```
> BACKUP DATABASE [AdventureWorks] TO  DISK =
> N'C:\Program Files\Microsoft SQL Server\
> MSSQL.1\MSSQL\Backup\AdvWorks20060301.bak'
> WITH NOFORMAT, NOINIT, SKIP, NOREWIND, NOUNLOAD, STATS = 10
> GO
> ```

5. Once you have set the path, click the OK button. Then click the OK button in the Backup dialog box. This will create a backup of the database in the specified location.

6. The next step is to restore the database. In the target server's Object Explorer, right-click the Databases folder and select Restore Database from the context menu. This will open the following dialog box:

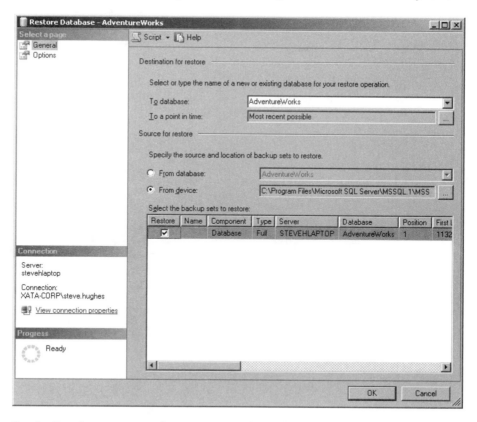

7. Set the Database name in the Restore Database dialog box.

8. Next, specify the source, as shown below. For this example, select From Device:. Set the path of the backup by clicking the expression builder button and setting the properties in the dialog box. From the Backup Media dropdown list, select File. Click the Add button to specify the path where you created the backup. Click the OK button when you are finished.

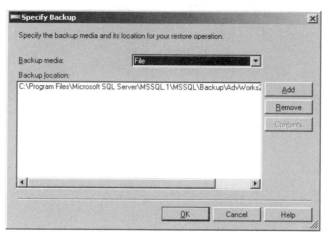

9. Next, select the backup set to restore by checking the box in the Restore column next to the set you created (the file in this case).

10. Now select the Options page from the Select A Page pane of the Restore Database dialog box, shown below. You will need to set the Restore options. If you are planning to overwrite the database on a regular basis on the target server, then you should select the Overwrite The Existing Database option.

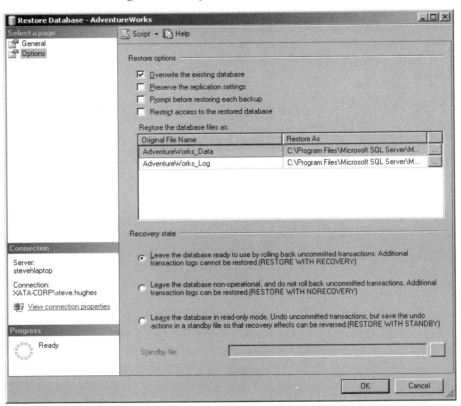

11. You will need to specify the file paths for the target server database files. If you do not select the Overwrite The Existing Database option, you will need to create a new file name in the Restore The Database Files As: section by clicking the expression builder button. (If you are making a copy of the database, be sure to give the database a different name on the General page of the Restore Database dialog box.)

12. Finally, select the first option, RESTORE WITH RECOVERY, in the Recovery State section. This option is used with full database restores as it makes the database available for use right away. The other options are used when you will be restoring additional backup files.

> **Note** At this point, you can click the Script button to script the restore process, which returns SQL similar to the following. This code is included in the sample files as FullRestoreScript.sql.
>
> ```
> RESTORE DATABASE [AdventureWorks2]
> FROM  DISK = N'C:\Program Files\Microsoft SQL Server\
> MSSQL.1\MSSQL\Backup\AdvWorks20060301.bak'
> WITH  FILE = 1,
> MOVE N'AdventureWorks_Data' TO N'C:\Program Files\Microsoft SQL Server\
> MSSQL.1\MSSQL\Data\AdventureWorks_Data2.mdf',
> MOVE N'AdventureWorks_Log' TO N'C:\Program Files\Microsoft SQL Server\
> MSSQL.1\MSSQL\Data\AdventureWorks_Log2.ldf',
> NOUNLOAD, REPLACE, STATS = 10
> ```

13. Click the OK button to finish restoring the database.

Backing Up All User Databases Using T-SQL

While the steps presented for creating a full backup allow you to do this process once, it is not an easily automated process. The following code, included in the sample files as BackupAllUserDBs.sql, will allow you more flexibility when scheduling backups and restores. (At the end of the chapter, we will cover automation and scheduling in greater detail.)

This code will back up all the user databases. Modify the script to best meet your needs. Note that some lines are split due to their length.

```
declare @DatabaseName varchar(300)
       ,@BackupSQL varchar(8000)
       ,@Timestamp varchar(30)
       ,@DirectoryPath varchar(2000)
       ,@FullPath varchar(2500)
       ,@RecoveryModel int

set @DirectoryPath = 'D:\MSSQL\BACKUP\'

-- create a timestamp for the backup file name
set @TimeStamp = convert(varchar, getdate(),112) +
    replace(convert(varchar, getdate(),108),':','')

-- get user databases only
declare Database_Cursor cursor for
    select d.name
    from sys.databases d
    where d.name not in('master','tempdb','model','msdb')

open Database_Cursor

fetch next from Database_Cursor
into @DatabaseName
```

```
while @@fetch_status = 0
    begin

        set @FullPath = ''
        set @FullPath = @DirectoryPath + @DatabaseName

        exec sys.xp_create_subdir @FullPath

        set @BackupSQL = ''
        set @BackupSQL = @BackupSQL + 'BACKUP DATABASE ' +
            @DatabaseName + ' TO  DISK = N''' + @FullPath + '\' +
            @DatabaseName + '_' + @TimeStamp + '.bak''
            WITH NOFORMAT, NOINIT, SKIP'

        exec (@BackupSQL)

        -- backups tlogs
        select @RecoveryModel = d.recovery_model from sys.databases
            as d where d.name = @DatabaseName
        -- only backup transaction logs for databases set for Full Recovery
        if @RecoveryModel = 1
            begin
                set @BackupSQL = ''
                set @BackupSQL = @BackupSQL + 'BACKUP LOG ' +
                    @DatabaseName + ' TO  DISK = N''' + @FullPath + '\'
                    + @DatabaseName + '_' + @TimeStamp + '.trn''
                    WITH NOFORMAT, NOINIT, SKIP'
                exec(@BackupSQL)
            end

        fetch next from Database_Cursor
            into @DatabaseName

    end

close Database_Cursor
deallocate Database_Cursor
```

Full Backup with Differential and Transaction Log Backups

When using differential backups or transaction log backups, you need to start with a full backup. Follow the first five steps of the procedure above to create the initial full backup. Do not continue on to the restore process. After creating a full backup, do the following:

Creating a Differential Backup

1. Repeat steps 1 through 5 above for creating a full backup, but in step 3 set the Backup Type to Differential. A Differential Backup will back up all the changes from the last full database backup.

2. The next step is to restore the full database backup as described above (steps 6 – 13), the only difference being that you need to set the Recovery State to RESTORE WITH NORE-

COVERY (step 12). This will leave the database in an unusable state. In the Object Explorer, you will see that the database is marked with a green arrow and the phrase "(Restoring...)." The database cannot be used until the restoration process is complete.

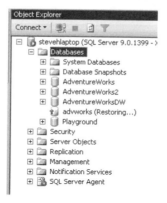

3. Next, restore the differential backup to the database by right-clicking the database you are restoring and selecting Tasks | Restore | Database from the context menu. This will open the Restore Database dialog box. Select the differential backup you created and choose RESTORE WITH RECOVERY. Click the OK button and the database will be ready for use once the restore is complete.

Creating a Transaction Log Backup

1. Once again you will need to start with a full database backup as described above. You can also use differential backups if you choose. Be sure that your database recovery model is set to FULL. For more information on recovery models, see Chapter 3.

> **Tip**   You can only use transaction backups if your database is using the full or bulk-logged recovery models. The simple recovery model regularly truncates the transaction log and therefore the transaction log cannot be backed up.

2. Once again, you will open the Backup Database dialog box, as in step 2 under Creating a Backup with SQL Server Management Studio earlier in the chapter. This time, change the Backup Type to Transaction Log. The rest of the settings are as before.

> **Tip**   It is common practice to use the .bak extension for full and differential backups and the .trn extension for the transaction log backups.

3. Normally, you will have more than one transaction log to restore. These logs are referred to collectively as a "log chain." So for this example, we will create a second transaction log backup. Follow the procedures above, but make sure to name the second backup clearly so that you know it is the second transaction log backup in the log chain.

4. Next, restore the full backup. As with the differential backup restore, you will need to set the recovery state to RESTORE WITH NORECOVERY.

5. Now restore the first of the two transaction log backups. This can be done by right-clicking the database that is in the process of restoring and selecting Tasks | Restore | Transaction Log from the context menus. This will open the Restore Transaction Log dialog box, shown here:

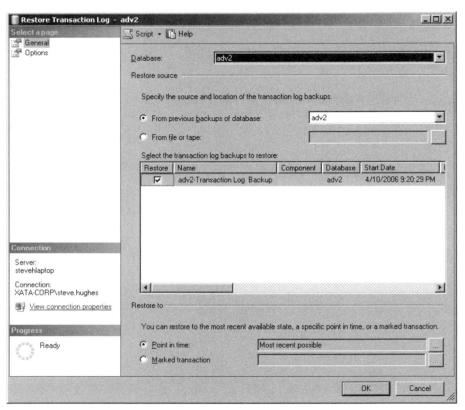

As you can see, this dialog box is similar to the normal Restore dialog box. The Restore To setting is an additional option at the bottom of the dialog box. For all of these examples, use the Point In Time option. Select the first transaction log backup in the log chain, setting the Recovery State to RESTORE WITH NORECOVERY. Click the OK button to restore this backup.

> **Tip**   If you have more transaction log backups, continue to restore the logs in the order they were backed up until you reach the last log backup in the log chain. You can also stop restoring at any point in the chain. Once you have restored all the files you want, continue on to the next step.

6. Now restore the second transaction log backup. This time, set the Recovery State to RESTORE WITH RECOVERY, which will make the database available for use.

> **Warning** You will not necessarily know what data is stored in a particular backup. You will need to estimate the data coverage based on the time of the backup. Even when using the transaction log backup, you only back up completed transactions.

> **Tip** There are a number of third-party tools that will compress your backups. This is a great option if you have to move significant amounts of data across a network, in particular, across a wide-area network.

Using Detach and Attach to Transfer Your Data

If you want to make sure that you know what data has been transferred and you are able to take your database offline for a period of time, using Detach and Attach to transfer data might be the right option for you. The major disadvantage of using the Detach/Attach method is that you have to make your database unavailable for a short period of time while it is detached. You need to make a copy of the .mdf file (mdf stands for master database file) and that can only be done while the database is detached. This means that your database will be unavailable as long as it takes you to make a copy of the database. If you have a large database, you may not be able to make the copy in a reasonable amount of time.

> **Tip** If you choose the Detach/Attach option, it may be to your advantage to investigate replication or high-speed copy options available via third parties.

If your business runs during a known set of hours with a specific period of down time, then Detach/Attach is more likely to be the best option for you. Once your business day is complete, you can detach the database, copy it to the desired location, attach it to the target server, and reattach it to the source server. Let's walk through this process.

Detaching a Database

1. From the Start Menu, select All Programs | Microsoft SQL Server 2005 | SQL Server Management Studio. Connect to the source server in Object Explorer.

2. Right-click the database you want to transfer and click Tasks | Detach in the context menu. This will open the Detach Database dialog box:

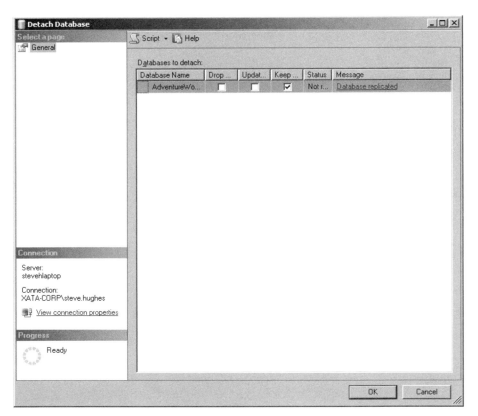

3. Select the Drop Connections checkbox and then click the OK button. This will detach the database, making the .mdf and .ldf files available to be moved or copied to the target server location. Copy the .mdf or .ldf files for your database to the target server now.

> **Tip**   Here is the T-SQL statement for detaching a database:
>
> ```
> EXEC sp_detach_db Adventureworks
> GO
> ```

Once you have detached your database, you can copy it to the target server. In order to bring the source and the target databases online, you will need to re-attach the original database on the source server and the copied database on the target server. To do so, follow the next set of steps in both locations.

Attaching a Database

1. In SQL Server Management Studio, right-click the Databases folder and select Attach from the context menu. This will open the Attach Database dialog box:

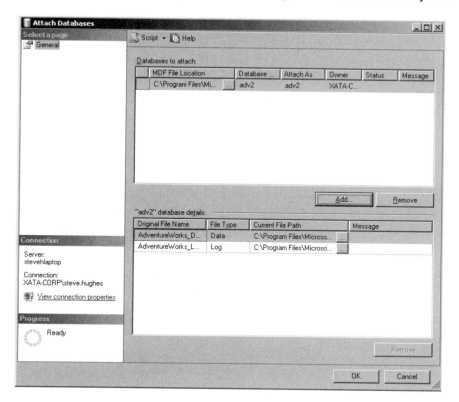

2. Click the Add button and then select the file or files to attach.

> **Note** If you use multiple files for your database structure, make sure all of the files are represented in the second list in the dialog box after you have added the .mdf file to the first list.

> **Tip** If you want to attach the copied database files to the source server, which would result in two initially identical databases on the same server, you can change the name of the database as you are attaching it. All you need to do is supply a different name in the Attach As column in the first listbox.

3. Click the OK button and you have successfully attached the database.

> **Tip** Here is the T-SQL statement for attaching a database:
>
> ```
> EXEC sp_attach_db @dbname = N'AdventureWorks',
>    @filename1 = N'd:\MSSQL\AdventureWorks.mdf',
>    @filename2 = N'd:\MSSQL\AdventureWorks_Log.ldf'
> GO
> ```

If you choose to use Detach/Attach to transfer data, make sure to reattach the database you originally detached. If you do not do this, the applications based on this database location will not function as expected if at all.

Using Replication to Transfer Your Data

Replication is a tried and true method for moving data between databases and servers. SQL Server 2005 supports three significant variations of replication. These replication methods have been part of the SQL Server platform for quite a while:

- Snapshot Replication
- Transactional Replication
- Merge Replication

SQL Server 2005 also supports a new concept called Peer-to-Peer Replication. This concept is actually a series of servers that are configured to use Transactional Replication to move data between servers.

Of the methods available for transferring databases, replication tends to be the least easily understood as well as the most difficult to design and maintain. Both the source and the target, referred to as the publisher and subscriber in replication lingo, must be set up correctly to replicate data. One of the advantages of replication over the previously described data transfer methods is that some variations of replication support writable targets and conflict resolution.

Complete coverage of the various methods of replication and the many configurations they each can employ is outside the scope of this book. For full information, see the SQL Server Books Online topic "Peer-to-Peer Transactional Replication." However, we will step through setting up Peer-to-Peer Replication between two servers so you can get a feel for the requirements for setting up replication in your environment.

Important   Look closely at the requirements for replication before deciding which of the data transfer methods is the best solution for your environment.

Configuring Peer-to-Peer Replication

1. Open SQL Server Management Studio.

2. Right-click the Replication node in Object Explorer and select Configure Distribution from the context menu. This will start the Configure Distribution Wizard, which you will need to run on both servers if you have not already configured them as distributors. In this exercise, you can accept the defaults in the wizard.

3. Next you will need to create a publication. Pick one of the servers on which to set up a publication. Expand the Replication node in Object Explorer and right-click on the

Local Publications folder. Select New Publication from the context menu to run the New Publication Wizard. This wizard will allow you to pick the database and set data you want to replicate. There are many options to set. You should specify the Publication Type as Transactional Publication, and then select one table for publication (for this example, select Address).

4. On the Snapshot Agent page, check the Create A Snapshot Immediately checkbox.

5. On the Agent Security page, enter a valid user for the Snapshot Agent to use when running.

6. Check the Create The Publication checkbox on the Wizard Actions page, then specify a name for your publication on the Complete The Wizard page.

7. Click the Finish button to finish the publication process. Now you have a publication ready.

8. Once you have a publication set up, you can configure it for Peer-to-Peer Replication. Select the Local Publications node in Object Explorer. You should now see your newly created publication displayed in the righthand window.

9. Right-click your new publication and select Properties from the context menu.

10. In the Publication Properties dialog box, select the Subscription Options page. Once here, you can set the Allow Peer-To-Peer Subscriptions option to True, as shown below. Click the OK button to close this dialog box.

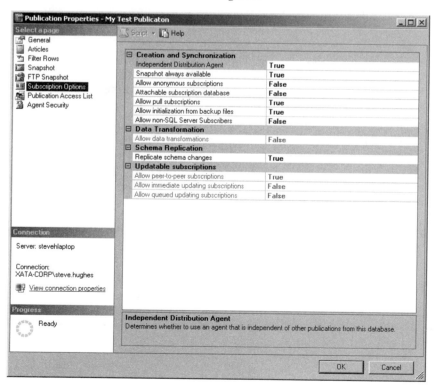

11. The next step is to make sure the schemas are the same on all of the databases. You can do this by creating a backup of the database on the source server and then restoring the database on the target server using the procedures explained earlier in this chapter.

12. Next you need to configure the peer-to-peer topology. You can do this by right-clicking your new publication and selecting Configure Peer-To-Peer Topology from the context menu. This will start a wizard that will set up the publications and subscriptions on the configured servers.

Once your SQL Servers are set up to participate in Peer-to-Peer Replication, any changes to data at either server will be replicated at the other server.

These are the basics of setting up Peer-to-Peer Replication. Snapshot and Transactional Replication are set up in similar ways. This information should give you an idea of how replication is configured and how it behaves so you can compare it with the other methods for transferring data described in this chapter.

Using SSIS to Transfer Your Data

Of all the methods for transferring databases, SQL Server Integration Services (SSIS) is the most flexible and robust. Not only can it transfer data, it can transform it. While this transformation capability is quite useful, it is not within the scope of this book. We will consider only the various options available in SSIS for moving data from your source system to your target system; we will not discuss any of the sophisticated data transformations that are possible with SSIS.

While the previously described methods required you to spend time in SQL Server Management Studio, in order to use SQL Server Integration Services, you will need to work in the Visual Studio 2005 IDE (Integrated Development Environment). SQL Server ships with a version of this IDE called the "SQL Server Business Intelligence Development Studio," also known as BIDS. If you already have Visual Studio 2005 installed on your development PC, then you will have two methods to get to the same features.

When you open either Visual Studio or BIDS, assuming you have installed the client and development tools from SQL Server on your PC, you will see a variety of project options. If you have installed any of the Visual Studio development tools, you will see them in either environment. The same is true for the SQL Server development tools. Either IDE reflects what you have installed.

Setting Up an SSIS Project

1. From the Start Menu, select All Programs | Microsoft SQL Server 2005 | SQL Server Business Intelligence Development Studio.

2. From the File menu, select New, then Project. This will open the New Project dialog box, shown below. This dialog box will contain all of the project types available to create. For

this exercise, select the Business Intelligence Projects node in the Project Types list and the Integration Services Project template from the Templates list. You can then change the name and path of the project and solution. When you have these settings the way you want them, click the OK button.

> **Tip**   A solution can contain many projects.

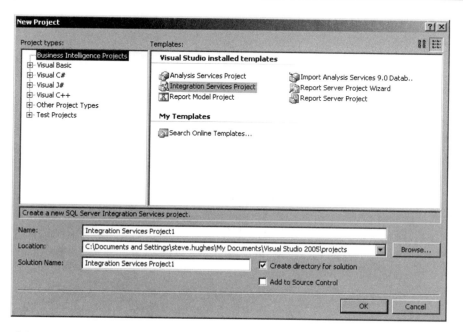

If this is your first time in either Visual Studio or BIDS, take some time to familiarize yourself with the interface. As you can see below, this is quite different from DTS (Data Transformation Services). The design interface has completely changed and has improved immensely. You will also see four tabs that are your design surfaces. In this example, you will use the Control Flow and Data Flow design surfaces only.

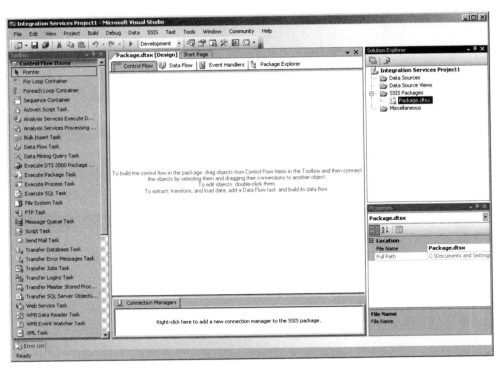

> **Tip** We are only touching the surface of SSIS's capabilities. I encourage you to fully explore this tool's capabilities.

3. Add a Data Flow Task to the Control Flow design surface. Drag-and-drop a Data Flow Task (shown here) from the Control Flow Items toolbox to the Control Flow design surface.

4. Once you add this task, you can either double-click the task or select the Data Flow tab to open the Data Flow design surface.

5. We are going to concentrate on getting data from the source to the target. In order to set this up, you will need to create two connection managers. Right-click in the Connection Managers pane and select the New OLE DB Connection option from the context menu. Set the Provider to Native OLE DB\SQL Native Client. Click the New button to create a new connection. Fill in the Server Name and select the database name. Click the OK button to create your first connection manager. You will need to do the same for the target server.

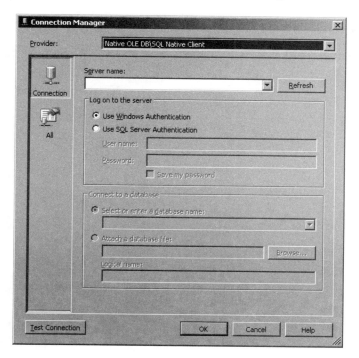

6. Once you have created the connection managers, drag-and-drop an OLE DB Source item (shown below) from the Data Flow toolbox to the Data Flow design surface.

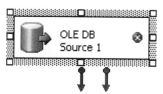

7. A red circle with an "X" in it on the OLE DB Source icon lets you know that you need to set up the source object. Double-click the icon to start the OLE DB Source Editor, shown below.

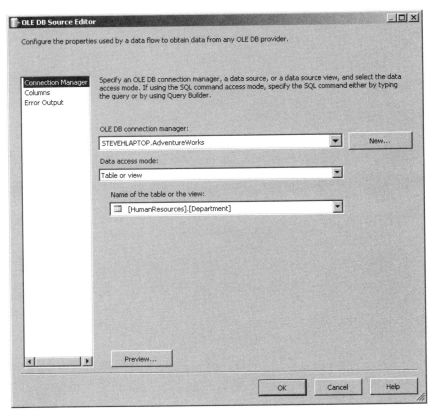

8.   Pick the connection manager for your source and pick the table to transfer. From here you can preview the data as well as modify the column list if necessary. The red circle disappears once you have properly set up the data flow source.

9.   Next, you will need to drag-and-drop an OLE DB Destination item (shown below) from the Data Flow Destinations section of the toolbox onto the Data Flow design surface.

Once again, a red circle appears on the icon until you have set up the source. However, with the *Destination* object, you will also need to set the input columns. Do this by selecting the OLE DB Source icon, then dragging the green arrow from the *Source* object to the *Destination* object, connecting the two.

10. Once you have made the connection, you can set up the source properties by right-clicking the OLE DB Destination icon and selecting Edit from the context menu. In the OLE DB Destination Editor, shown below, pick the connection manager, choose the Data Access Mode, select the destination table or view, and map the columns. There are a number of other properties that may be beneficial once you have tested your solution, including Table Lock and Rows Per Batch. You should look into these properties to determine whether or not they are appropriate for your situation.

Tip If you choose one of the Fast Load options for the Data Access Mode, you are utilizing the bulk load option in the data pump. When using this mode, you have additional options available at the bottom of the dialog box. These options are designed to improve the performance of the load process. See SQL Server Books Online for more information about these options.

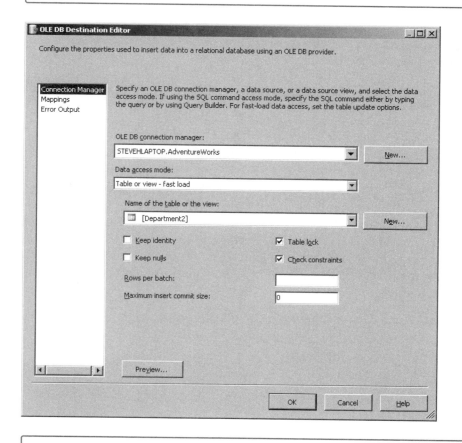

Tip You will need to set the column mappings before you can click the OK button. However, if the columns are named the same, you can click the Mappings item in the list on the left and the default mappings will be filled in for you.

11.   Repeat this process for each table or view you want to load. Once you have all of the tables ready to go, your *package*, that is, the list of data to be transferred, is ready to be deployed and scheduled. We will cover deployment and scheduling in the next section.

> **Tip**   If you want to test this project, you can debug the project as you would in any Visual Studio project by using the Debug menu option or the Debug button in the IDE.

You can use the RowCount Data Flow Transformation, shown below, as the destination, with a Data Viewer to view the data that is being moved.

SSIS gives you much more flexibility during the design and debug process than Data Transformation Services ever did. I encourage you to experiment with this tool as you might find many more uses for it.

The advantage of using SSIS is that you can filter the tables that you want to move around. Not only that, you can choose multiple destinations for your transfer, and you can even loop through multiple destinations as long as the schemas and loads are identical. If you need a flexible way to move your data around, this may be the best choice for you. For more information about SSIS, see the SQL Server Books Online topic "Integration Services Overview."

Automating and Scheduling the Transfer of Your Data

You can automate your data transfer using SQL Server Agent and SSIS. You can use Agent alone to schedule the various data movement techniques described above. SSIS can be used as well to graphically link various tasks and take advantage of the workflow engine that is built into it. In this section, we will walk through setting up a step for a backup procedure and then scheduling it.

Scheduling a Backup Operation Using SQL Server Agent

1.   In SQL Server Management Studio, open the SQL Server Agent node in Object Explorer and select the Jobs folder.

2.   Right-click the Jobs folder and select New Job from the context menu to open the New Job dialog box, shown below. This dialog box, like many SQL Server 2005 features, has been updated.

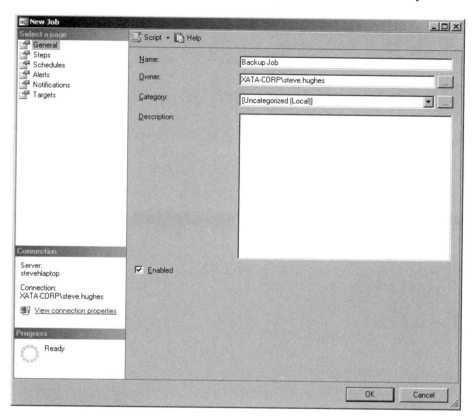

3. Next, set up the Steps required to execute the backup. Select the Steps page from the Select A Page pane to bring up a blank list of job steps. Click the New button to open up the New Job Step dialog box. Accept the default type, which is Transact-SQL Script (T-SQL) and the default database which is master. In the Command textbox, enter the backup script that we developed in the earlier section titled "Full Backup Only." This script is also included in the sample files as FullBackupScript.sql. Enter a name for the step, and click the OK button to close the New Job Step dialog box.

4. After the step or steps have been created, you will need to set the schedule. Go to the Schedules page and click the New button. This will open the New Job Schedule dialog box, shown below. In this dialog box, you can set the schedule to suit your needs. Choose the settings you want and click the OK button to close the New Job Schedule dialog box.

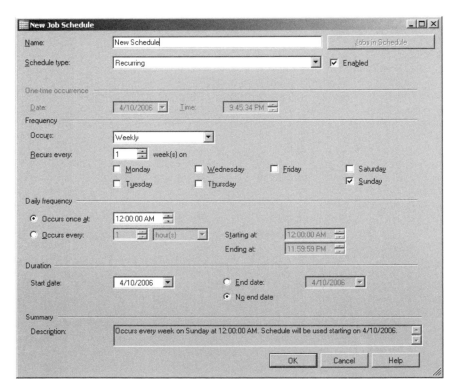

Tip   You can also click the Pick button on the Schedules page and select an existing schedule. If you have multiple jobs that need to run on the same or similar schedules, you can pick the schedule from a list of existing schedules on the server.

5. To finish, use the Alerts and Notifications pages to set up alerts or notifications to let you know whether the job or job steps were successful. Most commonly, you will use Notifications for this purpose. The Notifications page will also allow you to automatically delete the job when it runs if you want to run the job once only. Make appropriate Alerts and Notifications changes, and then click the OK button to close the New Job Schedule dialog box.

You can also schedule SSIS packages with SQL Server Agent. Agent jobs support deployed packages directly. (Deployed packages are packages that can be installed on a different server.) You can pick SQL Server Integration Services Package as the type in the New Job Step dialog box (shown below) and select the various package options, including configurations and execution options.

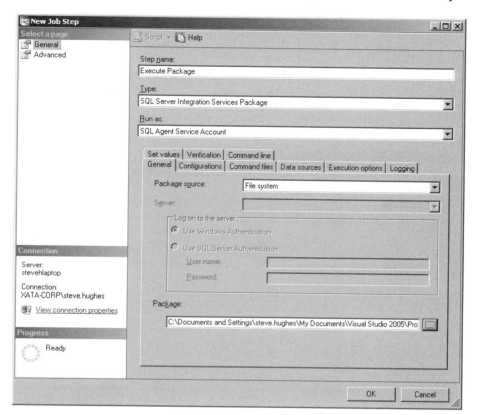

SQL Server Agent is a great tool for scheduling various tasks and jobs. However, SSIS can be used to create multiple workflows with various data sources and destinations. Using both Agent and SSIS together provides a powerful combination for moving data.

Conclusion

To transfer your database from one server to another, you can back it up and restore it on the target server, you can copy it while it is detached, and then attach the copy to the target server, you can use SQL Server's replication features, or you can use SSIS. Which method you choose depends on your application and your environment. You'll find the most versatility through a combination of SQL Server Agent and SSIS.

Chapter 4 Quick Reference

To	Do This
Create a database backup in SQL Server Management Studio	Right-click the database in Object Explorer, and select Tasks | Back Up.
Restore a database in SQL Server Management Studio	Right-click the Databases folder in Object Explorer, and select Restore Database.
Detach a database in SQL Server Management Studio	Right-click the database in Object Explorer, and select Tasks | Detach.
Attach a database in SQL Server Management Studio	Right-click the database in Object Explorer, and select Tasks | Attach.
Configure Peer-to-Peer Replication in SQL Server Management Studio	Right-click the Replication node in Object Explorer and select Configure Distribution from the context menu to run the Configure Distribution Wizard. Run this wizard on both servers in the replication group.
Set up an SSIS project	Open SQL Server Business Intelligence Development Studio (BIDS). Select File | New | Project, then select the Business Intelligence Projects node in the Project Types list and the Integration Services Project template from the Templates list. Add and configure connection managers, a data source, and a data destination.
Schedule a backup using SQL Server Agent	In SQL Server Management Studio, open the SQL Server Agent node in Object Explorer. Right-click the Jobs folder and select New Job from the context menu.

Part II
How to Query Data from SQL Server

Chapter 5
Computing Aggregates

After completing this chapter, you will be able to:

- Use aggregate functions in your applications to return totals and other summarizations from your data

- Use these functions to improve performance and enhance features of your applications

- Use CLR (common language runtime) aggregate functions to perform specialized calculations

In Part I of this book you learned how to design and build your database, to secure your database against unauthorized use and against unforeseen data loss, and to transfer your data to other locations. In Part II we'll look at how to manipulate the data in your database, starting in this chapter with how to compute totals and other summary information about data in a table.

Read this chapter with SQL Server Management Studio in front of you. Open a New Query window connected to your SQL Server and select AdventureWorks as your connected database.

As you read through the examples presented in this chapter, experiment with your own combinations and ideas. Aggregate functions perform read operations only, so there's no chance of damaging your database by trying something new.

Counting Rows

Sometimes in your applications, you need to tell the user how many items are in a data table.

If you look at a sampling of e-commerce sites on the Internet, you will see that many of them on the home page inform the reader about how many items the site has available for purchase. This kind of information might be obtained by using an algorithm like this:

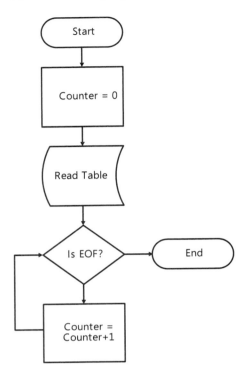

The same example written in Visual Basic looks like this:

```
Dim Counter As Integer = 0
While dataReader.Read
    Counter += 1
End While
dataReader.Close()
```

However, using this procedure in a table with many rows will take a very long time and require a great deal of resources. This slowdown occurs because the script must access each row, one at a time, to count them.

There is another way to get the number of rows in the same *DataReader* object, as shown here:

```
Dim Counter As Integer = dataReader.RecordsAffected()
```

However, this procedure uses the same amount of network resources as the previous one by connecting to the database.

As in other database-related tasks, system performance will be optimized by accessing data from within the database itself.

Using T-SQL Functions to Find the Number of Records

Transact-SQL (T-SQL) has special functions for aggregation (summarization of information about the data); these functions are scalar functions (which return only one value) and usually operate over a set of records.

Using COUNT

If you want to count the records in a table, you can use the following script:

```
SELECT COUNT(*) AS [Count] FROM Production.Product
```

> **Tip**   Yes! You can use * here (but only here).

Running a Visual Basic Sample Application that Utilizes the Count Function

1. On the sample cd, open Chapter05\Chapter 05.sln.

2. Microsoft Visual Studio will open. From the Build menu, select Build Chapter 05.

3. From the Debug Menu, select Start Debugging. This will open the application called Aggregate functions. It is important to note that you must have the AdventureWorks database attached locally at this point for the following steps to work.

4. From the Database menu, select Connect.

5. From the Demonstrations menu, select Counting Records. This will open the Counting Records application. You can now click three Run buttons to perform the three different aggregate functions and compare their runtimes.

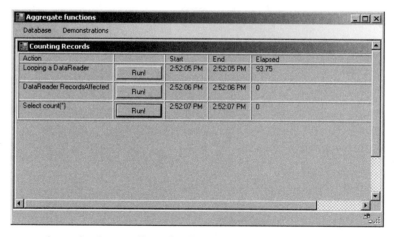

These time-elapsed values will not be the same each time the operations are performed. Other factors affect the results, like connection pooling and the size of the script cache. However, you can get an idea about the average length of time each operation takes to complete.

> **Important**   The most important lesson here is: always try to get the information directly from the database instead of making your own loops to get it.

You can use the *COUNT* function in several ways. The first way simply counts records. In this case, the *COUNT* function receives an asterisk (*) as argument.

However, sometimes you need to count only those records that do not have a NULL value in a particular field. In that case, you can use the name of the field as an argument.

The following sentence returns two different counts for the same table:

```
SELECT COUNT(*) AS [Count],
      COUNT(Class) AS [Classes with values]
FROM Production.Product
```

Table 5-1   Results

Count	Classes with Values
504	247

Perhaps you would like to know how many different credit card brands have been used by your customers to make their purchases. In this case, you need to count the number of distinct brands of credit cards, not the total number of credit card entries listed in the database. To do this, you need to apply the DISTINCT modifier to the *COUNT* function.

```
SELECT COUNT(DISTINCT CardType) AS [Different Credit Cards]  FROM Sales.CreditCard
```

> **Tip**   The *COUNT* function returns an int datatype, and the *COUNT_BIG* function performs the same aggregation but returns a bigint datatype. You have to use the *CONT_BIG* function when operating on tables containing billions of records.

Filtering Your Results

Sometimes, you have to query the database to answer questions like: "How many customers do we have from Seattle?" To answer this question, you can't use a simple *COUNT(*)* or a *COUNT*(DISTINCT field_name). You have to filter the counting process.

In fact, the aggregate syntax is simply a modification of the SELECT statement. If you consider this, you can filter the query using the WHERE clause just as in any other SELECT statement.

```
SELECT COUNT(*) AS [Customers In Seattle]
FROM Person.Address
WHERE (City = 'Seattle')
```

However, it would be better if you could give the user information for multiple cities instead of the count for just one city. Of course, you could repeat the query with a parameter in the WHERE clause so the user can specify the city they are interested in. What if you need to the answer the question: "How many customers do we have in *each* city?"

To answer this question, you have to change your SELECT statement by adding a GROUP BY clause. Look at this script and its result:

```
SELECT City, COUNT(*) AS [Count of Customers]
FROM Person.Address GROUP BY City
```

Table 5-2   Result

City	Count of Customers
Cheltenham	55
Kingsport	1
Baltimore	1
Reading	31
...	...

It is hard to find a specific city in a long list unless it is sorted. To sort the information for the users, do the following.

Creating a Sorted Totals Summary

1. From the Start Menu, select All Programs | Microsoft SQL Server 2005 | SQL Server Management Studio. Open a New Query window by clicking the New Query toolbar button. Enter and execute the following script to sort your results using the ORDER BY clause. (This script and all the other *COUNT* examples from this section are included in the sample files as CountExamplesFromText.sql in the \SqlScripts folder.)

   ```
   SELECT City, COUNT(*) AS [Count of Customers]
   FROM Person.Address
   GROUP BY City
   ORDER BY City
   ```

2. Perhaps you will be required to filter the data even further by answering the question: "How many customers do we have in each city, considering *only* those cities with more than 50 customers?" This is a special case because you have to filter the results of the *COUNT* aggregation after it performs the calculation. However, T-SQL has the solution for you. Click the New Query button, then enter and execute the following script to filter the *COUNT* aggregate with the HAVING clause:

   ```
   SELECT City, COUNT(*) AS [Count of Customers]
   FROM Person.Address
   GROUP BY City
   HAVING (COUNT(*) > 50)
   ORDER BY City
   ```

The difference between the WHERE clause and the HAVING clause is over what kind of information the filter is applied. The WHERE clause filters the original set of information from your table. The HAVING clause filters the information after the execution of the aggregation function and normally filters based on the results of the aggregate.

If we look at the estimated execution plan for one script using the WHERE clause and another using the HAVING clause, the difference between the two is very clear. View the estimated execution plan for the two previous queries using the following procedure. The two execution plans are shown in Figure 5-1 and Figure 5-2.

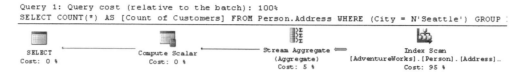

```
Query 1: Query cost (relative to the batch): 100%
SELECT COUNT(*) AS [Count of Customers] FROM Person.Address WHERE (City = N'Seattle') GROUP
```

SELECT   Compute Scalar   Stream Aggregate   Index Scan
Cost: 0 %   Cost: 0 %   (Aggregate)   [AdventureWorks].[Person].[Address]...
                                          Cost: 5 %   Cost: 95 %

Figure 5-1   Estimated execution plan for a T-SQL sentence using aggregates and the WHERE clause.

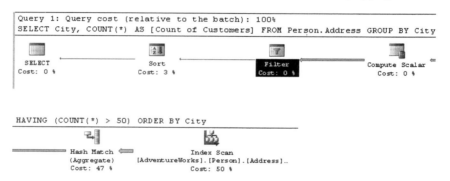

```
Query 1: Query cost (relative to the batch): 100%
SELECT City, COUNT(*) AS [Count of Customers] FROM Person.Address GROUP BY City
```

SELECT   Sort   Filter   Compute Scalar
Cost: 0 %   Cost: 3 %   Cost: 0 %   Cost: 0 %

```
HAVING (COUNT(*) > 50) ORDER BY City
```

Hash Match   Index Scan
(Aggregate)   [AdventureWorks].[Person].[Address]...
Cost: 47 %   Cost: 50 %

Figure 5-2   Estimated execution plan for a T-SQL sentence using aggregates and the HAVING clause.

Viewing the Estimated Execution Plan

1. Highlight the script whose execution plan you want to view.

2. Right-click the script, and select Display Estimated Execution Plan from the context menu.

> **Note**   The estimated execution plan shows you graphically how a query will be processed and how much each step influences the final cost of the query. See the SQL Server Books Online topic "How To: Display the Estimated Execution Plan" to learn about the meaning of each part of the graphical representation.

Computing Totals and Subtotals

You can use other aggregate functions to obtain summarizations and totals of data in your tables.

> **Tip**   All the modifiers you've learned to use for the *COUNT* function are available for any other aggregate function.

Computing Totals

You have to obtain totals to answer questions like: "How much money did we get from sales?" or "How many units have we sold of this product?" You could count records using a custom application. However, you will be able to get the desired information more efficiently by directly querying the database.

Using SUM

The *SUM* function does exactly what you would expect: it yields the sum of values in a column. The values have to be of numeric datatypes. In addition, the function will yield an error if it encounters a NULL value when trying to calculate a total. Let's examine the ways in which you can use the *SUM* function to give a variety of useful information. (The scripts in this section are included in the samples as SumExamplesFromText.sql in the \SqlScripts folder.)

Generating Totals

1. To total the LineTotal column from the SalesOrderDetail table in the AdventureWorks database, enter and execute the following script:

```
SELECT SUM(LineTotal) AS [Grand Total]
FROM Sales.SalesOrderDetail
```

2. Make the result given by this script more useful by displaying total sales by product by executing the following script:

```
SELECT ProductID, SUM(LineTotal) AS [Product Total]
FROM Sales.SalesOrderDetail
GROUP BY ProductID
```

3. This result is better, but the ProductID might not be meaningful enough for users. Improve this query by joining with the product table to display the product names as opposed to the product IDs using the following query:

```
SELECT Production.Product.Name,
SUM(Sales.SalesOrderDetail.LineTotal) AS [Product Total]
    FROM Sales.SalesOrderDetail
INNER JOIN Production.Product
    ON Sales.SalesOrderDetail.ProductID = Production.Product.ProductID
GROUP BY Production.Product.Name
ORDER BY Production.Product.Name
```

4. Now your results are much more useful to the user. Perhaps we could give the user some information about the Category and the SubCategory of each Product. To do so, run the following script:

```
SELECT C.Name AS Category,
    S.Name AS SubCategory,
    P.Name AS Product,
SUM(O.LineTotal) AS [Product Total]
FROM Sales.SalesOrderDetail AS O
    INNER JOIN
        Production.Product AS P
ON O.ProductID = P.ProductID
    INNER JOIN
        Production.ProductSubcategory AS S
ON P.ProductSubcategoryID = S.ProductSubcategoryID
    INNER JOIN
        Production.ProductCategory AS C
ON S.ProductCategoryID = C.ProductCategoryID
GROUP BY P.Name, C.Name, S.Name
ORDER BY Category, SubCategory, Product
```

We obtain these results:

Table 5-3   **Results**

Category	SubCategory	Product	Sales
Accessories	Bike Racks	Hitch Rack - 4-Bike	237096.16
Accessories	Bike Stands	All-Purpose Bike Stand	39591.00
Accessories	Bottles and Cages	Mountain Bottle Cage	20229.75
Accessories	Bottles and Cages	Road Bottle Cage	15390.88
Accessories	Bottles and Cages	Water Bottle - 30 oz.	28654.16
Accessories	Cleaners	Bike Wash - Dissolver	18406.97
Accessories	Fenders	Fender Set - Mountain	46619.58
Accessories	Helmets	Sport-100 Helmet, Black	16.869.52
...	...	...	...

Now, we are giving the user a very useful set of information.

Having too many items could make it difficult to analyze the results. In addition, it is possible that the users might need a summary on the SubCategory and Category fields. You can use the *ROLLUP* function to accomplish this.

Using ROLLUP to Compute Subtotals

T-SQL provides some operators for the GROUP BY clause that allow you to get information not only in detail, but also as a summary of each of the fields you define as arguments for the GROUP BY clause. (The scripts in this section are included in the samples as RollupExamplesFromText.sql in the \SqlScripts folder.)

Generating Subtotals

1. Alter the preceding SELECT statement to use only Category and SubCategory information. This will decrease the number of rows returned and make it a little easier to understand the data. We'll also add the WITH ROLLUP operator to the GROUP BY clause to see subtotals for both Category and SubCategory:

```
SELECT C.Name AS Category,
    S.Name AS SubCategory,
    SUM(O.LineTotal) AS Sales
FROM Sales.SalesOrderDetail AS O
    INNER JOIN Production.Product AS P
        ON O.ProductID = P.ProductID
        INNER JOIN Production.ProductSubcategory AS S
        ON P.ProductSubcategoryID = S.ProductSubcategoryID
        INNER JOIN Production.ProductCategory AS C
        ON S.ProductCategoryID = C.ProductCategoryID
GROUP BY C.Name, S.Name WITH ROLLUP
ORDER BY Category, SubCategory
```

Table 5-4   Results

Category	Subcategory	Sales
NULL	NULL	$ 109846381.40
Accessories	NULL	1272072.88
Accessories	Bike Racks	237096.16
Accessories	Bike Stands	39591.00
Accessories	Bottles and Cages	64274.79
Accessories	Cleaners	18406.97
Accessories	Fenders	46619.58
Accessories	Helmets	484048.53
Accessories	Hydration Packs	105826.42
Accessories	Locks	16240.22
Accessories	Pumps	13514.69
Accessories	Tires and Tubes	246454.53
Bikes	NULL	94651172.70
Bikes	Mountain Bikes	36445443.94
...	...	...

You can see from this result set that the overall total for sales is $109,846,381.40, the total sales for the Accessories Category is $1,272,072.88, the total sales for the Bike Racks SubCategory is $237,096.16, and so on. However, displaying the totals in this fashion is not the best way to present information.

2. To get more usefully structured result sets, you can use a special aggregate function called *GROUPING*. This function helps distinguish between total rows and detail rows. Add the *GROUPING* function to your script for the Category and the SubCategory fields

so that it will be easy to see the total rows in your result set by running the following script:

```
SELECT
    C.Name AS Category,
    S.Name AS SubCategory,
    SUM(O.LineTotal) AS Sales,
    GROUPING(C.Name) AS IsCategoryGroup,
    GROUPING(S.Name) AS IsSubCategoryGroup
FROM        Sales.SalesOrderDetail AS O
    INNER JOIN Production.Product AS P
        ON O.ProductID = P.ProductID
    INNER JOIN Production.ProductSubcategory AS S
        ON P.ProductSubcategoryID = S.ProductSubcategoryID
    INNER JOIN Production.ProductCategory AS C
        ON S.ProductCategoryID = C.ProductCategoryID
GROUP BY C.Name, S.Name WITH ROLLUP
ORDER BY Category, SubCategory
```

3. Now change the order of the rows in the result set by ordering by these grouping values. Doing so displays the information in a more appropriate style for a report.

```
SELECT
    C.Name AS Category,
    S.Name AS SubCategory,
    SUM(O.LineTotal) AS Sales,
    GROUPING(C.Name) AS IsCategoryGroup,
    GROUPING (S.Name) AS IsSubCategoryGroup
FROM Sales.SalesOrderDetail AS O
    INNER JOIN Production.Product AS P
        ON O.ProductID = P.ProductID
    INNER JOIN Production.ProductSubcategory AS S
        ON P.ProductSubcategoryID = S.ProductSubcategoryID
    INNER JOIN Production.ProductCategory AS C
        ON S.ProductCategoryID = C.ProductCategoryID
GROUP BY C.Name, S.Name WITH ROLLUP
ORDER BY
    IsCategoryGroup,
    Category,
    IsSubCategoryGroup,
    SubCategory
```

The result set for the above script is shown below. Note that some rows have been omitted to allow presentation within this text:

Table 5-5   Results

Category	SubCategory	Sales	IsCategory-Group	IsSubCategory-Group
Accessories	Bike Racks	$ 237096.16	0	0
Accessories	Bike Stands	39591.00	0	0
Accessories	NULL	1272072.88	0	1
Bikes	Mountain Bikes	36445443.94	0	0

Table 5-5   Results

Category	SubCategory	Sales	IsCategory-Group	IsSubCategory-Group
Bikes	Touring Bikes	$ 14296291.26	0	0
Bikes	NULL	94651172.70	0	1
Clothing	Bib-Shorts	167558.62	0	0
Clothing	Caps	51229.45	0	0
Clothing	NULL	2120542.52	0	1
Components	Bottom Brackets	51826.37	0	0
Components	Wheels	680831.35	0	0
Components	NULL	11802593.29	0	1
...	...	...	...	...
NULL	NULL	109846381.40	1	1

4. Finally, you can change the display of the NULL value to something more appropriate by using a CASE statement in the query:

```
SELECT
    CASE GROUPING(C.Name)
        WHEN 1 THEN 'Category Total'
        ELSE C.Name
    END AS Category,
    CASE GROUPING(S.Name)
        WHEN 1 THEN 'Sub-category Total'
        ELSE S.Name
    END AS SubCategory,
    SUM(O.LineTotal) AS Sales,
    GROUPING(C.Name) AS IsCategoryGroup,
    GROUPING(S.Name) AS IsSubCategoryGroup
FROM Sales.SalesOrderDetail AS O
    INNER JOIN Production.Product AS P
        ON O.ProductID = P.ProductID
    INNER JOIN Production.ProductSubcategory AS S
        ON P.ProductSubcategoryID = S.ProductSubcategoryID
    INNER JOIN Production.ProductCategory AS C
        ON S.ProductCategoryID = C.ProductCategoryID
GROUP BY C.Name, S.Name WITH ROLLUP
ORDER BY
    IsCategoryGroup,
    Category,
    IsSubCategoryGroup,
    SubCategory
```

You can decide whether to show the GROUPING values by including or excluding them from the SELECT clause of your script. Hidden GROUPING values can be used within the script in other clauses, such as the ORDER BY clause. If you obtain GROUPING values in your application, you can use them to add formatting for the total rows in reports or on screens.

Computing Running Totals

Sometimes you need to report cumulative values in order to display the progress of some kind of operation. For example, you might have to report on the daily progression of sales. The results would look something like this:

Table 5-6   Daily Progression of Sales

Date	Sales	Total Sales
7/1/2001	$ 665262.96	$ 665262.96
7/2/2001	15394.33	680657.29
7/3/2001	16588.46	697245.75
7/4/2001	7907.98	705153.72
7/5/2001	16588.46	721742.18
7/6/2001	15815.95	737558.13
7/7/2001	8680.48	746238.61
7/8/2001	8680.48	754919.10
7/9/2001	23105.31	778024.40
7/10/2001	11664.97	789689.37
7/11/2001	15815.95	805505.32
7/12/2001	15618.95	821124.28
7/13/2001	7907.98	829032.25
7/14/2001	27677.92	856710.17
7/15/2001	12409.84	869120.02
7/16/2001	15815.95	884935.97
...	...	...

As you can see, the Total Sales values are equal to all the previous dates' totals plus the current row's total. This type of total is called a running total because the total is calculated up to and including the current record.

The query for running totals has two parts. The first part is simple. Just sum the sales grouped by the date:

```
SELECT OrderDate,
SUM(TotalDue) AS Sales
FROM Sales.SalesOrderHeader AS A
GROUP BY OrderDate
ORDER BY OrderDate
```

We want to find the running total for one specific date using something like the following theoretical query:

```
--This is not valid SQL
SELECT SUM(TotalDue) AS Expr1
FROM Sales.SalesOrderHeader
WHERE (OrderDate <= <Specific_Date>)
```

Note that the above is not a valid T-SQL script; it is an explanation of how we might calculate a running total for a particular point in time. <Specific_Date> is not valid for T-SQL, but represents one specific date for our theoretical query. To turn this theory into useful T-SQL, we can use the OrderDate field as the specific date for each row. (The scripts in this section are included in the samples as RunningTotalsExamplesFromText.sql in the \SqlScripts folder.)

Calculating a Running Total Using a SubQuery

1. Use a sub-query to get all the values in the same result set. Save this query as SubQueryMethod.sql.

```
SELECT OrderDate,
SUM(TotalDue) AS Sales,
        (
            SELECT SUM(TotalDue)
            FROM Sales.SalesOrderHeader
            WHERE (OrderDate <= A.OrderDate)
        )
        AS [Actual Sales]
FROM Sales.SalesOrderHeader AS A
GROUP BY OrderDate
ORDER BY OrderDate
```

2. Look at the Estimated Execution Plan in SQL Server Management Studio. You will see two queries running in parallel to get the result sets.

Let us try something different. We can encapsulate the running total in a user-defined function.

Calculating a Running Total Using a User-Defined Function

1. First, create the user-defined function by executing the following script:

```
CREATE FUNCTION SalesToDate
    (
        @ThisDate datetime
    )
RETURNS money
AS
BEGIN
RETURN (SELECT SUM(TotalDue) AS Expr1
FROM Sales.SalesOrderHeader
WHERE (OrderDate <= @ThisDate))
END
```

2. Now execute the following query. Save the queries in step 1 and this step as UserDefFunctionMethod.sql.

```
SELECT OrderDate,
    SUM(TotalDue) AS Sales,
    dbo.SalesToDate(A.OrderDate) AS [Actual sales]
FROM Sales.SalesOrderHeader AS A
GROUP BY OrderDate
ORDER BY OrderDate
```

Which technique is better? To compare the two, use the following procedure.

Comparing the Performance of Two Queries

1. From SQL Server Management Studio, open the Query menu.

2. Select the Include Client Statistics menu item.

3. Execute the two sets of queries that you saved above a second time. You will now see the Client Statistics tab available along with the results. Use the information provided to learn about the costs of the two different kinds of queries.

The following table shows a subset of the statistics for the two queries.

> **Note**   The table shows only the part of the available statistics.

Table 5-7   Client Statistics Example

Sub-Query Method	Trial 1	Average
Client processing time	10375	10375.000
Total execution time	10835	10835.000
Wait time on server replies	460	460.000

User-Defined Function Method	Trial 1	Average
Client processing time	35677	35677.000
Total execution time	39502	39502.000
Wait time on server replies	3825	3825.000

As you can see, the running time for the query using the user-defined function is more than three times greater than the running time for the query using a sub-query.

Computing Statistical Values

Counting and summing are not the only aggregate options that you have available. You can also use both basic and advanced statistical functions in your queries. As before, these functions allow you to work directly with the database to obtain results, yielding excellent processing efficiency.

You can use these functions in the same way that you used the *SUM* function. Filters and grouping can be added to suit your needs. When you filter or group these functions, the resulting value of each function will vary according to its definition. (The scripts in this section are included in the samples as StatisticalExamplesFromText.sql in the \SqlScripts folder.)

Using AVG

The *AVG* function returns the average of the values contained in the column used as the argument. The *AVG* function ignores NULL values, so the presence of NULLs in your data will not change the meaning of the average value returned.

AVG accepts any expression that returns a numeric value as an argument. The argument can be the name of a column or a calculation. However, sub-queries or other aggregate functions are not allowed as arguments.

This is a simple SELECT statement that yields the average selling price for each product:

```
SELECT Production.Product.Name AS Product,
    AVG(Sales.SalesOrderDetail.UnitPrice) AS [Avg Price]
FROM Sales.SalesOrderDetail
    INNER JOIN
        Production.Product
        ON
        Sales.SalesOrderDetail.ProductID = Production.Product.ProductID
GROUP BY Production.Product.Name
ORDER BY Production.Product.Name
```

Here we have another SELECT statement, yielding the average prices for each product by month and the general average by product.

```
SELECT
    CASE GROUPING(Production. Product .Name)
        WHEN 1 THEN 'Global Average'
        ELSE
            Production. Product .Name
    END AS Product,
    CASE GROUPING(
        CONVERT(nvarchar(7), Sales.SalesOrderHeader.OrderDate, 111))
        WHEN 1 THEN 'Average'
        ELSE
            CONVERT(nvarchar(7),Sales.SalesOrderHeader.OrderDate, 111)
    END AS Period,
    AVG(Sales.SalesOrderDetail.UnitPrice) AS [Avg Price]
FROM Sales.SalesOrderDetail
    INNER JOIN Production.Product
        ON Sales.SalesOrderDetail.ProductID =
            Production.Product.ProductID
    INNER JOIN Sales.SalesOrderHeader
        ON Sales.SalesOrderDetail.SalesOrderID = Sales.SalesOrderHeader.SalesOrderID
GROUP BY
    Production.Product.Name,
    CONVERT(nvarchar(7), Sales.SalesOrderHeader.OrderDate, 111)
        WITH ROLLUP
ORDER BY
    GROUPING(Production.Product.Name),
    Production.Product.Name,
    Period
```

Using MIN and MAX

These two functions return the minimum or maximum value from an expression. Once again, the expression used as an argument for these functions can be a column name or other calculation, and you can use GROUP or ROLLUP to format the results. Execute the following script to see the *MIN* and *MAX* functions in action:

```
SELECT Production.Product.Name,
    MIN(Sales.SalesOrderDetail.UnitPrice) AS [Min Price],
    MAX(Sales.SalesOrderDetail.UnitPrice) AS [Max Price],
    AVG(Sales.SalesOrderDetail.UnitPrice) AS [Avg Price]
FROM Sales.SalesOrderDetail
INNER JOIN Production.Product
    ON Sales.SalesOrderDetail.ProductID = Production.Product.ProductID
GROUP BY Production.Product.Name
ORDER BY Production.Product.Name
```

Using Complex Statistical Functions

Sometimes, it is necessary to analyze the data in a database more deeply than the functions we have studied so far allow. For instance, demographic analysis and population estimation, used mostly in social or medical applications, require a more in-depth analysis of the collected data. Some of the more complex statistical functions you can use for further analysis of data are *STDEV, STDEVP, VAR* and, *VARP*.

> **Note**   These are very specialized functions. If you're not sure how to apply them, for now just be aware that the functions are available.

Using VAR

The *VAR* function returns the statistical variance for the numeric values in the specified expression.

Using VARP

This function returns the statistical variance for the population for all values in the specified expression.

Using STDEV and STDEVP

STDEV returns the statistical standard deviation of the values in a specified expression, while *STDEVP* returns the statistical standard deviation of the population of values in a specified expression.

Please, refer to statistical documentation for more information about the meaning of these statistical functions.

Using the DISTINCT Keyword

All of the aggregate functions accept the DISTINCT modifier, which causes the aggregate calculation to be performed only on each unique occurrence of a value.

```
SELECT Production.Product.Name,
    MIN(DISTINCT Sales.SalesOrderDetail.UnitPrice) AS [Min Price],
    MAX(DISTINCT Sales.SalesOrderDetail.UnitPrice) AS [Max Price],
    AVG(DISTINCT Sales.SalesOrderDetail.UnitPrice) AS [Avg Price]
FROM Sales.SalesOrderDetail
INNER JOIN Production.Product
    ON Sales.SalesOrderDetail.ProductID = Production.Product.ProductID
GROUP BY Production.Product.Name
ORDER BY Production.Product.Name
```

In the following table, you can compare the results from the above script run with and without the DISTINCT keyword. Notice that the MIN and MAX values do not change, but the AVG is different in most cases.

Table 5-8   Results With and Without the Distinct Keyword

	With DISTINCT			Without DISTINCT		
	Min	Max	AVG	Min	Max	AVG
All-Purpose Bike Stand	$ 159.00	$ 159.00	$ 159.00	$ 159.00	$ 159.00	$ 159.00
AWC Logo Cap	4.32	8.99	5.37	4.32	8.99	7.67
Bike Wash - Dissolver	3.98	7.95	5.14	3.98	7.95	6.94
Cable Lock	14.50	15.00	14.75	14.50	15.00	14.99
Chain	11.74	12.14	11.94	11.74	12.14	12.14
Classic Vest, L	38.10	63.50	50.80	38.10	63.50	62.74
Classic Vest, M	34.93	63.50	43.34	34.93	63.50	47.06
...	...	...	...	...	...	...

Designing Your Own User-Defined Aggregates Using the CLR

> **Tip**   To practice the steps in this section, CLR Integration must be enabled on your SQL Server. To learn about this setting, see the SQL Server Books Online topic "Surface Area Configuration for Features."

SQL Server 2005 allows you to create new aggregate functions written directly using CLR (common language runtime) languages. For example, imagine that you need to calculate the average elapsed time between orders. This is not a very practical example, but it will show you how to work with the Date, Time, and TimeSpan datatypes, which can be hard to manage using only T-SQL.

Creating an Aggregate Function Stub

1. From the Start menu, select All Programs | Microsoft Visual Studio 2005 | Microsoft Visual Studio 2005.

2. From the File menu, select New, and then Project. This will open the New Projects dialog box, as shown below.

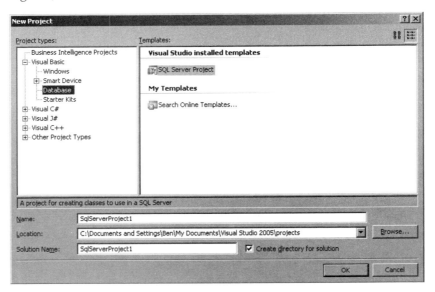

3. In the Project Types pane, expand the Visual Basic node and select the Database project type. In the Templates pane, select SQL Server Project. Specify a name and file path for this project, and click the OK button to create it.

4. The Add Database Reference dialog box, shown below, will open. Choose the database reference you wish to use and click the OK button to connect. If you do not have any database references set up, you will be prompted to create a new one. When choosing or creating a reference, be sure to specify AdventureWorks as the database to connect to.

5. If you are prompted as shown below to enable SQL/CLR debugging, click the Yes button to enable SQL/CLR debugging.

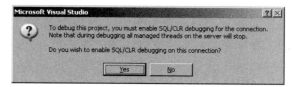

6. From the View menu, select Solution Explorer. Within Solution Explorer, right-click your project and select Add, and then select Aggregate from the context menus, as shown here:

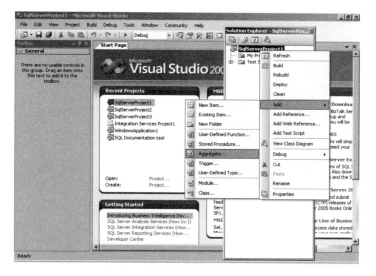

7. In the Add New Item dialog box, name the aggregate function WAVG.vb (for weighted average) as shown below and click the Add button.

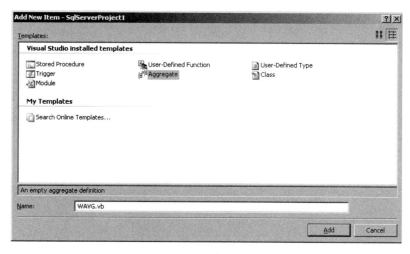

8. When you add the WAVG.vb item, Visual Studio adds the following code stub to the aggregate structure.

```
<Serializable()> _
<Microsoft.SqlServer.Server.SqlUserDefinedAggregate(Format.Native)> _
Public Structure WAVG
Public Sub Init()
    ' Put your code here
End Sub
Public Sub Accumulate(ByVal value As SqlString)
    ' Put your code here
End Sub
Public Sub Merge(ByVal value As WAVG)
    ' Put your code here
End Sub
Public Function Terminate() As SqlString
    ' Put your code here
    Return New SqlString("")
End Function
' This is a place-holder field member
Private var1 As Integer
End Structure
```

There are four procedures defined in this structure: *Init*, *Accumulate*, *Merge*, and *Terminate*. You will have to add the appropriate code to them to ensure that your function will execute properly.

Before you start, you have to define what datatype the aggregate will manage. For this example, because we will operate over dates and times, define the datatype as SqlDateTime.

Because you will be working with elapsed times, a TimeSpan datatype might seem like the right type to return. However, this datatype is not usable in SQL Server. Instead, you will have to return a string with a representation of the time span.

To calculate the weighted average, you need to total all the time spans for a set of records and then divide this total by the number of records in the set.

Adding Code to the Stubs

1. To perform the required calculation, first create three local variables within the *WAVG* function. Enter the declarations as shown below:

```
Public Structure WAVG
    Private Ticks As Long 'Cumulate the ticks between dates
    Private Previous As SqlDateTime 'Store the previous dates
                                    'to obtain the elapsed time
    Private Count As Integer 'Qty of records processed
```

2. Aggregate functions normally execute over grouped sets of records. For each group, the executor will call the *Init* procedure before processing the first record. In the *Init* procedure, you need to initialize your variables using the following code:

```
Public Sub Init()
    Count = 0
```

```
        Previous = Nothing
        Ticks = -1 'To detect the first record
    End Sub
```

3. For each record in the group, the executor will call the *Accumulate* procedure, which is detailed below. Note that you need to change the argument for this procedure from the default datatype of SqlString to a SqlDateTime.

```
Public Sub Accumulate(ByVal value As SqlDateTime)
    Dim span As New TimeSpan(0)
    If Ticks > -1 Then
        span = New TimeSpan(Ticks)
        span = span.Add(value.Value.Subtract(Previous.Value))
    Else
        Ticks = 0
    End If
    Previous = value
    Count += 1
    Ticks = span.Ticks
End Sub
```

The first time the executor calls this procedure, we will have no previous date. Therefore, the number of *Ticks* between the date currently being examined and the previous date will be zero. The code stores the actual date in the *Previous* variable in order to make our calculation the next time *Accumulate* is called. Also, we add one to the *Count* variable to keep track of the number of records we have examined.

Subsequent calls of the *Accumulate* procedure calculate the different time spans between dates. Since the *Ticks* variable is no longer equal to -1, the procedure creates a *TimeSpan* and adds to it the difference between the actual date and the previous one. It also can preserve the date in the *Previous* variable and increments the *Count* variable as before.

4. When there are no more records for the set, the executor calls the *Terminate* function. Enter it as detailed below:

```
Public Function Terminate() As String
    If Ticks <= 0 Then
        Return New TimeSpan(0).ToString
    Else
        Dim Resp As Long = CLng(Ticks / Count)
        Dim RespDate As New System.TimeSpan(Math.Abs((Resp)))
        Return RespDate.ToString
    End If
End Function
```

If no time spans were calculated, the *Ticks* variable will be zero. In this case, we would return the string representation of a new *TimeSpan* with zero ticks.

If time spans are calculated, then we divide the sum of these differences by the count of records processed and then create a new *TimeSpan* variable to hold the result. Then, we return the string representation of that *TimeSpan*.

> **Note**   SQL Server might also separate the work into smaller pieces whose results need to be combined by calling the *Merge* method. In a real application, you will need to implement this function appropriately.

5. To test the function, edit the Test.sql file that Visual Studio automatically added to your project. This file can be found under the Test Scripts folder in Solution Explorer. In this file, enter the following SELECT statement that uses your function.

```
SELECT CONVERT(nvarchar(7), OrderDate, 111) AS Period,
    dbo.WAVG(OrderDate) as Span
FROM Sales.SalesOrderHeader
GROUP BY CONVERT(nvarchar(7), OrderDate, 111)
```

6. Then select Build <ProjectName> from the Build menu, and select Start Debugging from the Debug menu to run the script.

Below you can see part of the result set.

Table 5-9   Results

Period	Span
2001/07	03:54:46.9565217
2001/08	03:07:00.7792208
2001/09	03:22:43.1067961
2001/10	03:34:55.5223881
2001/11	02:41:14.1312741
2001/12	02:24:57.9865772
2002/01	03:09:28.4210526
2002/02	02:35:31.2000000
2002/03	02:44:15.5133080
2002/04	02:51:08.8524590
2002/05	02:24:28.8963211
2002/06	02:28:05.1063830
2002/07	02:12:55.3846154
2002/08	01:42:51.4285714
2002/09	02:15:08.7378641
2002/10	02:23:02.7814570
2002/11	02:08:05.8895706
...	...

If you take a closer look at the *Accumulate* procedure, you will notice that it creates a *TimeSpan* variable each time it runs; meanwhile it stores the value that it calculates in the *Ticks* variable. Why not just use a *TimeSpan* variable? The problem here is that the CLR aggregate functions have to be serialized between calls. The way this serialization occurs is defined by one attribute in the declaration of the function. For example, look at the declaration below:

```
<Microsoft.SqlServer.Server.SqlUserDefinedAggregate(Format.Native)> _
Public Structure WAVG
```

The Format argument establishes the serialization format. In the Native format, you can only serialize Value types, not Reference types like CLR classes (including System.String) or your own classes. In this example, we can translate the value we need to preserve between calls by storing its representation in the *Ticks* variable of datatype long. However, if you need to use Reference types, you can change the Format argument to Format.UserDefined. If you make this change, however, you will have to implement your own serialization mechanism. Refer to the SQL Server Books Online topic "Invoking CLR User-Defined Aggregate Functions" for more information about serialization mechanisms.

The complete example of this CLR aggregate function is included in the sample files for this chapter in the WAVG folder.

Conclusion

Aggregates are powerful tools for organizing and interpreting data. SQL Server provides a wide array of common aggregates for you to use, and you can apply them in various flavors by adding keywords to the aggregates. If exactly the right aggregate isn't already built into SQL Server, you can easily create your own aggregate function through Visual Studio, then call your custom-designed aggregate through a SQL query.

Chapter 5 Quick Reference

To	Do this
Count the records in a table	SELECT COUNT(*) FROM <Table_Name>
Count the number of records with values that are not null in a field	SELECT COUNT (<Field_Name>)
	FROM <Table_name>
Count the records that meet a specified condition	SELECT COUNT (*)
	FROM <Table_Name>
	WHERE <condition>
Count the records with the same value in one of the fields	SELECT <Field_Name>, COUNT(*)
	FROM <Table_Name>
	GROUP BY <Field_Name>
Sum the values contained in a column	SELECT SUM(<Field_name>)
	FROM <Table_Name>
Obtain the minimum value in a column	SELECT MIN(<Field_Name>)
	FROM <Table_Name>

To	Do this
Obtain the maximum value in a column	SELECT MAX(<Field_Name>) FROM <Table_Name>
Obtain the average for the values in a column	SELECT AVG(<Field_Name>) FROM <Table_Name>
Obtain subtotals and grand totals for the values	SELECT <Field_Name>, <FUNCTION_NAME>(<Field_Name>) FROM <Table_Name> GROUP BY <Field_Name> WITH ROLLUP
Obtain results only for values that are not repeated	SELECT <FUNCTION_NAME> (DISTINCT <Field_Name>) FROM <Table_Name>
Define your own aggregate function	Create a CLR aggregate function using Visual Studio

Chapter 6

Improving Query Performance

After completing this chapter, you will be able to:

- Generate query plans

- Read query plans

- Design your database so data is stored efficiently for how it will be used

- Use clustered and nonclustered indexes

- Index XML columns

- Index views

- Defragment indexes

- Use the Database Engine Tuning Advisor

In the previous chapter, you learned how to retrieve summary information about data in your database. SQL Server can return results, including summary information, quickly and efficiently if the data is stored appropriately in the database. This chapter will explain the different ways SQL Server stores data, how it retrieves data, and what you should consider when designing your database to achieve the most efficient performance from SQL Server.

Understanding Query Plans

Whenever SQL Server executes a query, it first has to determine the best way to execute it. This decision involves deciding how and in which order to access and join the data, how and when to perform calculation and aggregations, and so on. This is done by a subsystem called the Query Optimizer. The Query Optimizer uses statistics about data distribution, the metadata relating to the database objects involved, index information, and other factors to calculate multiple possible query plans. For each of these plans, it estimates the cost based on statistics about the data and chooses the plan with the minimal cost for execution. Of course, SQL Server does not calculate all possible plans for every query because, for some queries this calculation might itself take longer than executing the least efficient query plan. Therefore, SQL Server has complex algorithms to find an execution plan with reasonable costs close to the minimum possible costs. After the execution plan is generated it is stored in a buffer cache (where SQL Server allocates most of its virtual memory). It is then executed in the way the execution plan instructs the database engine.

> **Note**   Execution plans in a buffer cache can be re-used when the same or a similar query is executed. Therefore, execution plans are kept in the cache as long as possible. To learn more about execution plan caching, see the whitepaper titled: "Batch Compilation, Recompilation, and Plan Caching Issues in SQL Server 2005" at *http://www.microsoft.com/technet/prodtechnol/sql/2005/recomp.mspx*.

Whether or not SQL Server Query Optimizer can produce an efficient plan for a given query depends on the following factors:

- **Indexes**   Like an index in a book, a database index provides the ability to quickly find specific rows in tables. Many indexes can exist on each table. With indexes on tables, SQL Server Query Optimizer can optimize data access by finding the right indexes to use. Without an index, the Query Optimizer has only one choice, which is to scan all the data in the table to find the right data rows. Later in this chapter, you will learn how indexes work and how to design and create them.

- **Data distribution statistics:**   SQL Server keeps statistics about data distribution. If these statistics are missing or out of date, the Query Optimizer will not be able to calculate efficient query plans. In most cases, statistics are generated and updated automatically. You will see later in this chapter how this generation works and how the statistics can be managed.

As you can see, execution plan generation is a crucial function for SQL Server performance since the effectiveness of a query plan determines whether it completes within milliseconds, seconds, or even minutes. Query execution plans of poorly performing queries can be analyzed to determine whether indexes are missing, statistics are out of date or missing, or SQL Server has chosen an inefficient plan (this doesn't occur very often).

> **Note**   Of course, it's also possible that a poorly performing query was executed with a good query plan. In these cases, query optimization is not the problem. The problem most likely lies in another area, like the query design, contention, disk I/O (input/output), memory, CPU, the network, and so on. To learn more about these kinds of problems you can read the whitepaper "Troubleshooting Performance Problems in SQL Server 2005" which can be found at *http://www.microsoft.com/technet/prodtechnol/sql/2005/tsprfprb.mspx*.

Viewing Query Execution Plans

1. From the Start menu, select All Programs | Microsoft SQL Server 2005 | SQL Server Management Studio. Click the New Query button to open a New Query window and change the database context to AdventureWorks by selecting it from the Available Databases dropdown menu.

2. Execute the following SELECT statement. The code for this example is included in the sample files as Viewing Query Plans.sql.

```
SELECT SalesOrderID, OrderQTY
    FROM Sales.SalesOrderDetail
WHERE ProductID = 712
ORDER BY OrderQTY DESC
```

3. To show the execution plan of this query, press Ctrl+L or choose Display Estimated Execution Plan from the Query menu. The execution plan is shown below.

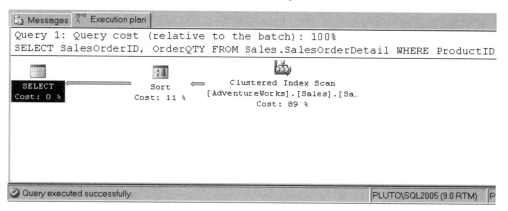

The estimated execution plan is produced without actually executing the query. The query is optimized by Query Optimizer, but not executed. This facet of Query Optimizer is advantageous when dealing with queries that have long runtimes because it is not necessary to wait until the query completes to see the query plan. The graphical query plan has to be read from right to left and from top to bottom. Every icon represents one operator in the plan, and the data exchanged between these operators is represented by arrows. The thickness of the arrows represents the amount of data that flows between the operators. We won't go into detail explaining every available operator, but the ones you see in this query plan are:

- SQL Server accesses the data using a Clustered Index Scan. This scan is the actual data access operation and will be discussed in more detail later.

- The data comes to the Sort operator, which sorts the data based on the ORDER BY clause of the statement.

- The data is sent to the client.

We will discuss the most important operators that SQL Server uses when you learn about indexes and joins. A complete list of operators can be found in the SQL Server Books Online topic "Graphical Execution Plan Icons."

The cost percentage under each operator icon shows the percentage of the total cost of this query that the operation represents. This number can give you a good idea of which operation uses the most resources to execute. In our case, the Clustered Index Scan is the most costly operation, accounting for 89% of the total cost of the query.

4. Let the mouse pointer hover over the Clustered Index Scan operator. You will see a yellow window appear, as in the graphic below.

Clustered Index Scan
Scanning a clustered index, entirely or only a range.

Physical Operation	Clustered Index Scan
Logical Operation	Clustered Index Scan
Estimated I/O Cost	0.917199
Estimated CPU Cost	0.133606
Estimated Operator Cost	1.0508 (89%)
Estimated Subtree Cost	1.0508
Estimated Number of Rows	3382
Estimated Row Size	17 B
Ordered	False
Node ID	1

Predicate
[AdventureWorks].[Sales].[SalesOrderDetail].
[ProductID]=(712)
Object
[AdventureWorks].[Sales].[SalesOrderDetail].
[PK_SalesOrderDetail_SalesOrderID_SalesOrderDetailID]
Output List
[AdventureWorks].[Sales].
[SalesOrderDetail].SalesOrderID, [AdventureWorks].
[Sales].[SalesOrderDetail].OrderQty

This window provides you with detailed information about the operation. Until now, you only knew that SQL Server was retrieving data using a scan operation. But in this window, you can see that it performs a Clustered Index Scan operation (which will be explained in detail later) on the clustered index of Sales.SalesOrderDetail table and that it searches for ProductID 712. This information is found in the Predicates section. Also, the estimated costs and the estimated number of rows and row size is shown. While the number of rows are estimated based on the statistics SQL Server has for this table, the cost numbers are found based on statistics and on numbers from a reference system. Therefore, cost numbers cannot be used to calculate how long a query will take on a computer. They can only be used to distinguish if one operation is cheaper or more expensive than another.

5. This operator information can also be seen in the Properties window of SQL Server Management Studio. To open the Properties window, right-click one of the operator icons and select Properties from the context menu.

6. Query plans can also be saved. To save a query plan, right-click the plan and choose Save Execution Plan As from the context menu. The plan will be saved using an XML format with the extension of .sqlplan. It can be opened with SQL Server Management Studio by choosing Open | File from the File menu.

7. What you have seen up to now is the estimated execution plan of a query, but it is also possible to show the actual execution plan of a query. The actual execution plan is similar to the estimated execution plan, but it also includes actual numbers (not estimations) for the number of rows, the number of rewinds, etc. To include the actual execution plan in the query, press Ctrl+M or select Include Actual Execution Plan from the Query menu. Then press F5 to execute the query. The query results are displayed as usual, but you will also see the execution plan displayed on the Execution Plan tab.

Creating Indexes to Provide Faster Query Execution

Now we will have a look at how indexes work and how they improve query performance. In SQL Server, it is possible to define two different types of indexes: clustered indexes and non-clustered indexes. To understand how indexes can improve data access and which index type to use for a given situation, it is essential to understand how data and indexes are stored in data files and how SQL Server accesses data in data files.

Heap Structures

A data file in a SQL Server database is divided in 8k pages. Every page can contain data, indexes, or other types of data that SQL Server needs to maintain the data files. However, the majority of the pages are data or index pages. Pages are the units that SQL Server writes and reads from the data files. Every page contains data or index information for only one database object. So on each data page, you'll find the data of a single object, and on each index page, you'll find information for only one index. In SQL Server 2000, it was not possible for a data row to be split between pages, which meant that a data row had to fit on one page, limiting the row size to about 8060 bytes (with the exception of large object data). In SQL Server 2005, this restriction no longer exists for varying-length datatypes like nvarchar, varbinary, CLR, and so on. With varying-length datatypes, data rows can span several pages, but all the fixed-length datatypes of a row still have to fit on one page.

When you create a table without any index and fill it with data, SQL Server searches for unused pages on which to store the data. To keep track of which pages hold the data for the table, SQL Server has one or more IAM (Index Allocation Map) pages for every table. These IAM pages point to the pages where the table's data is stored. Since the data for this table is stored on the pages without any index and is only kept together through IAM pages, the table is called a heap. To access data in a heap, SQL Server has to read the IAM page of that table and then scan all pages pointed to by the IAM page. Such an operation is called a table scan. Table scans read all of the data without any order. If a query searches for one particular row, a table scan of a heap will have to read all the rows in the table just to find it, which is a very inefficient operation.

Examining Heap Structures

1.   Open SQL Server Management Studio. Open a New Query window and change the database context to AdventureWorks.

2.   In the following examples, you will create two tables called dbo.Orders and dbo.OrderDetails. Type and execute the following statements to build the tables and populate them with data. The code for this entire example is included in the sample files as Examining Heap Structures.sql.

```
USE AdventureWorks
GO

CREATE TABLE dbo.Orders(
    SalesOrderID int  NOT NULL,
```

```
    OrderDate datetime NOT NULL,
    ShipDate datetime NULL,
    Status tinyint NOT NULL,
    PurchaseOrderNumber dbo.OrderNumber NULL,
    CustomerID int NOT NULL,
    ContactID int NOT NULL,
    SalesPersonID int NULL
    );

CREATE TABLE dbo.OrderDetails(
    SalesOrderID int NOT NULL,
    SalesOrderDetailID int NOT NULL,
    CarrierTrackingNumber nvarchar(25),
    OrderQty smallint NOT NULL,
    ProductID int NOT NULL,
    UnitPrice money NOT NULL,
    UnitPriceDiscount money NOT NULL,
    LineTotal  AS (isnull((UnitPrice*((1.0)-UnitPriceDiscount))*OrderQty,(0.0)))
    );

INSERT INTO dbo.Orders
SELECT SalesOrderID, OrderDate, ShipDate, Status, PurchaseOrderNumber,
    CustomerID, ContactID, SalesPersonID
FROM Sales.SalesOrderHeader;

INSERT INTO dbo.OrderDetails(SalesOrderID, SalesOrderDetailID, CarrierTrackingNumber,
OrderQty,
    ProductID, UnitPrice, UnitPriceDiscount)
SELECT SalesOrderID, SalesOrderDetailID, CarrierTrackingNumber,OrderQty,
    ProductID, UnitPrice, UnitPriceDiscount
FROM Sales.SalesOrderDetail;
```

3. Now you have built the two tables with the heap storage structure. Type the following statements to query the dbo.Orders table. Include the actual execution plan by pressing Ctrl+M prior to execution or by selecting Include Actual Execution Plan from the Query menu. Execute the query.

```
SET STATISTICS IO ON;

SELECT * FROM dbo.Orders

SET STATISTICS IO OFF
```

The SET STATISTICS IO option turns on a feature that causes SQL Server to send messages about the I/O performed while executing a statement back to the client. This is an excellent feature to use to determine the I/O cost of queries.

4. Switch to the Messages tab. You will see a message similar to the following

```
(31465 row(s) affected)
Table 'Orders'. Scan count 1, logical reads 178, physical reads 0, read-ahead reads 0,
lob logical reads 0, lob physical reads 0, lob read-ahead reads 0.

(1 row(s) affected)
```

This output tells us that SQL Server needed to scan the data of the table one time and needed to perform 178 page reads (logical reads) for this operation. The output also shows us that no physical reads were used (physical reads or read-ahead reads) to perform the operation. There were no physical reads because, in this case, the data was already in the buffer cache. If your Messages window indicates that there were physical reads with that query, execute the query again and you should see that the number of physical reads is lower than before. This is because SQL Server keeps recently accessed data pages in the buffer cache to increase performance.

5. Switch to the Execution Plan tab. In the execution plan, shown below, you see that SQL Server used a Table Scan operation to access the data since that was its only choice.

```
Query 1: Query cost (relative to the batch): 100%
SELECT * FROM dbo.Orders
```

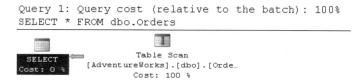

6. Now change the query a little bit to retrieve a specific row.

```
SET STATISTICS IO ON;

SELECT * FROM dbo.Orders
WHERE SalesOrderID =46699;

SET STATISTICS IO OFF;
```

7. Examine the message output and the graphical execution plan. You will see that SQL Server still needed 178 page reads and used a Table Scan operation for the query. The table scan is used because SQL Server has no index and therefore needs to scan all data in the table to find the right row.

You can see that SQL Server uses table scans to access tables without any index. This scan forces SQL Server to scan all data regardless of the size of the table. In a very large table, a table scan could take a long time.

Indexes on Tables

To improve data access performance, you should define indexes on columns. The columns where an index is defined are called the index key columns. An index built on a column is similar to a book index. It includes the sorted values from that column and pointers to the pages where the actual rows of data can be found.

To find the rows where the indexed column has a specific value, SQL Server has to search the index for that value and then follow the pointer to read the row. This operation is much easier and cheaper than scanning all of the data as we did when using the table scan.

Indexes in SQL Server are built in a tree structure called a balanced tree. The general structure of a balanced tree can be seen in Figure 6-1. As you can see, the bottom level is called the leaf level. You can think of the leaf level as a book index. It includes an entry for every data row, sorted by the index column. To find values quickly within the index, a tree is built upon it using the < (less than) and > (greater than) comparison operations. The number of index levels depends on the number of rows and the size of the index key. In reality, an index page would contain many more entries than you see in Figure 6-1. Since a page is 8k in size, SQL Server can point to hundreds of pages from one index page. Therefore, indexes normally don't have many levels, even when the table contains millions of rows. This fact makes it possible to find specific values very quickly.

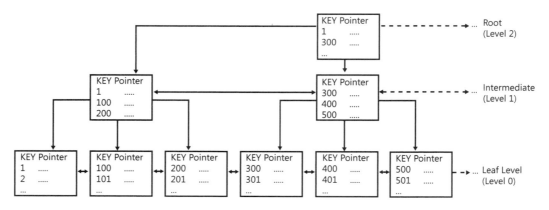

Figure 6-1   The general structure of a B-tree.

As mentioned before, SQL Server has two types of indexes: clustered and nonclustered indexes. Both types are balanced trees, but each is built differently. Let us now have a look at what the differences are.

Clustered Indexes

Clustered indexes are a special kind of balanced tree. The difference from what you have seen before is found in the leaf level of the index. In a clustered index, the leaf level does not include the index key and a pointer; instead, the leaf level is the data itself. This difference means that the data is not stored in a heap structure anymore. It is now stored in the leaf level of the index, sorted by the index key. This design has two advantages:

■ SQL Server doesn't need to follow a pointer to access the data. The data is stored directly in the index.

■ The data is sorted by the index key, which is the main advantage. Whenever SQL Server needs the data sorted by the index key, performing a sort operation is no longer necessary because it is sorted already.

Because the data is included in a clustered index, it is only possible to define one clustered index per table. To create a clustered index, the following syntax is used:

```
CREATE [ UNIQUE ] CLUSTERED INDEX index_name
    ON <object> ( column [ ASC | DESC ] [ ,...n ] )
```

As you can see, it is possible to define indexes as unique, which means that no two rows are permitted to have the same index key value.

> **Note** SQL Server builds a unique index when a primary or unique constraint is created on a table. When a primary key is defined it builds a clustered index by default if no clustered index exists on the table. The kind of index SQL Server should use when creating a primary or unique constraint can be defined within the CREATE or ALTER TABLE statements with the CLUSTERED or NONCLUSTERED keyword.

Creating and Using Clustered Indexes

1. Open SQL Server Management Studio. Open a New Query window and change the database context to AdventureWorks.

2. Type and execute the following statement to create a unique clustered index on the Orders table. The code for this example is included in the sample files as Creating And Using Clustered Indexes.sql.

   ```
   CREATE UNIQUE CLUSTERED INDEX CLIDX_Orders_SalesOrderID
       ON dbo.Orders(SalesOrderID)
   ```

3. Now execute the same two SELECT statements as before and examine the differences. Be sure to include the actual query plan when executing.

   ```
   SET STATISTICS IO ON;

   SELECT * FROM dbo.Orders;

   SELECT * FROM dbo.Orders
   WHERE SalesOrderID =46699;

   SET STATISTICS IO OFF;
   ```

4. Switch to the Execution Plan tab.

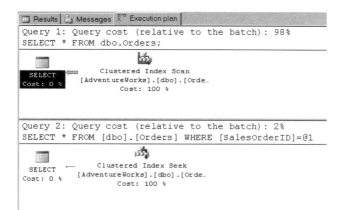

What you see here is that SQL Server is no longer using table scans. Now SQL Server performs index operations, because the data is no longer stored in a heap structure. The query execution plan shows that you are using the two main index operations that exist:

- **Index scan**   A scan through the leaf level of the index, reading all the data of the table. Because the first SELECT statement has no WHERE clause, SQL Server knows that it needs to retrieve all data, which is stored in the leaf level of the index.

- **Index seek**   An operation in which SQL Server searches for a particular value by passing through the branches of the index, beginning at the root of the index.

These two operations can also be combined to retrieve particular ranges of data. In this type of partial scan operation, SQL Server seeks to get to the beginning of the range and then scans until the end of the range.

5. Switch to the Messages tab, shown below.

```
(31465 row(s) affected)
Table 'Orders'. Scan count 1, logical reads 180, physical reads 0, read-ahead reads 0,
lob logical reads 0, lob physical reads 0, lob read-ahead reads 0.

(1 row(s) affected)

(1 row(s) affected)
Table 'Orders'. Scan count 0, logical reads 2, physical reads 0, read-ahead reads 0,
lob logical reads 0, lob physical reads 0, lob read-ahead reads 0.

(1 row(s) affected)
```

What you see is that the first SELECT statement produced almost the same amount of page reads as the table scan did when you had the heap structure. This is not surprising because the SELECT statement requests all data and therefore SQL Server has to retrieve all data. But the second query only produced two page reads, which is a major improvement over the 178 page reads you saw before. SQL Server only needed to seek through the index, which requires much less I/O than searching through every page of data.

6. Enter the following SELECT statements, which retrieve the data in a sorted form, and press Ctrl+L to get the estimated execution plan.

```
SELECT * FROM dbo.Orders
ORDER BY SalesOrderID;

SELECT * FROM dbo.Orders
ORDER BY OrderDate;
```

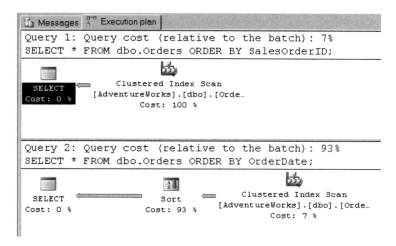

You can see here that the first statement performs only a clustered index scan and doesn't sort the data. This is because the data is already sorted by SalesOrderID because this column is the clustered index key. Therefore, SQL Server only needs to scan the data on the leaf level and return the result to get the rows in the right order.

For the second query, the data has to be sorted after it is retrieved. Therefore, you see a Sort operation after the clustered index scan where the data is sorted by the OrderDate column. Since sorting is a very expensive operation, the second query produces 93% of the total query costs of both queries. Thus, it is a good practice to define clustered indexes on columns that are frequently used as sort columns, or as the grouping criteria of an aggregate, because aggregating data requires SQL Server to sort the data according to the grouping criteria first.

Now you will build a *composite index* on the OrderDetails table. A composite index is an index that is defined for more than one column. The index keys will be sorted by the first index key column, then by the second, and so on. Such an index is useful when two or more columns are used together as search arguments in a query or when the uniqueness of a row has to be determined throughout more than one column.

Building a Composite Clustered Index

1. In SQL Server Management Studio, enter and execute the following statement to create a composite clustered index on the OrderDetails table.

```
CREATE UNIQUE CLUSTERED INDEX CLIDX_OrderDetails
    ON dbo.OrderDetails(SalesOrderID,SalesOrderDetailID)
```

2. Now enter the two following SELECT statements. The first searches for a specific Sales-OrderID and the second for a SalesOrderDetailID. Both of these columns are index columns of our CLIDX_OrderDetails index. Press Ctrl+L to show the estimated execution plan.

```
SELECT * FROM dbo.OrderDetails
WHERE SalesOrderID = 46999
```

```
SELECT * FROM dbo.OrderDetails
WHERE SalesOrderDetailID = 14147
```

You can see that in the first query, which searches for a value from the first column of the composite index, SQL Server uses an index seek to find the row. In the second query it uses an index scan, which is a much more expensive operation. This index scan is used because it is not possible to seek only for a value from the second column of a composite index since the index is initially sorted by the first column. Thus, it is important to consider the order of the index columns in your composite indexes. Remember, composite indexes should only be used when the additional columns are always searched in combination with the first column or when uniqueness must be enforced.

Nonclustered Indexes

In contrast with clustered indexes, nonclustered indexes do not include all of the data rows in the leaf level of the index. Instead, all of the key columns and a pointer to the row in the table is stored on the leaf level. How the pointer is written and used depends on whether the base table is a heap or has a clustered index:

- **Heap**   If the table has no clustered index, SQL Server stores a pointer to the physical row (file id, page id, and row id within the page) at the leaf level of the nonclustered index. To find a specific row in this case, SQL Server seeks through the index and follows the pointer to retrieve the row.

- **Clustered index**   When a clustered index exists, SQL Server stores the clustering index keys of the rows as pointers in the leaf level of the nonclustered index. If SQL Server retrieves a row by means of a nonclustered index, it seeks through the nonclustered index, retrieves the appropriate clustering key, and then seeks through the clustered index to retrieve the row.

Since nonclustered indexes don't include whole data rows, it is possible to create up to 249 nonclustered indexes per table. The syntax to create them is very much the same as for clustered indexes:

```
CREATE [ UNIQUE ] NONCLUSTERED INDEX index_name
    ON <object> ( column [ ASC | DESC ] [ ,...n ] )
```

Creating and Using Nonclustered Indexes

1. Open SQL Server Management Studio. Open a New Query window and change the database context to AdventureWorks.

2. Enter the following SELECT statement and press Ctrl+L to show the estimated execution plan. The code for this example is included in the sample files as Creating And Using Nonclustered Indexes.sql.

```
SELECT DISTINCT SalesOrderID, CarrierTrackingNumber
    FROM dbo.OrderDetails
    WHERE ProductID = 776
```

SQL Server performs a clustered index scan operation because it has no index on ProductID. To speed up this query, SQL Server would need an index on ProductID. Because a clustered index is already defined on the OrderDetails table, you must use a nonclustered index.

> **Note** The Sort operator is used in this query plan to make the result distinct.

3. Enter and execute the following statement to create a nonclustered index on the ProductID table of the OrderDetail table.

```
CREATE INDEX NCLIX_OrderDetails_ProductID
    ON dbo.OrderDetails(ProductID)
```

4. Use the same SELECT statement as before and press Ctrl+L to show the estimated execution plan.

```
SELECT DISTINCT SalesOrderID, CarrierTrackingNumber
    FROM dbo.OrderDetails
    WHERE ProductID = 776
```

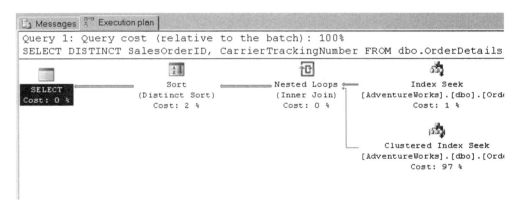

When you let the mouse hover over the upper Index Seek operator, you can see that SQL Server performs an index seek on NCLIX_OrderDetails_ProductID to retrieve the pointers to the actual rows. Because a clustered index exists on that table, it receives the list of clustering keys as pointers. This list is the input of the Nested Loops operator, which is a type of Join operator (joins will be discussed later in the chapter). The Nested Loops operator uses an index seek on the clustered index to retrieve the actual rows of data, which then go to the distinct Sort operator to make the result distinct. This is how SQL Server retrieves rows with the help of a nonclustered index when a clustered index exists.

5. Now let's look at how SQL Server accesses data when a nonclustered index exists on a table with no clustered index. Enter and execute the following DROP INDEX statement to drop the clustered index from the OrderDetails table.

```
DROP INDEX OrderDetails.CLIDX_OrderDetails
```

6. Enter the same SELECT statement as before and press Ctrl+L to show the estimated execution plan.

```
SELECT DISTINCT SalesOrderID, CarrierTrackingNumber
    FROM dbo.OrderDetails
    WHERE ProductID = 776
```

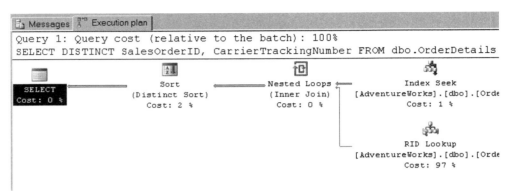

You can see that SQL Server now uses a RID Lookup operator because the pointers SQL Server receives from the index seek are pointers to the physical rows of data, not the clustering key. The RID Lookup operator is the operator that SQL Server uses to retrieve rows directly from a page.

7. Enter and execute the following statement to create the clustered index again.

```
CREATE UNIQUE CLUSTERED INDEX CLIDX_OrderDetails
    ON dbo.OrderDetails(SalesOrderID,SalesOrderDetailID)
```

Using Covered Indexes

It is not always necessary for SQL Server to retrieve the whole row as a second step when using nonclustered indexes. This situation arises when the nonclustered index includes all the data of the table SQL Server needs to perform the operation. When this happens, we call the index a covered index because that index covers the entire query. Covered indexes can speed up query performance tremendously, as you can see from the two query plans in the previous example. In those queries, operators that retrieve the actual data rows cost 97% of the whole query. In other words, the query would be about 32 times faster without that operation. Let's have a look how covered indexes work.

Using a Covered Index

1. Open SQL Server Management Studio, open a New Query window, and change the database context to AdventureWorks.

2. The idea of a covered index is that it includes all data necessary for the query. If you have a look at the first query below, which you used in the previous example, you can see that SQL Server needs the columns SalesOrderID, CarrierTrackingNumber, and ProductID.

The nonclustered index NCLIX_OrderDetails_ProductID you created before includes the ProductID because it is built on that column and also SalesOrderID because this column is the key of the clustered index. Because of this, SalesOrderID is the pointer SQL Server uses in the nonclustered index. Therefore, SQL Server needs to retrieve the data row by seeking the clustered index only to get the CarrierTrackingNumber. In the second query, the CarrierTrackingNumber is not in the SELECT list. Type and execute the statement with the actual execution plan included to see the difference. The code for this example is included in the samples files as Using Covered Indexes.sql.

```
SET STATISTICS IO ON
--not covered
SELECT DISTINCT SalesOrderID, CarrierTrackingNumber
    FROM dbo.OrderDetails
    WHERE ProductID = 776
--covered
SELECT DISTINCT SalesOrderID
    FROM dbo.OrderDetails
    WHERE ProductID = 776
SET STATISTICS IO OFF
```

You can see in the graphic shown below that SQL Server needs no access to the clustered index for the second query because the index covers the query when Carrier-TrackingNumber is not selected. Because accessing the clustered index for every row is very costly, the second query uses only 1% of the total batch cost. Looking at the Messages tab, you will see that for the covered query, SQL Server needs only 2 page reads as opposed to 709 for the first query.

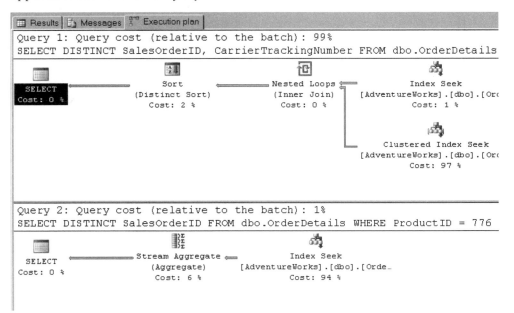

You have seen now how big the benefit from a covered index can be. Of course, it is not possible to eliminate columns from queries if they are needed in the result. But as a general rule, retrieve only the columns you truly need in order to have a higher likelihood of using a covered index. It is not a good practice to use * in the SELECT statement just because it is easier to write.

3. Suppose the CarrierTrackingNumber is needed in the query, but for performance reasons a covered index should be used. It is possible to include the column in the nonclustered index in SQL Server 2005. Included columns are stored with the index keys on the leaf level of the nonclustered index, making it unnecessary to retrieve from the clustered index. To include the CarrierTrackingNumber in your nonclustered index, enter and execute the following statements to DROP the index and CREATE the index again with the included column.

```
DROP INDEX dbo.OrderDetails.NCLIX_OrderDetails_ProductID

CREATE INDEX NCLIX_OrderDetails_ProductID
    ON dbo.OrderDetails(ProductID)
    INCLUDE (CarrierTrackingNumber)
```

4. Execute the former uncovered query to see whether it is now covered.

```
SET STATISTICS IO ON
SELECT DISTINCT SalesOrderID, CarrierTrackingNumber
    FROM dbo.OrderDetails
    WHERE ProductID = 776
SET STATISTICS IO OFF
```

Looking at the execution plan, you can see that no clustered index access is needed anymore. On the Messages tab you can see that the query needs only five page reads now as opposed to the 709 it needed before.

> **Note**   Included columns produce overhead for SQL Server when data changes because SQL Server has to change it in every index and because more space in the data files is needed. Therefore, including columns in nonclustered indexes is a good way to improve query performance, but it is not a good practice to create indexes with included columns for all queries in an application. This feature should be used selectively to speed up problematic queries.

Indexes on Computed Columns

In the dbo.OrderDetails table, you have the computed column LineTotal, which represents the LineTotal of the row and is calculated by the formula below.

```
(isnull(([UnitPrice]*((1.0)-[UnitPriceDiscount]))*[OrderQty],(0.0)))
```

Each time this column is accessed, SQL Server calculates the values from the values of the original rows referenced by the calculation. This process is not a problem as long as LineTotal is used in the SELECT clause, but it is an issue when LineTotal is used as a search predicate in the WHERE clause or in aggregation functions, like MAX or MIN. When computed columns are used for searches, SQL Server has to calculate the value for every row of the table and then search within the result for the requested rows. This is a very inefficient process because it always requires a table or full clustered index scan. For these types of queries, it is possible to build indexes on computed columns. When an index is built on a computed column, SQL Server calculates the result in advance and builds an index over them.

> **Note**   There are some restrictions on building indexes on computed columns. The main restrictions are that the computed column has to be deterministic and precise. For more information on these restrictions, see the SQL Server Books Online topic "Creating Indexes on Computed Columns."

Creating and Using Indexes on Computed Columns

1. Open SQL Server Management Studio. Open a New Query window and change the database context to AdventureWorks.

2. Imagine you want to retrieve all SalesOrderIDs where LineTotal has a specific value. Enter the query below and press Ctrl+L to see the estimated query plan when no supporting index on the computed column exists. As you can see, SQL Server needs to do a clustered index scan, compute the column values, and filter for the required rows. The code for this example is included in the sample files as IndexesOnComputedColumns.sql.

```
SELECT SalesOrderID
FROM OrderDetails
WHERE LineTotal = 27893.619
```

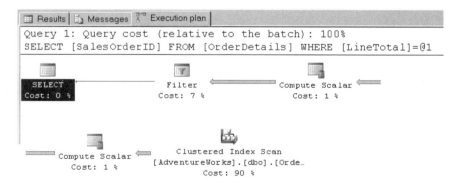

3. Enter and execute the following CREATE INDEX statement to build an index on the computed column.

```
CREATE NONCLUSTERED INDEX NCL_OrderDetail_LineTotal
ON dbo.OrderDetails(LineTotal)
```

4. Highlight the first query and press Ctrl+L to show the new query plan with the index on the computed column. As shown below, you see that SQL Server uses the newly built index to retrieve the data, making the query much faster than before.

```
SELECT SalesOrderID
FROM OrderDetails
WHERE LineTotal = 27893.619
```

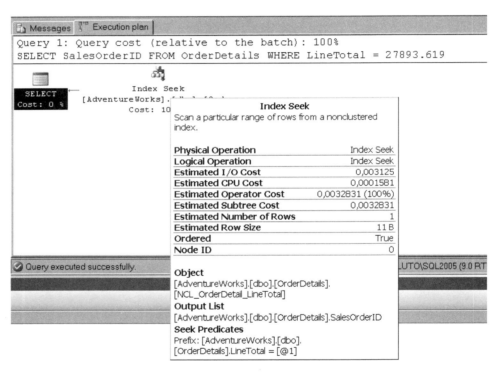

5. Close SQL Server Management Studio.

Indexes on XML Columns

SQL Server 2005 has a native XML datatype. XML instances in XML datatypes are stored as binary large objects (BLOBs) and can have a size up to 2 GB per instance. XML data can be queried using XQuery, but querying XML datatypes can be very time consuming without an index. This is true especially of large XML instances because SQL Server has to shred the binary large object containing the XML at runtime to evaluate the query.

To improve query performance on XML datatypes, XML columns can be indexed. XML indexes fall in two categories: primary XML indexes and secondary XML indexes.

Creating and Using Primary XML Indexes

The first index to create on an XML column is the primary XML index. When creating that index, SQL Server shreds the XML content and creates several rows of data that include information like element and attribute names, the path to the root, node types and values, and so on. With this information, SQL Server can support XQuery requests more easily. To build a primary XML index, a primary key with a clustered index has to exist on the base table. The syntax to build a primary XML index is shown below:

```
CREATE PRIMARY XML INDEX index_name
    ON <object> ( xml_column_name )
```

Creating a Primary XML Index

1. Open SQL Server Management Studio. Open a New Query window and change the database context to AdventureWorks.

2. Enter and execute the following statements to create a table to use in the following procedures. The code for this is included in the sample files as CreatingAndUsingPrimary-XMLIndexes.sql.

    ```
    CREATE TABLE dbo.Products(
        ProductID int NOT NULL,
        Name dbo.Name NOT NULL,
         CatalogDescription xml NULL,
    CONSTRAINT PK_ProductModel_ProductID PRIMARY KEY CLUSTERED
    ( ProductID ));

    INSERT INTO dbo.Products  (ProductID,Name,CatalogDescription)
    SELECT ProductModelID, Name, CatalogDescription
    FROM Production.ProductModel;
    ```

3. Use the following CREATE INDEX statement to create a primary index on the Catalog-Description Column of the Production.ProductModel table.

    ```
    CREATE PRIMARY XML INDEX PRXML_Products_CatalogDesc
        ON dbo.Products (CatalogDescription);
    ```

4. The following statement uses an XQuery method to retrieve only XML data when a specific path exists within the XML document. Enter and execute this statement, and be sure to include the query execution plan.

    ```
    WITH XMLNAMESPACES
    ('http://schemas.microsoft.com/sqlserver/2004/07/adventure-works
    /ProductModelDescription' AS "PD")

    SELECT ProductID, CatalogDescription
    FROM dbo.Products
    WHERE CatalogDescription.exist ('/PD:ProductDescription/PD:Features') = 1
    ```

5. In the following execution plan, you can see that SQL Server uses the index on the XML column to find the right rows and retrieves the actual data row with a Nested Loop oper-ator. SQL Server then uses an index seek against the clustered index in the same manner that you observed with nonclustered indexes.

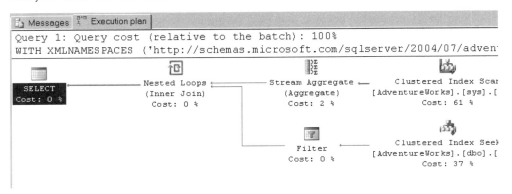

6. Close SQL Server Management Studio.

Secondary XML Indexes

Although primary XML indexes improve XQuery performance because the XML data is shredded, SQL Server still needs to scan through the shredded data to find the queried data. To improve query performance even more, it is possible to create secondary XML indexes on top of primary XML indexes. There are three types of secondary XML indexes, and each type supports specific query types against XML columns, providing the functionality to create only the index types needed for a specific scenario. The three types of secondary XML indexes are:

- **Path**   Secondary XML indexes, which are useful when using the *.exist* methods to deter-mine whether a specific path exists.

- **Value**   Secondary XML indexes, which are used when performing value-based queries where the full path is unknown or includes wildcards.

- **Property**   Secondary XML indexes, which are used to retrieve values when the path to the value is known.

The general syntax for creating secondary XML indexes is:

```
CREATE XML INDEX index_name
    ON <object> ( xml_column_name )
    USING XML INDEX xml_index_name
    FOR { VALUE | PATH | PROPERTY }
```

Creating and Using Secondary XML Indexes

1. Open SQL Server Management Studio. Open a New Query window and change the database context to AdventureWorks.

2. Enter and execute the following statement to create secondary path, value, and property indexes on the XML column CatalogDescription. The code for this example is included in the sample files as CreatingAndUsingSecondaryXMLindexes.sql.

```
CREATE XML INDEX IXML_Products_CatalogDesc_Path
    ON dbo.Products (CatalogDescription)
    USING XML INDEX PRXML_Products_CatalogDesc FOR PATH


CREATE XML INDEX IXML_Products_CatalogDesc_Value
    ON dbo.Products (CatalogDescription)
    USING XML INDEX PRXML_Products_CatalogDesc FOR VALUE


CREATE XML INDEX IXML_Products_CatalogDesc_Property
    ON dbo.Products (CatalogDescription)
    USING XML INDEX PRXML_Products_CatalogDesc FOR PROPERTY
```

3. Enter the following statements, which use XQuery methods, and request the estimated execution plans by pressing Ctrl+L. Examine the different ways SQL Server uses these newly created indexes.

```
WITH XMLNAMESPACES ('http://schemas.microsoft.com/sqlserver/2004/07/adventure-works/
ProductModelDescription' AS "PD")
SELECT *
    FROM dbo.Products
    WHERE CatalogDescription.exist
    ('/PD:ProductDescription/@ProductModelID[.="19"]') = 1;


WITH XMLNAMESPACES ('http://schemas.microsoft.com/sqlserver/2004/07/adventure-works/
ProductModelDescription' AS "PD")
SELECT *
    FROM dbo.Products
    WHERE CatalogDescription.exist ('//PD:*/@ProductModelID[.="19"]') = 1;


WITH XMLNAMESPACES ('http://schemas.microsoft.com/sqlserver/2004/07/adventure-works/
ProductModelDescription' AS "PD")
SELECT
    CatalogDescription.value('(/PD:ProductDescription/@ProductModelID)[1]',
    'int') as PID
FROM dbo.Products
WHERE
    CatalogDescription.exist ('/PD:ProductDescription/@ProductModelID') = 1;
```

4. Close SQL Server Management Studio.

Indexes on Views

A view without an index doesn't need any storage space, and when it is used in a statement, SQL Server merges the view definition with the statement, optimizes it, produces a query plan, and retrieves the data. The overhead of this process can be significant when the view processes or joins a large number of rows. In such a situation, it can be helpful to index the view if it is queried frequently.

When a view is indexed, it is processed and the result is stored in the data file just like a clustered table. SQL Server automatically maintains the index when data in the base table changes. Indexes on views can speed up data access through the view tremendously, but of course indexing does involve overhead when data in the base table changes. Therefore, consider using indexed views when the view processes many rows, as with aggregate functions, and when the data in the base table does not change frequently.

With SQL Server 2005 Enterprise, Developer, or Evaluation Edition, indexed views can speed up queries that don't reference the view directly. When the query being processed includes an aggregate, for example, and SQL Server Optimizer finds an indexed view where the aggregate is already included, it retrieves the aggregate from the index rather than recalculating it.

To create an indexed view, use the following steps:

Creating an Indexed View

1. Create a view with SCHEMABINDING. The view has to meet several requirements. For instance, it can only reference base tables that exist in the same database. All referenced functions have to be deterministic; rowset functions, derived tables, and sub-queries are not allowed at all. The full list of requirements can be found in the SQL Server Books Online topic "Creating Indexed Views."

2. Create a unique clustered index on the view. The leaf level of this index consists of the full result set of the view.

3. Create nonclustered indexes on top of the clustered index as needed. Nonclustered indexes can be created as usual.

Creating and Using Indexed Views

1. Open SQL Server Management Studio. Open a New Query window and change the database context to AdventureWorks.

2. Enter and execute the following statement to create a view that aggregates the LineTotal grouped by the month of the order. The code for this example is included in the sample files as CreatingAndUsingIndexedViews.sql.

```
CREATE VIEW dbo.vOrderDetails
    WITH SCHEMABINDING
AS
    SELECT DATEPART(yy,Orderdate) as Year,
        DATEPART(mm,Orderdate) as Month,
        SUM(LineTotal) as OrderTotal,
        COUNT_BIG(*) as LineCount
    FROM dbo.Orders o INNER JOIN dbo.OrderDetails od
        ON o.SalesOrderID = od.SalesOrderID
    GROUP BY DATEPART(yy,Orderdate),
        DATEPART(mm,Orderdate)
```

3. Enter and execute the following SELECT statement. On the Messages tab, you can see that SQL Server needs almost 1000 page reads to execute the statement.

```
SET STATISTICS IO ON
SELECT Year, Month, OrderTotal
    FROM dbo.vOrderDetails
    ORDER BY YEAR, MONTH
SET STATISTICS IO OFF
```

4. Enter and execute the following CREATE INDEX statement to create a unique clustered index on the vOrderDetails view.

```
CREATE UNIQUE CLUSTERED INDEX CLIDX_vOrderDetails_Year_Month
ON dbo.vOrderDetails(Year,Month)
```

5. Execute the following SELECT statement. Notice that SQL Server now needs only two page reads because the result is already calculated and stored in the index.

```
SET STATISTICS IO ON
SELECT Year, Month, OrderTotal
    FROM dbo.vOrderDetails
    ORDER BY YEAR, MONTH
SET STATISTICS IO OFF
```

6. If you have SQL Server 2005 Enterprise, Developer, or Evaluation editions installed, type and execute the following SELECT statement, which does not reference the view, and press Ctrl+L to request the estimated execution plan, which is shown below.

```
SELECT DATEPART(yy,Orderdate) as Year,
       SUM(LineTotal) as YearTotal
    FROM dbo.Orders o INNER JOIN dbo.OrderDetails od
        ON o.SalesOrderID = od.SalesOrderID
    GROUP BY DATEPART(yy,Orderdate)
```

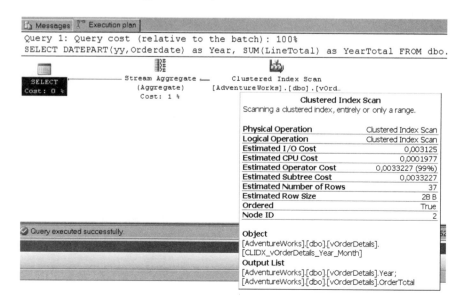

7. The preceding query plan shows that SQL Server uses the clustered index on the view to retrieve the data because it is more efficient to create the YearTotal aggregate by summing up the monthly aggregates found in the view. Thus, you can see that the presence of indexed views makes it possible to speed up a query without recoding the query itself.

8. Close SQL Server Management Studio.

Indexes that Speed Up Join Operations

Join operators are used to join together tables or intermediate results. SQL Server uses three types of join operators.

- Nested Loop Joins use one join input as the inner input table and the other join input as the outer input table. Nested loops scan once through the each inner input row and search for the corresponding row in the outer input. When an index exists on the columns of the join condition of the outer input, SQL Server can use an index seek to find the rows in the outer input. If no index exists, SQL Server has to use scan operators to find matching rows in the outer input for every row of the inner input. Nested loops are always used when the inner input has only a few rows because, in that case, it is the most efficient join operation.

- Merge Joins are used when the join inputs are sorted on their join columns. In a merge join operation SQL Server scans once through the sorted inputs and merges the data together, like closing a zipper. The merge join operation is very efficient, but data has to be sorted in advance, which means that indexes have to exist on the join columns. If no index exists, SQL Server can decide to sort the input first, but this is not done very often because sorting data is generally inefficient.

- Hash Joins are used on large, unsorted, non-indexed inputs. Hash joins use hashing operations on join columns to join inputs together. To calculate and store the result of a hash operation, SQL Server needs more memory and CPU processing than other join operations.

Examining Join Operations

1. Open SQL Server Management Studio. Open a New Query window and change the database context to AdventureWorks.

2. Enter and execute the following statement, and don't forget to include the actual execution plan. The code for this example is included in the sample files as Examining Join Operations.sql. The query plan of this statement is shown below. You can see that SQL Server uses an index seek to retrieve the rows of the inner input (data from the OrderDetails table) and then uses a Nested Loop Join operator because there is only one matching row in the outer input (data from the Orders table). The matching rows of the outer input are retrieved with an index seek as well because a matching index exists. SQL Server only needs five page reads to retrieve the data, as you can see on the Messages tab.

```
SET STATISTICS IO ON
```

```
SELECT o.SalesOrderID, o.OrderDate, od.ProductID
FROM dbo.Orders o INNER JOIN dbo.OrderDetails od
ON o.SalesOrderID = od.SalesOrderID
WHERE o.SalesOrderID = 43659
```

```
Query 1: Query cost (relative to the batch): 100%
SELECT o.SalesOrderID, o.OrderDate, od.ProductID FROM dbo.Order
```

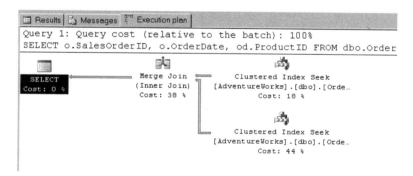

3. Change the query to retrieve more than one SalesOrderID. In this case, SQL Server uses a merge join because the sorted rows exist in an index and the inner input has many rows. Enter and execute the following query. You will see that SQL Server needs 19 page reads to execute this query.

```
SELECT o.SalesOrderID, o.OrderDate, od.ProductID
FROM dbo.Orders o INNER JOIN dbo.OrderDetails od
ON o.SalesOrderID = od.SalesOrderID
WHERE o.SalesOrderID BETWEEN 43659 AND 44000
```

```
Results   Messages   Execution plan
Query 1: Query cost (relative to the batch): 100%
SELECT o.SalesOrderID, o.OrderDate, od.ProductID FROM dbo.Order
```

```
SELECT            Merge Join          Clustered Index Seek
Cost: 0 %        (Inner Join)       [AdventureWorks].[dbo].[Orde...
                 Cost: 38 %              Cost: 18 %

                                        Clustered Index Seek
                                     [AdventureWorks].[dbo].[Orde...
                                        Cost: 44 %
```

4. Enter and execute the following batch, which drops the supporting indexes.

```
DROP INDEX CLIDX_Orders_SalesOrderID
ON dbo.Orders

DROP INDEX CLIDX_OrderDetails
ON dbo.OrderDetails
```

5. Re-execute the SELECT statements you used before (shown again below) and examine how the query plans and I/O have changed.

```
SELECT o.SalesOrderID, o.OrderDate, od.ProductID
FROM dbo.Orders o INNER JOIN dbo.OrderDetails od
ON o.SalesOrderID = od.SalesOrderID
```

```
WHERE o.SalesOrderID = 43659

SELECT o.SalesOrderID, o.OrderDate, od.ProductID
FROM dbo.Orders o INNER JOIN dbo.OrderDetails od
ON o.SalesOrderID = od.SalesOrderID
WHERE o.SalesOrderID BETWEEN 43659 AND 44000
```

```
Query 1: Query cost (relative to the batch): 48%
SELECT o.SalesOrderID, o.OrderDate, od.ProductID FROM dbo.Ord
```

```
         [  ]                    [  ]                        [  ]
      SELECT          Nested Loops  ─────         Table Scan
      Cost: 0 %       (Inner Join)          [AdventureWorks].[dbo].[Orde...
                      Cost: 8 %                  Cost: 17 %

                                                     [  ]
                                               Table Scan
                                         [AdventureWorks].[dbo].[Orde...
                                               Cost: 75 %
```

```
Query 2: Query cost (relative to the batch): 52%
SELECT o.SalesOrderID, o.OrderDate, od.ProductID FROM dbo.Ord
```

```
         [  ]                    [  ]                        [  ]
      SELECT          Hash Match  ─────          Table Scan
      Cost: 0 %       (Inner Join)          [AdventureWorks].[dbo].[Orde...
                      Cost: 15 %                 Cost: 16 %

                                                     [  ]
                                               Table Scan
                                         [AdventureWorks].[dbo].[Orde...
                                               Cost: 69 %
```

The preceding query plan shows that SQL Server uses a nested loop join again for the first query, because the inner input is small, and a hash join for the second query, because the input data is no longer sorted. Because no supporting indexes exist, SQL Server has to scan the entirety of the base tables in both cases, which requires about 1000 page reads for both queries.

As you have seen in this section, it is very important to have supporting indexes for joins. As a general rule, all foreign key constraints should be indexed because they are the join conditions for almost all queries.

Data Distribution and Statistics

In the last example, you saw that SQL Server chooses different Join operators based on the input size for the joins. Also, for other operations, like index seeks or scans, SQL Server needs to know how many rows are affected to determine the best operator to use. This determination is made based on statistics because SQL Server needs to make it before actually accessing the data. These statistics are created and updated automatically on a column basis by SQL Server using the steps detailed below:

1.   A query is submitted to SQL Server.

2. SQL Server Query Optimizer starts by determining which data has to be accessed.

3. SQL Server looks for statistics on the columns accessed.

   ❑ If statistics already exist and are up to date, SQL Server can proceed.

   ❑ When no statistics exist, SQL Server generates new statistics.

   ❑ When statistics exist but they are not up to date, SQL Server calculates new statistics for the data.

4. SQL Server Optimizer proceeds with generating the query plan.

This is the default behavior, and it is the best choice for most databases. You can use the ALTER DATABASE statement to tell SQL Server that it should update statistics asynchronously, which means that it won't wait for the new statistics when generating a query plan. Of course, this means that the query plan generated may not be optimal because old statistics were used to create it. In special situations, it can be desirable to generate or update statistics manually. This can be done with the CREATE STATISTICS or UPDATE STATISTICS statements. It is also possible to turn off automatic index creation and updating with the ALTER DATABASE statement at the database level. All of these options should be used only in special situations because the default behavior works best in most cases. To learn more about these options, read the whitepaper "Statistics Used by the Query Optimizer in Microsoft SQL Server 2005" at *http://www.microsoft.com/technet/prodtechnol/sql/2005/qrystats.mspx.*

Viewing Data Distribution Statistics

1. Open SQL Server Management Studio. Open a New Query window and change the database context to AdventureWorks.

2. To get information on which statistics exist, you can query the *sys.stats* and *sys.stats_columns* views. Enter and execute the following query to find out which statistics exist for the dbo:OrderDetails table. The code for this example is included in the sample files as DataDistributionStatistics.sql.

```
SELECT NAME, COL_NAME ( s.object_id , column_id ) as CNAME
FROM sys.stats s INNER JOIN sys.stats_columns sc
ON s.stats_id = sc.stats_id
AND s.object_id = sc.object_id
WHERE s.object_id = OBJECT_ID('dbo.OrderDetails')
ORDER BY NAME;
```

The result tells us the names of the statistics, and the columns for which they are calculated. Statistics for indexed columns are named like the corresponding index. The statistics with names starting with _WA_Sys_ are statistics SQL Server created automatically for columns without indexes.

3. To get statistics information from a statistic the DBCC SHOW_STATISTICS statement can be used. Enter and execute the following statement to show the statistics for the LineTotal column of the dbo.OrderDetails table.

```
DBCC SHOW_STATISTICS('dbo.OrderDetails', 'NCL_OrderDetail_LineTotal')
```

The results pane shown below displays part of the output of the DBCCSHOW_ STATISTICS statement. The first part displays general information, such as creation date, the number of rows in the table, and how many of the rows are sampled. Data density information is also displayed. Density is a value that shows how distinct values in the column are. Besides this general information SQL Server defines ranges within the data called steps and stores distribution statistics for these steps. With these distribution statistics SQL Server can estimate the number of rows affected when searching for a specific value by using the statistics for the range the specific values belong to. For every step, SQL Server stores the following information:

- RANGE_HI_KEY is the upper boundary value of the step.

- EQ_ROWS is the number of rows that are equal to the RANGE_HI_KEY.

- RANGE_ROWS is the number of rows in the range, without the boundaries.

- DISTINCT_RANGE_ROWS is the number of distinct values within the range.

- AVG_RANGE_ROWS is the average number of duplicate values within the range.

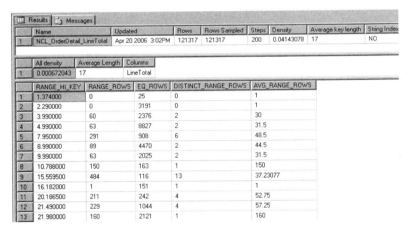

4.   Close SQL Server Management Studio.

Index Fragmentation

When a clustered index is created, the data is stored in the leaf level in a sorted order. In nonclustered indexes, the index keys are sorted and stored in the leaf level. To get the best performance from the leaf level, pages of indexes are ordered not only logically, but also physically. SQL Server stores these index pages in the appropriate physical order to be able to read the data as fast as possible from the disk. The most expensive part of reading data from disks is moving the arm of the disk. When the data pages to be read are ordered sequentially, the amount of arm movement needed is minimized, thus optimizing read performance.

When data is inserted into a table, it is stored at a specific page of a clustered index leaf-level page. The index keys of the nonclustered index also have to be inserted onto the right pages of the nonclustered index leaf-level pages. If this page is full, SQL Server has to perform a page split, which means allocating a new page and linking the new page to the appropriate index. This situation leads to index fragmentation, which means that the logical order of the data pages no longer matches the physical order. Index fragmentation can also happen as a result of UPDATE and DELETE statements.

To reduce fragmentation, the FILLFACTOR option can be used at index creation, which defines to what percentage leaf-level pages of indexes should be filled when the indexes are created. With a lower FILLFACTOR, fragmentation is less likely to occur because more entries can be made into a leaf-level page without the page splitting. On the other hand, a lower FILL-FACTOR will yield a larger index because less data is initially stored on each leaf-level page.

When the table being indexed is not a read-only table, its indexes will fragment sooner or later. Fragmented indexes can be defragmented to improve the speed of data access by using the ALTER INDEX statement. There are two options for defragmentation:

- **REORGANIZE**   Reorganizing an index means that the leaf-level pages are sorted using a bubble sort operation. REORGANIZE sorts only the data pages, not the entries within the page, which means that a FILLFACTOR cannot be used while reorganizing.

- **REBUILD**   Rebuilding an index means that the whole index is rebuilt. This takes longer than reorganizing the index, but has better results. A FILLFACTOR option can be supplied to fill the pages to the desired percentage again. If no FILLFACTOR option is supplied, leaf-level pages are filled completely. The ONLINE option can also be supplied when rebuilding indexes. When the option is not supplied, the rebuild is performed offline, which means that the table is locked throughout the rebuild. Offline rebuilding is faster than online rebuilding, but because it locks the data, it cannot be used during times when data access is required.

Maintaining Indexes

1. Open SQL Server Management Studio. Open a New Query window and change the database context to AdventureWorks.

2. To retrieve fragmentation information, use the rowset function sys.dm_db_physical_stats. Enter and execute the following statement to retrieve the list of indexes with a fragmentation over 50%. The code for this section is included in the sample files as IndexFragmentation.sql.

```
SELECT object_name(i.object_id) as object_name ,i.name as IndexName
    ,ps.avg_fragmentation_in_percent
    ,avg_page_space_used_in_percent
FROM sys.dm_db_index_physical_stats(db_id(), NULL, NULL, NULL , 'DETAILED') as ps
INNER JOIN sys.indexes as i
ON i.object_id = ps.object_id
    AND i.index_id = ps.index_id
WHERE ps.avg_fragmentation_in_percent > 50
AND ps.index_id > 0
ORDER BY 1
```

3. To perform an online rebuild of the PK_Employee_EmployeeID index, enter and execute the following statement.

```
ALTER INDEX PK_Employee_EmployeeID
ON HumanResources.Employee
REBUILD
WITH (ONLINE = ON)
```

4. Close SQL Server Management Studio.

> **Note**   Usually the process of index defragmentation will be automated. This can be done using a maintenance plan (see the SQL Server Books Online topic titled "How to: Create a Maintenance Plan") or through writing your own scripts, which can be scheduled using SQL Server Agent.

Tuning Queries Using the Database Engine Tuning Advisor

Creating the right indexes for a database project is not an easy job. To do this, a lot of factors must be considered:

■ The data model of the database

■ The amount and distribution of the data within the tables

■ Which queries are performed against the database

■ How often the queries occur

■ How often the data is updated

To help in designing indexes, SQL Server offers a tool called the Database Engine Tuning Advisor. The Database Engine Tuning Advisor requires a workload file, which can be a text file with the statements to be optimized, or a trace file, which can be produced with SQL Server Profiler. The Database Engine Tuning Advisor then optimizes the database using the SQL Server Query Optimizer and the existing database to suggest changes in physical design structures, like creating, changing, or removing various indexes.

Using the Database Engine Tuning Advisor

1. Start SQL Server Management Studio. Open a New Query window and change the database context to AdventureWorks.

2. Enter the following statements, which you will optimize with the Database Engine Tuning Advisor. The code for this example is included in the sample files as UsingDatabaseEngineTuningAdvisor.sql.

```
USE AdventureWorks;

SELECT o.SalesOrderID, o.OrderDate, od.ProductID
```

```
    FROM dbo.Orders o INNER JOIN dbo.OrderDetails od
    ON o.SalesOrderID = od.SalesOrderID
    WHERE o.SalesOrderID = 43659;

SELECT o.SalesOrderID, o.OrderDate, od.ProductID
    FROM dbo.Orders o INNER JOIN dbo.OrderDetails od
    ON o.SalesOrderID = od.SalesOrderID
    WHERE o.SalesOrderID BETWEEN 43659 AND 44000;
```

3. To save this script as a workload file, open the File menu and select Save As. Save the query as dta.sql.

4. From SQL Server Management Studio, select Database Engine Tuning Advisor from the Tools menu. Connect to your SQL Server instance.

5. Choose the file you saved in step 3 as the workload file and choose AdventureWorks as the database to tune as shown below:

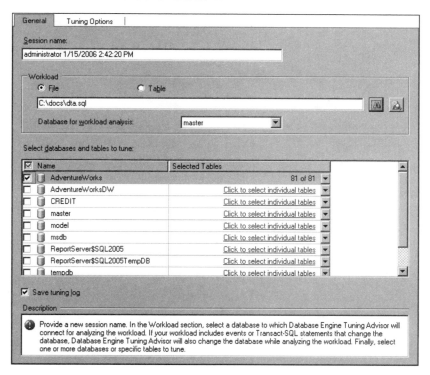

6. Press the Start Analysis button on the toolbar.

7. After the analysis finishes, the window displays the recommendations, as shown here:

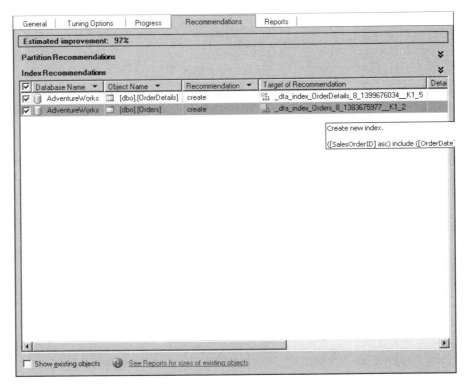

8. Database Engine Tuning Advisor recommends building two indexes. To save the script for generating the indexes, select Save Recommendations from the Actions menu.

9. Close Database Engine Tuning Advisor.

As you can see, SQL Server tries to optimize the two queries as well as it can. This is beneficial only if these queries should be optimized without concern for the effects of optimization on other database operations. To optimize all database indexes, it is a good idea to use a SQL Server Profiler trace, which provides the Database Engine Tuning Advisor with a normal workload for the whole database. With this information, Database Engine Tuning Advisor can optimize queries with other workloads on the database. After analyzing a workload, be sure to save and review the recommendations.

Conclusion

In this chapter, you have learned how SQL Server stores and accesses data with and without indexes. Through analyzing query plans and I/O statistics, you have seen how important it is that the right indexes exist to optimize performance. You have learned when and how to use different index types (summarized in the table opposite) and how to maintain them.

Index Types

Clustered index	Stores the table data rows in the leaf level of the indexes. Provides fast sorted and range access based on the index keys. Only one clustered index can exist on a table.
Nonclustered index	Provides fast index seek operations based on index keys and can be created as covered indexes. Up to 249 can exist on a table.
Computed column index	Stores computed columns and provides fast access when the computed column is used as a search argument.
XML column index	Provides fast XQuery access to XML columns.
Indexed views	Stores the result of a view and provides faster access to the view. Useful when the view is queried often, especially with aggregates.

You have seen that it is important to find the right index design and that the Database Engine Tuning Advisor can be a great help in building the index design.

Chapter 6 Quick Reference

To	Do This
View an estimated query execution plan	Press Ctrl+L or choose Display Estimated Execution Plan from the Query menu.
View the actual query execution plan	Press Ctrl+M or choose Include Actual Execution Plan from the Query menu. The actual execution plan is displayed on the Execution Plan tab.
Create a clustered index	`CREATE UNIQUE CLUSTERED INDEX <index_name>` `    ON <table>(<column>)`
Create a nonclustered index	`CREATE [ UNIQUE ] NONCLUSTERED INDEX index_name` `    ON <object> ( column [ ASC | DESC ] [ ,...n ] )`
Create a primary XML index	`CREATE PRIMARY XML INDEX index_name` `    ON <object> ( xml_column_name )`

Create a secondary XML index	`CREATE XML INDEX index_name`
	`    ON <object> ( xml_column_name )`
	`    USING XML INDEX xml_index_name`
	` FOR { VALUE
		PATH	PROPERTY }`

View data distribution	Query the sys.stats and sys.stats_columns views. For a specific column, use `DBCC SHOW_STATISTICS(<table>, <column>)`
Retrieve fragmentation information	Use the rowset function sys.dm_db_physical_stats.

Rebuild and defragment an index	`ALTER INDEX <index>`
	`ON <table>.<column>`
	`REBUILD`

Use the Database Engine Tuning Advisor	In the SQL Server Management Studio, select Database Engine Tuning Advisor from the Tools menu.

Chapter 7
Building Queries Dynamically

After completing this chapter, you will be able to:

- Build a query using SQL Server Management Studio's Query Builder
- Retrieve information about a database from the database's system tables
- Create simple queries dynamically, based on user input
- Format user input to sort and filter sophisticated dynamic queries
- Parse and reformat dates for use in a filter
- Protect your database from a "SQL-injection" attack
- Use *sp_executeSql* to submit a query

In the previous chapter, you learned how to increase the performance of your queries. Now you know how to create an efficient set of queries to give your users the most important information from your application using predefined queries in stored procedures or views.

However, in all but the simplest applications, there's no way to figure out ahead of time all the possible variations on what information your users will need or how they'll want it filtered and organized. Rather than try to plan for every possibility, you can give the users control over the information the application provides. This chapter will show you how to build queries dynamically based on choices that the user makes at runtime.

A User Interface for Building Queries

SQL Server Management Studio includes a sophisticated user interface for building queries. Let's take a quick tour of this query-building interface to give you an idea of how dynamic queries can be built. Your application won't need all the bells and whistles that SQL Server Management Studio provides. In fact, you will want to consider carefully how best to limit the choices your users can make.

Build a Query in SQL Server Management Studio's Query Builder

1. In SQL Server Management Studio, attach the AdventureWorks database if necessary, then expand the database in Object Explorer, as shown here:

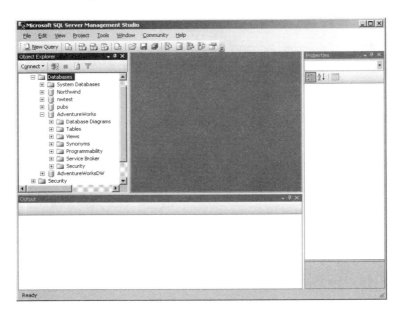

> **Tip**   Chapter 4, "Transferring Your Database to Other Systems," explains how to attach a database.

2. Expand the Tables node in the Object Explorer tree.

3. Scroll to find the Sales.Customer table. Right-click the table and choose Open Table from the context menu. The table will appear, as shown below. (The Properties window has been closed in this screenshot.)

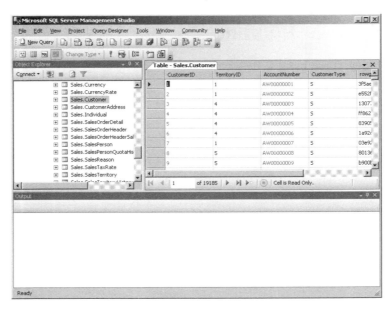

4. SQL Server Management Studio adds the Query Designer toolbar, shown below. The first three buttons on this toolbar display the tables for your query, the list of selected columns, and the actual SQL your query has generated, respectively.

5. Click the first (Show Diagram Pane) button, then select the CustomerID and Account-Number columns.

6. Click the second (Show Criteria Pane) button. Uncheck the Output checkbox in the * row. Click in the Sort Type column on the CustomerID row and select Ascending from the dropdown list.

7. Scroll to the right if necessary to see the Filter column. Again, on the CustomerID row, enter <10 and press the Enter key.

8. Click the third (Show SQL Pane) button. Your screen will look similar to the following:

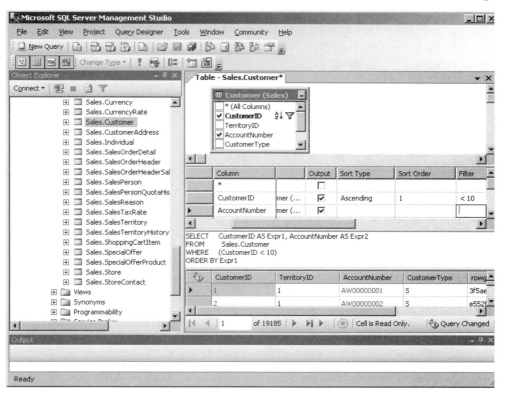

9. Notice the SQL query string that SQL Server Management Studio has generated for you in the SQL pane. Click the Execute SQL toolbar button. Nine records will be retrieved in your Results pane.

Your application's users will typically have nothing to do with the query string. They don't know anything about SQL. It's your job to create the query string correctly, either at design time or through your application's code at runtime. Constructing the query string dynamically at runtime allows you to base the query string on user input.

Retrieving Information about the Tables in a Database

To provide your user with a list of options your application will probably need to get information about the tables in your database. There are several ways to get that information. The most important method is to use the INFORMATION_SCHEMA schema. This schema is standard in every database.

Using INFORMATION_SCHEMA

INFORMATION_SCHEMA is a special schema contained in every database. It contains the definition for several objects inside the database.

INFORMATION_SCHEMA conforms to an ANSI standard that provides for retrieving information from any ANSI-compatible database engine. In the case of SQL Server, INFORMATION_SCHEMA consists of a set of views that query the database's sys* tables, which contain information about the database structure. You can query these tables directly, just as you can query any database table. In most cases, however, it is better to use the INFORMATION_SCHEMA views to retrieve information from the sys* tables.

> **Note**   INFORMATION_SCHEMA sometimes queries tables that you do not really need, which adversely affects performance. In the examples in this chapter, this isn't especially important because the application also has to wait for user input. You should keep this in mind, however, if speed is an important concern for your application.

The basic T-SQL code used to get information about the columns belonging to a table is:

```
SELECT TABLE_SCHEMA,
    TABLE_NAME,
    COLUMN_NAME,
    ORDINAL_POSITION,
    DATA_TYPE
FROM INFORMATION_SCHEMA.COLUMNS
WHERE TABLE_NAME = '<TABLE_NAME>')
```

Notice that you select the TABLE_SCHEMA field to obtain the schema for the table. This will be important for creating the appropriate query later. To experiment with the techniques in this chapter, start a new project in Visual Studio.

Starting a New Visual Studio Project

1.   Click Start | Programs | Microsoft Visual Studio 2005 | Microsoft Visual Studio 2005.

2. Choose File | New | Project from the Visual Studio menu.

3. Select the Visual Basic node in the Project Types pane and select the Windows Application template in the Templates pane. Name the project Chapter7 and click the OK button.

4. The application for this example is included in the sample files in the \Chapter7\DynQuery folder. You can cut and paste the code for the procedures that follow from the file Form1.vb.

Obtaining a List of Tables and Views

Typically, you will want to let the user choose the table in addition to the columns for a dynamic query, so you will have to give the user a list of tables from which to choose. Using the following query you can get the necessary information:

```
SELECT TABLE_SCHEMA, TABLE_NAME, TABLE_TYPE
    FROM INFORMATION_SCHEMA.TABLES
```

You can use this query in your application as follows.

Obtaining the Table List

1. Double-click the Form1 form that Visual Studio created for you. You will see the *Form1_Load* procedure. Declare two global variables and add a call to the *RetrieveTables* procedure in the *Form1_Load* procedure, so it looks like this:

```
Public Class Form1
    Dim SchemaName As String = "", TableName As String = ""
    Private Sub Form1_Load(ByVal sender As System.Object,
        ByVal e As System.EventArgs) Handles MyBase.Load
        RetrieveTables()
    End Sub
```

2. Now add the *RetrieveTables* procedure shown here beneath the *Form1_Load* procedure. For this code to work, you must have the AdventureWorks database attached to your SQLExpress Server. To learn about attaching databases to servers, see Chapter 4.

```
Sub RetrieveTables()
    Dim FieldName As String
    Dim MyConnection As New SqlClient.SqlConnection( _
        "Data Source=.\SQLExpress;" & _
        "Initial Catalog=AdventureWorks;Trusted_Connection=Yes;")
    Dim com As New SqlClient.SqlCommand( _
        "SELECT TABLE_SCHEMA, TABLE_NAME, TABLE_TYPE " & _
        "FROM INFORMATION_SCHEMA.TABLES", _
        MyConnection)
    MyConnection.Open()
    Dim dr As SqlClient.SqlDataReader = com.ExecuteReader
    With dr
        Do While .Read
            'You must preserve the information to use it in a Form or Page
            SchemaName = .GetString(0)
            TableName = .GetString(1)
            FieldName = .GetString(2)
```

```
            Console.WriteLine("{0} {1} {2}", _
                SchemaName, TableName, FieldName)
        Loop
        .Close()
    End With
    'Assume user has chosen the following schema and table:
    SchemaName = "Sales"
    TableName = "Customer"
End Sub
```

> **Note**   In a real application, the connection string and the SQL string would be main-
> tained in application resources or in the application config file.

3. Choose Start Debugging from the Debug menu to build and run your project. A blank
    form will appear and the schema information will be written to the Output pane in the
    Visual Studio window.

4. Close the form to end the application.

The preceding Visual Basic code initializes a *SqlCommand* object named *com* with the SQL
string you want to execute, then executes the *SqlCommand* object. This is the simplest way to
execute a T-SQL sentence from an application.

As an exercise, you can place the schemas and tables retrieved during the form's *Load* procedure into a user interface on the form so that the user can choose the schema and table to
work with. For the example in this chapter, we'll assume the user has selected the Sales
schema and the Customer table.

Once the user chooses the table, you can retrieve the list of columns for that table using the
same method but with the user's input as the name of the table in the query. To do that, you
can code a placeholder in the query string, then replace the placeholder through a call to
String.Format. In the code below, the placeholder in the query string is *{0}*.

Obtaining the Column List

1. Add the following *RetrieveColumns* procedure beneath the *RetrieveTables* procedure.

```
Sub RetrieveColumns(ByVal TableName As String)
    Dim MyConnection As New SqlClient.SqlConnection( _
        "Data Source=.\SQLExpress;" & _
        "Initial Catalog=AdventureWorks;Trusted_Connection=Yes;")
    Dim sqlStr As String
    sqlStr = "SELECT TABLE_SCHEMA, TABLE_NAME, COLUMN_NAME, " + _
            "ORDINAL_POSITION, DATA_TYPE " + _
            "FROM INFORMATION_SCHEMA.COLUMNS " + _
            "WHERE (TABLE_NAME = '{0}')"
    Dim tableColumns As New DataTable
    Dim da As New SqlClient.SqlDataAdapter( _
        String.Format(sqlStr, TableName), MyConnection)
    da.Fill(tableColumns)
    For i As Integer = 0 To tableColumns.Rows.Count - 1
        With tableColumns.Rows.Item(i)
```

```
                Console.WriteLine("{0} {1} {2}", _
                    .Item(1), .Item(2), .Item(3))
            End With
        Next
    End Sub
End Sub
```

2. In the *Form1_Load* procedure, add the following call to the *RetrieveColumns* procedure after the *RetrieveTables* procedure.

    ```
    RetrieveColumns(TableName)
    ```

3. Choose Start Debugging from the Debug menu to build and run the project. A blank form appears and the table and column information is written to the Output pane in the Visual Studio window.

4. Close the form to end the application.

The *DataTable* in the *RetrieveColumns* procedure can be used to fill a CheckListBox control or a ListView control with CheckBoxes enabled to let the user select the desired fields.

Add a ListView Control to the Form

1. Select the Form1.vb [Design] tab in the Visual Studio window.

2. Choose Toolbox from the View menu.

3. Drag and drop a Label control from the Toolbox onto your form. Right-click the label and select Properties from the context menu. In the Properties window, change the Label's text to *Columns*.

4. Now drag and drop a ListView control from the Toolbox onto your form. Your screen should look similar to this:

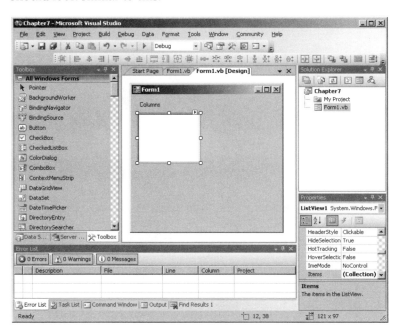

5. Drag the right border of the ListView to make the list wider. Right-click the ListView and select Properties from the context menu. In the Properties window, set the CheckBoxes property to True and set the View property to List.

6. Right-click the form and choose View Code from the context menu to return to your code. In the *RetrieveColumns* procedure, replace the *Console.WriteLine* statement with the following code:

```
ListView1.Items.Add(.Item(2))
```

7. Build and run your project. You will see a list of columns with checkboxes in the list on your form, as shown here:

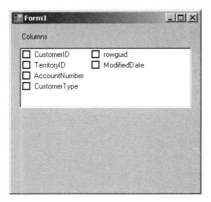

8. Close the form to end the application.

Once the user selects the table and columns they want to view, your application can create the query. The basic structure of a selection query includes a comma-separated list of columns, like this:

```
SELECT <Column1>, <Column2>, <Column3>
   FROM <Table_Name>
```

You can easily create the list of columns from your ListView control.

Format User Input for the Dynamic Query

1. Select the Form1.vb [Design] tab in the Visual Studio window.

2. Drag and drop a Button control below your ListView control. In the Properties window change the text to *Run Query*.

3. Double-click the button. Visual Studio creates a procedure called *Button1_Click*. Add the following code to this procedure:

```
Private Sub Button1_Click(ByVal sender As System.Object, _
    ByVal e As System.EventArgs) Handles Button1.Click
    Dim baseSQL As String = "SELECT {0} FROM {1}"
```

```
Dim sbFields As New System.Text.StringBuilder
Dim numChecked As Integer = 0
With sbFields
    For Each el As ListViewItem In ListView1.Items
        If el.Checked Then
            numChecked = numChecked + 1
            If .Length <> 0 Then
                .Append(",")
            End If
            Console.WriteLine(el.Text)
            .AppendFormat("[{0}]", el.Text)
        End If
    Next
End With
Console.WriteLine(sbFields)
End Sub
```

> **Note**   When you have to manipulate a string more than two times, it is better to use a *StringBuilder* object to achieve your result than to use string concatenation.

4. Build and run the project. Select some columns in the ListView control, click the Run Query button, and examine the comma-delimited list of columns displayed in the Output pane.

5. Close the form to end the application.

6. Finally, you can create the complete dynamic query statement by adding the column list and the name of the table. Because the tables can belong to a schema, it is a good idea to use the fully qualified name of the table in the query.

> **Tip**   In your application, if security is not an issue, you might want to display the query string in a TextBox control and let the user modify it before executing it. See the section "Parameters and Security in Dynamic Queries" for information about the security risks involved in allowing a user to directly modify query strings.

Build and Execute the Dynamic Query

1. Replace the *Console.WriteLine* statement at the end of the *Button1_Click* procedure with the following code, which builds the dynamic query string:

```
Dim tblsql As String
Dim txtsql As String
tblsql = String.Format("{0}.{1}", SchemaName, TableName)
txtsql = String.Format(baseSQL, _
    sbFields.ToString, tblsql)
```

2. Now add the following code at the end of the *Button1_Click* procedure to execute the dynamic query. For this example, the first 100 rows of the results are displayed in the Output pane. In a real application, you would use the *DataTable* as a *DataSource* for a

DataGridView control. DataGridView controls are ideal for displaying query results to the user.

```
Dim MyConnection As New SqlClient.SqlConnection( _
    "Data Source=.\SQLExpress;" & _
    "Initial Catalog=AdventureWorks;Trusted_Connection=Yes;")
Dim com As New SqlClient.SqlCommand(txtsql, MyConnection)
Dim tableResults As New DataTable
tableResults.Clear()
Dim da As New SqlClient.SqlDataAdapter(com)
da.Fill(tableResults)
For i As Integer = 0 To tableResults.Rows.Count - 1
    With tableResults.Rows.Item(i)
        Dim rowstr As New System.Text.StringBuilder
        For j As Integer = 0 To numChecked - 1
            rowstr.Append(.Item(j))
            rowstr.Append(" ")
        Next
        Console.WriteLine(rowstr)
    End With
    If i > 100 Then Exit For
Next
```

3. Build and run the project. Select some columns in the ListView control and click the Run Query button. The results of the dynamic query are displayed in the Output pane. You can select different columns and click the button again to build and execute a different dynamic query.

4. Close the form to end the application.

Executing a Dynamic Query on Behalf of Another Account

One of the best security practices is to deny READ permission on tables to avoid unauthorized access, so sometimes an application needs to execute a query dynamically generated by the user but using other credentials.

In SQL Server 2005, you can use the EXECUTE command to act as another user for a particular command. The syntax for the EXECUTE command is:

```
EXECUTE ('<dynamic query>') as USER='<User Name>'
```

Caution   This is a very dangerous idea. As you will see later in the chapter, it leads to a potential security risk. To avoid security breaches, your application has to be sure what kind of query it is executing.

Sorting and Filtering Dynamically

If a query returns a large set of records, the results will be more useful if the user can define the order in which the rows are returned and which rows should be filtered out.

Adding a Sort Order to a Dynamic Query

To sort a dynamic query, just append the ORDER BY clause followed by a list of columns in the order indicated by the user. If the user wants to get the information in descending order, also append the DESC keyword.

In the following code, the order selections are stored in a special collection called *SortInfo*, a custom class designed to store all the information needed for each order selection.

```
Public Class SortInfo
    Public SchemaName As String
    Public TableName As String
    Public ColumnName As String
    Public SortOrder As SortOrder
    Public SortPosition As Integer
End Class
```

To create the order list, the code goes through this list, adding the definition into a String-Builder, and in case some ordering is defined, adds the ORDER TO clause at the beginning of the StringBuilder content.

```
For Each o As System.Collections.Generic.KeyValuePair( _
            Of Integer, SortInfo) In OrderList
    With sbOrderBy
        If .Length <> 0 Then
            .Append(",")
        End If
        .AppendFormat("[{0}].[{1}]", o.Value.TableName, _
                o.Value.ColumnName)
        If o.Value.SortOrder = SortOrder.Descending Then
            .Append(" DESC")
        End If
    End With
Next
If sbOrderBy.Length > 0 Then
    sbOrderBy.Insert(0, " ORDER BY ")
End If
```

Filtering a Dynamic Query

Adding filtering to a query is a bit more complicated than adding a sort order. You have to take into account the many different operators and datatypes. The results, however, are worth the effort. Again, our starting point is the base syntax of the WHERE clause filtering expression in a SELECT statement:

```
SELECT <Field_List>
FROM <Table_Name>
WHERE <Condition_List>
ORDER BY <Order_List>
```

The condition list has to be constructed using the following guidelines:

- Use the <ColumnName> <compare operator> <value> pattern.

- Match the value datatype with the column datatype.

- Add additional filters to the Condition_List using the AND or OR keywords.

You have to implement a user interface for the user to specify values and comparison operators for each filter. The goal is to take the user's input and create a string with the filter conditions that you can then insert into the dynamic query.

A Full-Fledged Dynamic Query Sample Application

The following examples are based on The Dynamic Queries sample application included in the Filters folder in the Chapter 7 sample files. The Dynamic Queries sample application is a fleshed-out version of the application you've created so far in this chapter. It includes a List-View control that shows all the selections made by the user in order to construct a dynamic query, as shown in Figure 7-1. To try this yourself, perform the procedure below.

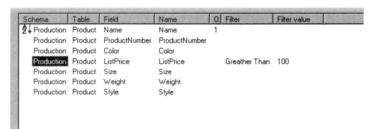

Figure 7-1   ListView control with information about the query the user wants to create.

Run the Dynamic Queries Sample Application

1. Double-click the Ch07.sln file in the Chapter07\Filters folder to open the project in Visual Studio.

2. Choose Start Debugging from the Debug menu. Select your server and click the OK button. Visual Studio builds and runs the project, displaying an initial form, as shown here:

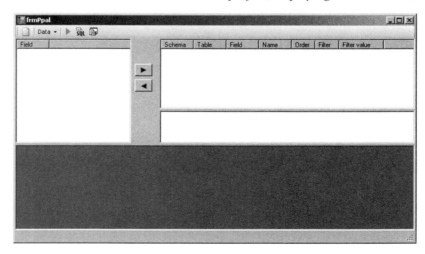

3. In the frmPpal form, click the Data dropdown list on the toolbar, then select Table | Sales | Customer.

4. Select the CustomerID, TerritoryID, and AccountNumber items in the listbox and click the right-arrow icon in the middle of the form.

5. Click the Build Query button on the toolbar. Your screen now displays the fields you've selected in the upper right and the corresponding SQL query in the lower right, like this:

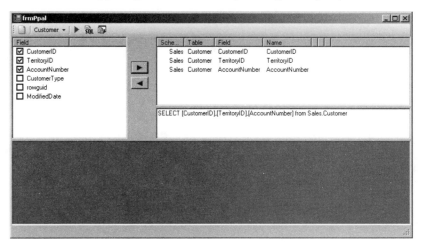

6. Right-click in the CustomerID row and choose Order | Ascending from the context menu.

7. Right-click again in the CustomerID row and choose Filter from the context menu. In the Filter dialog box, choose Less_Than in the dropdown list and enter *20* in the text-box. Click the OK button.

8. Again click the Build Query button on the toolbar. The dynamic query now looks like this:

```
SELECT [CustomerID],[TerritoryID],[AccountNumber]
FROM Sales.Customer WHERE [CustomerID] < 20
ORDER BY [Customer].[CustomerID]
```

9. Click the Execute Query button to execute the dynamic query. The screen will display the results:

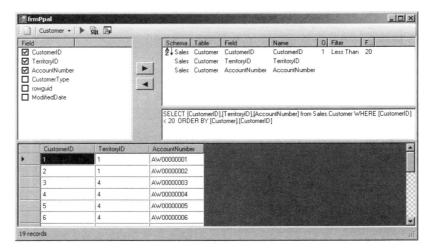

How the Sample Application Builds Its Filter String

The application stores the different values shown in the upper right of the form in a ListView control, named *lvUseFields*, as shown in Table 7-1.

Table 7-1   **Fields in the *lvUseFields* ListView**

Property	Contains
Text	Schema name
SubItems(1)	Table name
SubItems(2)	Field name
SubItems(3)	Name (Alias for the result column)
SubItems(4)	Order position
SubItems(5)	Filter operator
SubItems(6)	Filter value

When you click the Build Query button on the toolbar, the following code builds the dynamic query using the contents of the *lvUseFields* ListView control. Pay particular attention to the section of code shown in bold, which demonstrates how to build the WHERE clause for filtering the dynamic query.

```
Private Sub tsbGen_Click(ByVal sender As System.Object, _
    ByVal e As System.EventArgs) Handles tsbGen.Click
    Dim baseSQL As String = "SELECT {0} from {1}"
    'List of Fields to show
    Dim sbFields As New System.Text.StringBuilder
    'List of columns order
    Dim sbOrderBy As New System.Text.StringBuilder("")
    'Filters
    Dim sbFilter As New System.Text.StringBuilder("")
    With sbFields
        For Each el As ListViewItem In lvUseFields.Items
            If .Length <> 0 Then
```

```vb
        .Append(",")
End If
'Add the Column in the list of fields
.AppendFormat("[{0}]", _
    el.SubItems(UseFieldsColumnsEnum.Field).Text)
'If the Name is different than the column name, add the Alias
If el.SubItems(UseFieldsColumnsEnum.Name).Text <> _
    el.SubItems(UseFieldsColumnsEnum.Field).Text Then
    .AppendFormat(" AS [{0}]", _
        el.SubItems(UseFieldsColumnsEnum.Name).Text)
End If
'If there is a filter...
If el.SubItems(UseFieldsColumnsEnum.Filter).Text <> "" Then
    With sbFilter
        If .Length > 0 Then
            .Append(" AND ")
        End If
        'Add the column name to the list of filters
        .AppendFormat("[{0}]", el.SubItems( _
            UseFieldsColumnsEnum.Field).Text)
        'Add the operator
        Select Case CType([Enum].Parse( _
            GetType(FilterTypeEnum), _
            el.SubItems(UseFieldsColumnsEnum.Filter _
            ).Text.Replace(" ", "_")), FilterTypeEnum)
            Case FilterTypeEnum.Equal
                .Append(" = ")
            Case FilterTypeEnum.Not_Equal
                .Append(" <> ")
            Case FilterTypeEnum.Greather_Than
                .Append(" >")
            Case FilterTypeEnum.Less_Than
                .Append(" < ")
            Case FilterTypeEnum.Like
                .Append(" LIKE ")
            Case FilterTypeEnum.Between
                .Append(" BETWEEN ")
        End Select
        'Get the Data type from the columns definition
        Dim Typename As String = _
            tableColumns.Select(String.Format("COLUMN_NAME='{0}'", _
            el.SubItems(UseFieldsColumnsEnum.Field).Text))(0).Item( _
            "DATA_TYPE").ToString
        'When the data type is one with characters values,
        'the value must be enclosed by apostrophes
        If Typename.ToUpper.IndexOf("CHAR") > -1 _
            OrElse Typename.ToUpper.IndexOf("TEXT") > -1 Then
            .Append("'")
        End If
        .Append(el.SubItems(UseFieldsColumnsEnum.Filter_Value).Text)
        'If the operator is Like, append the wildcard '%'
        If CType([Enum].Parse(GetType(FilterTypeEnum), _
        el.SubItems(UseFieldsColumnsEnum.Filter).Text.Replace( _
            " ", "_")), FilterTypeEnum) = FilterTypeEnum.Like Then
            .Append("%")
```

```
                              End If
                              If Typename.ToUpper.IndexOf("CHAR") > -1 _
                              OrElse Typename.ToUpper.IndexOf("TEXT") > -1 Then
                                    .Append("'")
                              End If
                        End With
                  End If
            Next
      End With
      'Add the Order
      For Each o As System.Collections.Generic.KeyValuePair( _
                  Of Integer, SortInfo) In OrderList
            With sbOrderBy
                  If .Length <> 0 Then
                        .Append(",")
                  End If
                  .AppendFormat("[{0}].[{1}]", o.Value.TableName, o.Value.ColumnName)
                  If o.Value.SortOrder = SortOrder.Descending Then
                        .Append(" DESC")
                  End If
            End With
      Next
      If sbOrderBy.Length > 0 Then
            sbOrderBy.Insert(0, " ORDER BY ")
      End If
      If sbFilter.Length > 0 Then
            sbFilter.Insert(0, " WHERE ")
      End If
      'The query string has to be: SELECT columns FROM table,
      'then WHERE and finally ORDER
      txtsql.Text = _
            String.Format(baseSQL, _
            sbFields.ToString, _
            String.Format("{0}.{1}", SchemaName, TableName)) & _
            sbFilter.ToString & " " & sbOrderBy.ToString
End Sub
```

Considerations for Formatting a Filter String

As you build the filter, for each column whose datatype is one that contains characters (char, nchar, varchar, nvarchar, text, or ntext), the values compared to that column must be enclosed by apostrophes (').

When filtering a smalldatetime or datetime datatype, your code depends on the country and cultural settings for your user's machine. Can you assume that the date "11/10/05" is November 10, 2005, or is it October 11, 2005, or could it be October 5, 2011? This can be a real problem in any application, but it is even more significant issue if you are constructing an application for the Web. In that case, you must consider users from all around the world.

The simplest solution can be instructing the user about how to enter dates. It would be better to have a solution so that users don't have to be trained. SQL Server uses the date formats defined by the cultural settings in the server's host operating system. Nevertheless, it always recognizes the ISO format, which matches the following pattern: yyyy-mm-dd.

If you use the CultureInfo setting on the user's machine, you can get a DateTime value. Use that value to create the appropriate comparison value in your filter. In addition, just to be sure you are sending the appropriate string to SQL Server, you can also use the *CONVERT* function. Here's how to do all this:

```
Dim theDate As Date = DateTime.Parse(el.SubItems(1).Text, _
    System.Globalization.CultureInfo.CurrentCulture.DateTimeFormat)
sparam = String.Format("Convert(datetime,'{0}-{1}-{2}',120)", _
    theDate.Year, _
    theDate.Month, _
    theDate.Day)
```

The *tsbGen_Click* procedure generates the following dynamic query using the fields shown in Figure 7-1.

```
SELECT [Name],
    [ProductNumber],
    [Color],
    [ListPrice],
    [Size],
    [Weight],
    [Style]
FROM Production.Product
WHERE [ListPrice] >100
ORDER BY [Product].[Name]
```

Parameters and Security in Dynamic Queries

Creating queries using values entered by the user is a significant security risk, especially if the application is a public Web site, in which case you don't know who the user is or how much knowledge the user has. If the user knows about SQL syntax, they can break into your database using a technique known as a "SQL-injection" attack.

How SQL-Injection Attacks Work

Let's consider a very simple example. Imagine a public Web site that lets the user search for products online. In the site, the application allows the user to find products using part of the name, so it builds and uses a simple dynamic query like this:

```
SqlDataSource1.SelectCommand = _
    "SELECT ProductNumber, Name,  ListPrice " _
    "FROM Production.Product WHERE Name LIKE '" _
    & TextBox1.Text & "%'"
Me.GridView1.DataBind()
```

The user can enter the first characters of a name in a Search By textbox and the code will search for products whose name begins with those characters, as shown in Figure 7-2.

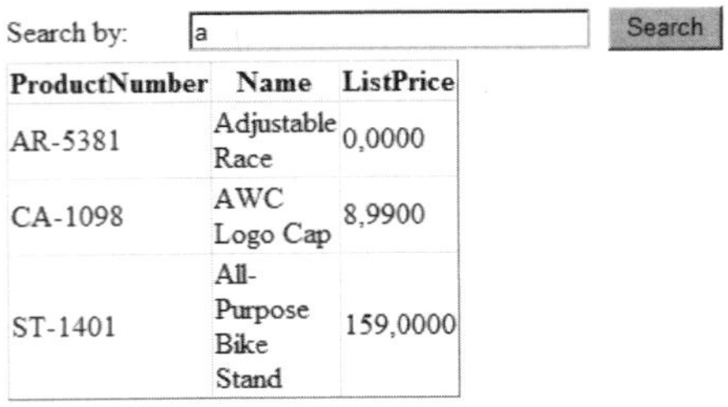

ProductNumber	Name	ListPrice
AR-5381	Adjustable Race	0,0000
CA-1098	AWC Logo Cap	8,9900
ST-1401	All-Purpose Bike Stand	159,0000

Figure 7-2 A simple application that uses text from a textbox to build a dynamic query.

Well, as a SQL expert, even if you know nothing about the application, you can imagine that behind the scenes it is running code similar to what you've learned in this chapter. You can check if you're right. What happens if you enter the following in the Search By textbox?

```
a' UNION select @@Version, @@SERVERNAME, 0;--
```

In fact, you will get the result shown in Figure 7-3 because the unsophisticated application turns the user's input into the following SQL statements:

```
SELECT
    ProductNumber,
    Name,
    ListPrice
FROM Production.Product
WHERE Name LIKE 'a'
UNION
select @@Version,@@SERVERNAME,0;--%'
```

Notice the close-quote character (') and the comment characters (- -)that the sneaky user has used to transform the dynamic query into multiple valid SQL statements.

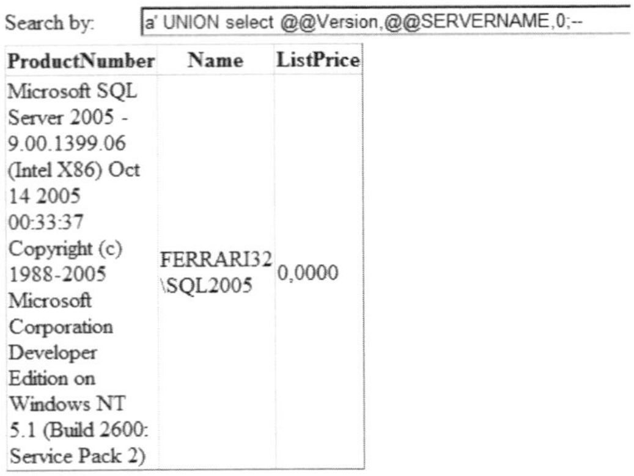

ProductNumber	Name	ListPrice
Microsoft SQL Server 2005 - 9.00.1399.06 (Intel X86) Oct 14 2005 00:33:37 Copyright (c) 1988-2005 Microsoft Corporation Developer Edition on Windows NT 5.1 (Build 2600: Service Pack 2)	FERRARI32 \SQL2005	0,0000

Figure 7-3 The user has performed a SQL-injection attack by entering a SQL command in the textbox.

Now you know which database engine is running on the server and you know its name, but more importantly, you know that the server can execute your commands. If you want to give yourself maximum permission on the server, you can create your own user!

> **Tip** If you can't remember the exact syntax for a particular command, you can use SQL Server Management Studio to create a script that you can use to refresh your memory.

The following code creates the user BadBoy and adds it to the server role sysadmin!

```
USE [master]
CREATE LOGIN [BadBoy] WITH PASSWORD='Mad', DEFAULT_DATABASE=[master],
CHECK_EXPIRATION=OFF, CHECK_POLICY=OFF
EXEC master.sp_addsrvrolemember @loginame = 'BadBoy',
    @rolename = 'sysadmin'
```

If you enter this in the textbox with a close-quote (') to end the WHERE clause and comment characters to eliminate the application-supplied close-quote, you will cause the application to generate and execute the following code to create a new user:

```
SELECT
    ProductNumber,
    Name,
    ListPrice
FROM Production.Product
WHERE Name LIKE 'a';
USE [master];
CREATE LOGIN [BadBoy] WITH
    PASSWORD='Mad',
    DEFAULT_DATABASE=[master],
    CHECK_EXPIRATION=OFF,
CHECK_POLICY=OFF;
EXEC master..sp_addsrvrolemember
    @loginame = 'BadBoy',
    @rolename = 'sysadmin';
--%'
```

In addition, you can check whether your user has been created by entering the following in the textbox:

```
a'
UNION
SELECT name,
    CONVERT(nvarchar(1), sysadmin) AS IsAdmin,
    0 AS Expr1
FROM sys.syslogins
WHERE (name = 'BadBoy')--%'
```

Doing so creates the following SQL statements:

```
SELECT ProductNumber,
    Name,
    ListPrice
```

```
FROM Production.Product
WHERE Name LIKE 'a'
UNION
SELECT name,
    CONVERT(nvarchar(1), sysadmin) AS IsAdmin,
    0 AS Expr1
FROM sys.syslogins
WHERE (name = 'BadBoy')--%'
```

How to Prevent SQL-Injection Attacks

Now you have a clear idea about what can occur, so take the time and effort to protect your database from this sort of attack by following a few simple guidelines.

- Avoid constructing a SQL sentence; use parameterization instead. In the same application as shown in Figure 7-2, use the following SQL sentence, which has a parameter, and link the parameter with the Search By textbox so that the text in the textbox will be treated strictly as a string. Any commands in the text will not be processed.

```
SELECT ProductNumber,
    Name,
    ListPrice
FROM Production.Product
WHERE (Name LIKE @Param1 + '%')
```

- Keep the queries inside Stored Procedures whenever possible.
- Use *sp_ExecuteSql* to submit your query to SQL Server. This system stored procedure is explained in the next section.

How to Use sp_ExecuteSql

The *sp_executeSql* system stored procedure allows you to execute dynamically defined T-SQL sentences in the same way the EXECUTE command does. However, *sp_executeSql* requires you to define the parameters and their datatypes as well as the values for those parameters.

The first time *sp_executeSql* executes your query, it creates and preserves a query plan. Since the parameter definition is required, each time the sentence is executed subsequently, *sp_executeSql* simply updates the parameter values and uses the same query plan.

Because this system stored procedure needs a parameter definition, you can create complex queries not only for a SELECT statement, but for any database action your application requires. Your statements can even include output parameters.

Assume that you need to define a new reason for delayed production in the AdventureWorks database, and you are required to assign the new reason to all the work orders for which the due date is greater than the end date. You can use the following T-SQL script to accomplish both tasks in a single batch. This code is included in the sample files as newReason.sql.

```
--Variable for the T-SQL statement
DECLARE @sql nvarchar(300);
SET @sql='INSERT INTO [AdventureWorks].[Production].[ScrapReason]
            ([Name]
            ,[ModifiedDate])
     VALUES
            (@NewNameSQL
            ,GetDate()); '
SET @sql=@sql + 'SET @NewIdSQL=(SELECT ScrapReasonID ' +
                'FROM [AdventureWorks].[Production].[ScrapReason] ' +
                'WHERE Name=@NewNameSQL)'
-- Variable to get the new Id
DECLARE @NewId int;
-- Parameters declaration
DECLARE @Params nvarchar(200);
SET @Params='@NewNameSQL nvarchar(100), @NewIdSQL int OUTPUT';
-- New Name to add
DECLARE @NewName nvarchar(100);
SET @NewName='Delayed Production';
-- Execute the insert into ScrapReason
EXEC sp_executeSql @sql,@params,@NewNameSQL=@NewName,
    @NewIdSQL=@NewId OUTPUT;

/*
Change the T-SQL statement to update the ScrapReasonID
to this new one, for all the records with End Date greater than
Due Date
*/

SET @sql='UPDATE [AdventureWorks].[Production].[WorkOrder] ' +
         'SET ScrapReasonID=@NewIdSQL ' +
         'WHERE (EndDate > DueDate) AND (ScrapReasonID IS NULL)';
-- Define the parameter for this new sentence
SET @Params='@NewIdSQL int ';
EXEC sp_executeSql @sql, @params, @NewIdSQL=@NewId;
GO
```

As you can see, *sp_executeSql* allows you to apply parameters to dynamic SQL statements other than simple SELECT queries.

Conclusion

You now know how to gather user input and format it to build a query dynamically. You're aware of some of the pitfalls in constructing dynamic queries as well as some of the security risks.

Keep your database secure by constructing parameterized queries and executing them through the *sp_executeSql* stored procedure. You can even use these techniques to accomplish tasks beyond simply returning data to the user.

Chapter 7: Quick Reference

TO	DO THIS
Build a query in SQL Server Management Studio's Query Builder	Right-click a table in the Object Explorer, then choose Open Table from the context menu. Use the buttons on the Query Designer toolbar and the related panes to design your query.
Obtain a list of tables and views in a database	Execute the SQL statement `SELECT TABLE_SCHEMA, TABLE_NAME, TABLE_TYPEFROM INFORMATION_SCHEMA.TABLES`
Create queries dynamically	Concatenate the SELECT keyword followed by a list of column names and then the FROM keyword followed by a table name.
Sort the results	Add an ORDER BY clause followed by a list of column names. Add the DESC statement to arrange the information in descending order.
Filter the results	Add a WHERE clause (before the ORDER BY clause, if there is one), followed by the filter conditions.
Prevent SQL-injection attacks	Always use parameterized queries. Try to perform all the operations under an appropriate security context.
Enhance dynamic query execution	Use *sp_executeSql* to persist the query plan in the cache.

Chapter 8

Working with Data from Remote Data Sources

After completing this chapter, you will be able to:

- Open ad hoc connections to a variety of data sources using T-SQL
- Configure a linked server using T-SQL
- Configure a linked server using Microsoft SQL Server Management Studio
- Update data in remote data sources

In Chapter 4, "Transferring Your Database to Other Systems," you learned how to transfer local data to remote database servers, how to use the different replication options that SQL Server 2005 offers, and how to use SQL Server Integration Services to communicate with a variety of data sources.

In real-world applications, when you need to work with data from a remote data source, it is not always possible or desirable to set up a replication scheme; sometimes you just want to execute a single query or to extract the information in real time and not wait for replicated data.

In this chapter, we are going to focus on how to read data from remote data sources and how to write data to remote data sources in real time. These data sources can be either another SQL Server instance or a different data source, like a Microsoft Office Excel file or Microsoft Exchange Server.

When you want to read data from a remote data source, you need a way to declare the destination data source that you want to communicate with and what data you want to extract.

In applications that connect to a single database server, this is usually implemented using ADO.NET's *Connection* class. This chapter focuses on connecting to a remote data source from within SQL Server using T-SQL code when there is no ADO.NET available.

Reading Data from Remote Sources at the Middle Tier

Let's go back for a moment to using ADO.NET. To read data from remote sources from a middle-tier component, you need to open a *Connection* object to each of the different data sources that you want to communicate with and query each one of them independently for the data that you want to extract.

As Figure 8-1 shows, when taking this approach, the middle-tier code has to deal with querying each of the different data sources using each data source's access API and merging the collected result sets into a single result set.

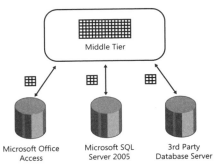

Figure 8-1   Architectural model for reading data from remote sources at the middle tier.

Reading Data from Remote Data Sources Using ADO.NET at the Middle Tier

Your middle-tier application must connect to each of the different data sources using the appropriate data access provider. For example:

- To connect to an Oracle database using ADO.NET:

```
'Connect to pacific sales
Dim oracleConn As OracleConnection = New OracleConnection()
oracleConn.ConnectionString = "Data Source=MyOracleDB;Integrated Security=yes"
Dim oracleDA As New OracleDataAdapter("SELECT * FROM PacificSales", oracleConn)
```

- To connect to an Excel file using ADO.NET:

```
'Connect to central sales
Dim excelConn As New OleDbConnection()
excelConn.ConnectionString = "Provider=Microsoft.Jet.OLEDB.4.0;" &_
    "Data Source=C:\CentralSales.xls;Extended Properties=""Excel 8.0"""
Dim excelDA As New OleDbDataAdapter("SELECT * FROM [Sales$]", excelConn)
```

- To connect to a SQL Server database using ADO.NET:

```
'Connect to atlantic sales
Dim sqlConn As New SqlConnection()
sqlConn.ConnectionString = _
    "Data Source=MySQLServer; Initial Catalog=MySQLDB; Integrated Security=SSPI"
Dim sqlDA As New SqlDataAdapter("SELECT * FROM AtlanticSales", sqlConn)
```

Then your middle-tier application must use a *DataSet* object to hold all the data coming from the different data sources, as in the following code snippet. (The code in this section is included in the sample files as MiddleTier.vb.txt.)

```
Dim salesData as New DataSet()
oracleDA.Fill(salesData)
excelDA.Fill(salesData)
sqlDA.Fill(salesData)
```

To summarize, by implementing the remote access at the middle tier, every time the sales data is required, the application needs to:

1. Open a different connection to each of the remote data sources.

2. Bring the data to the middle tier and merge all of the results into a single result.

The middle tier deals with the fact that the data is distributed in different physical locations.

Sometimes merging the data in the middle tier is not as easy as shown in this example because it might come in different formats and representations. The code needed to manipulate heterogeneous data sources is not always the same in .NET Framework programming. For example, if you need to retrieve data from a text file, you probably would use the classes inside the *System.IO* namespace, but if you need to retrieve data from Active Directory, you probably would use the classes inside the *System.DirectoryServices* namespace. The programming model for the classes inside these two namespaces is very different.

Reading Data from Remote Sources in SQL Server

A second possible approach would be for the middle tier to query a view created inside SQL Server. The view should be responsible for communicating with all the different data sources, merging the results and providing a single result set to the calling application.

As shown in Figure 8-2, by moving the responsibility of merging the results to SQL Server, we can take advantage of the following facts:

■ The middle tier doesn't have to be coupled to the physical implementation.

■ SQL Server can provide a single result set, regardless of its physical distribution, so the middle-tier code is much easier to write and less risky in terms of security, maintenance, concurrency control, and communication.

■ By processing the intermediate result sets from each of the different data sources in SQL Server, we can take advantage of the relational search engine and T-SQL constructions to make this a simpler, easier, and more maintainable solution.

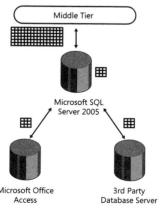

Figure 8-2   Architectural model for reading data from remote sources in SQL Server.

SQL Server 2005 offers two different approaches for managing connections to remote data sources:

- Open an ad hoc connection to the external data source; or
- Manage the connection configuration information statically by setting up a linked server.

Both approaches require the remote data source to support an OLE DB data access provider. This means that you could potentially connect to another SQL Server database, the Windows File System, Microsoft Exchange Server, Windows Active Directory Service, Microsoft Excel, or any other data source with an OLE DB provider available.

Reading Data from a Remote Data Source Using Ad Hoc Queries

Ad hoc queries provide the ability to open a connection to a remote data source and query it from within T-SQL code. This one-time connection lives just throughout the duration of the operation currently being executed.

Enabling Support for Ad Hoc Queries

In SQL Server 2005, support for ad hoc queries is disabled by default as a security measure. Follow the procedure below to use the *sp_configure* stored procedure to configure support for ad hoc queries, or use the second procedure below to accomplish the same thing through the SQL Server Surface Area Configuration tool.

Enabling Ad Hoc Queries Using T-SQL

1. From the Start menu, select All Programs | Microsoft SQL Server 2005 | SQL Server Management Studio. Open a new query window, and enter the following code (included in the sample files as EnableAdHoc.sql in the SqlScripts folder):

```
sp_configure 'show advanced options', 1;
GO
RECONFIGURE;
GO
sp_configure 'Ad Hoc Distributed Queries', 1;
GO
RECONFIGURE;
GO
```

2. Click the Execute button.

Enable Ad Hoc Queries Using the SQL Server Surface Area Configuration Tool

1. From the Start menu, select All Programs | Microsoft SQL Server 2005 | Configuration Tools | SQL Server Surface Area Configuration.

2. From the main screen, shown below, click on the Surface Area Configuration For Features link at the bottom.

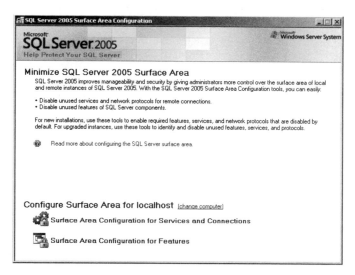

3. In the Surface Area Configuration For Features window, select the View By Instance tab on the left side of the screen

4. Select the SQL Server instance you would like to configure and open the Database Engine tree view.

5. Choose Ad Hoc Remote Queries from the list on the left side of the screen.

6. Select the Enable OPENROWSET And OPENDATASOURCE Support checkbox, as shown below:

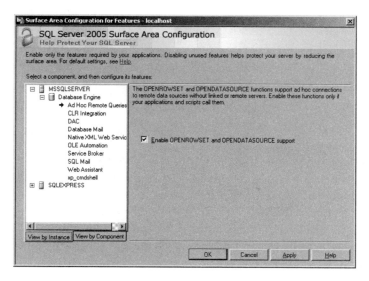

Using the OPENROWSET Function to Connect to Any Data Source

Use the *OPENROWSET* function to open any relational or nonrelational data source. SQL Server will always connect to the remote data source using OLE DB interfaces. The remote data source must support OLE DB, otherwise the connection will fail.

OPENROWSET allows you to specify connection configuration settings to control how SQL Server connects to the remote data source. You can also use a provider-specific query string that allows you to specify which resource you are requesting.

Connecting to a Microsoft Office Access Database by Using the OPENROWSET Function

1. Open SQL Server Management Studio and open a New Query window.

> **Note**   Northwind.mdb and Employees.xls are installed with the sample files to the following path by default:
>
> C:\Documents and Settings\User\My Documents\Microsoft Press\
>
> Sql2005SBS_AppliedTechniques\Chapter08
>
> If you installed your sample files to a different location, you will have to modify the code accordingly.

2. Enter the following script in the New Query window. (Modify the file path to match the location of the Northwind.mdb file on your computer. This example is included in the sample files as OPENROWSET.sql in the SqlScripts folder.)

```
SELECT OrderInfo.OrderID, OrderInfo.CustomerID, OrderInfo.EmployeeID
FROM OPENROWSET(
   'Microsoft.Jet.OLEDB.4.0',
   'C:\Documents and Settings\User\My Documents\Microsoft Press
     \Sql2005SBS_AppliedTechniques\Chapter08\Northwind.mdb'; 'Admin';'',
   'SELECT OrderID, CustomerID, EmployeeID FROM Orders')
As OrderInfo
```

3. Execute the script.

The OPENROWSET result set can be used anywhere in T-SQL where a table is expected.

Using SQL Server to Read Data from Multiple Data Sources

The following steps define a view with functionality similar to the ADO.NET method presented at the beginning of the chapter for connecting to multiple data sources from the middle tier. This time, however, the code will use SQL Server to read data from multiple data sources. The code for this example is included in the sample files as ReadDataFromMultipleSources.sql in the SqlScriptExamples folder. You will need to modify the following steps to match data sources that actually exist on your network (an Access database, a SQL Server database, and an Oracle database).

1. Open SQL Server Management Studio and connect to the SQL Server 2005 server and database where the view will be created.

2. Type the necessary T-SQL code to declare a view:

```
CREATE VIEW GlobalSalesData
AS
```

3. Open an ad hoc connection to the Microsoft Access PreSalesDB database; notice that the full path to the database file needs to be written.

```
SELECT PreSales.CustomerID, PreSales.Date, PreSales.Amount
FROM OPENROWSET(
'Microsoft.Jet.OLEDB.4.0',
'D:\PreSalesDB.MDB';'Admin';'Pass@word1',
'SELECT CustomerID, Date, Amount, Quarter FROM Opportunities
ORDER BY Date DESC') As PreSales
UNION
```

Microsoft.Jet.OLEDB.4.0 is the data access provider used to access the remote data source. Replace the file path, file name, user, and password with appropriate values for your environment.

4. Open an ad hoc connection to the Microsoft SQL Server 2005 server that hosts the SalesDB database:

```
SELECT Orders.CustomerID, Orders.Date, Orders.Amount
FROM OPENROWSET(
'SQLOLEDB',
'Server=Sales; Trusted_Connection=yes;',
'SalesDB.Sales.Orders') As Orders
UNION
```

SQLOLEDB is the data access provider used to access the remote SQL Server data source. Setting *Trusted_Connection* to *yes* means that the code authenticates the user using Windows credentials for the remote server. Replace the server and database name with appropriate values for your environment.

5. Open an ad hoc connection to a third-party database server (in this example, an Oracle OLE DB provider is used) that hosts the PostSalesDB database:

```
SELECT PostSales.CustomerID, PostSales.Date, PostSales.Amount
FROM OPENROWSET(
'msdaora',
'Data Source=PostSalesDB;User Id=LowPrivilegeUser; Password=SomePwd;',
'SELECT CustomerID, Quarter, Date, Amount from Support') As PostSales
```

Here, msdaora is the data access provider used to access the remote data source. Replace the data access provider, data source, user, and password with appropriate values for your environment.

The results of each query are unioned to return the complete result set.

Reading Objects with the OPENROWSET Function

The *OPENROWSET* function accepts two different sets of parameters to specify the connection string configurations:

■ The first syntax allows you to reuse the same connection string used in any application that uses OLE DB to connect to the data source. Specify the connection string with the syntax defined by the OLE DB provider:

```
OPENROWSET('provider name', 'provider specific string', 'object|query')
```

■ In the second syntax, you specify separately the data source, user id, and password to use:

```
OPENROWSET('provider name', 'datasource'; 'user_id'; 'password', 'object|query')
```

The last parameter (shown as object|query in the previous code examples) indicates to the remote data source what it needs to return as a response. You could specify that you want to retrieve a data object, for example a table or a view, or you could specify that you want to retrieve the result of a given query, as shown here in bold. (The code in this section is included in the sample files as OPENROWSETSyntaxExamples.sql in the SqlScriptExamples folder.)

```
SELECT PostSales.CustomerID, PostSales.Date, PostSales.Amount
FROM OPENROWSET(
'msdaora',
'Data Source=PostSalesDB;User Id=LowPrivilegeUser; Password=SomePwd;',
'SELECT CustomerID, Quarter, Date, Amount from Support') As PostSales
```

You could also specify a resource to retrieve by using a three-part name, as shown below in bold, where SalesDB identifies the catalog (or database), Sales identifies the schema, and Orders identifies the table (or view) to retrieve.

```
SELECT Orders.CustomerID, Orders.Date, Orders.Amount
FROM OPENROWSET(
'SQLOLEDB',
'Server=Sales; Trusted_Connection=yes;',
'SalesDB.Sales.Orders') As Orders
WHERE Orders.Quarter = @Quarter
```

> **Important**   Fully qualified names are used to correctly identify the resource or object you would like to retrieve in data sources that organize their data in catalogs, schemas, and data objects.
>
> Fully qualified names are made of four identifiers:
>
> *<ServerName>.<CatalogName>.<SchemaName>.<ResourceName>*

Using the OPENDATASOURCE Function to Connect to Any Data Source

The *OPENDATASOURCE* function also allows you to connect to data sources that expose data organized in catalogs, schemas, and data objects. The main difference from the *OPENROWSET* function is the way *OPENDATASOURCE* is invoked. They both return an OLE DB result set.

The *OPENDATASOURCE* function takes the place of the <ServerName> in a fully qualified (four-part) name to identify the object you want to retrieve from the remote data source, as shown below. Keep in mind that you must modify these examples to match your own servers and databases. The following code is included in the sample files as UseOPENDATASOURCE ToConnectToAnotherServer.sql in the SqlScriptExamples folder.

```
SELECT Orders.CustomerID, Orders.Date, Orders.Amount
FROM OPENDATASOURCE(
'SQLOLEDB',
'Server=Sales; Trusted_Connection=yes;').SalesDB.dbo.Orders
WHERE Orders.Quarter = @Quarter
```

In the above example, the *OPENDATASOURCE* function is substituted for the name of the server in the fully qualified name for the Orders table.

The following code shows how data can be extracted from an Excel file. This sample is included in the sample files as UseOPENDATASOURCEtoExtractXL.sql in the SqlScripts folder.

```
SELECT
    Employees.FirstName,
    Employees.LastName,
    Employees.Title,
    Employees.Country
FROM OPENDATASOURCE(
    'Microsoft.Jet.OLEDB.4.0',
    'Excel 8.0;DATABASE=C:\Documents and Settings\User\My Documents\
        Microsoft Press\Sql2005SBS_AppliedTechniques\
        Chapter08\EmployeeList.xls')...[Employees$] AS Employees
WHERE LastName IS NOT NULL
ORDER BY Employees.Country DESC
```

Note   Even when opening an Excel file, the four-part name syntax is used. In the SQL code above, the catalog and schema are omitted, but the dot (.) separator must still be present. That is why the query requires the "..." before the Excel page name (Employees$).

Reading Data from a Remote Data Source Using Linked Servers

Notice that every time the *OPENROWSET* or *OPENDATASOURCE* functions are used, you need to specify the connection configuration information.

In the following example, the *OPENROWSET* function and the *OPENDATASOURCE* function are both used to retrieve results from the same remote data source. This code is included in the sample files as OPENROWSETandOPENDATASOURCEUsedTogether.sql in the SqlScript Examples folder.

```
SELECT Orders.CustomerID, Orders.Date, Orders.Amount
FROM
OPENROWSET( 'SQLOLEDB', 'Server=Sales; Trusted_Connection=yes;',
SalesDB.Sales.Orders) As Orders
INNER JOIN
OPENDATASOURCE('SQLOLEDB', 'Server=Sales;
Trusted_Connection=yes;').SalesDB.Sales.OrderDetails
ON Orders.OrderID = OrderDetails.OrderID
WHERE Sales.Quarter = 3
```

Even when connecting to the same server, *OPENROWSET* and *OPENDATASOURCE* require you to specify the connection configuration settings every time.

Using Linked Servers to Connect to Any Data Source

Instead of repeating the same connection configuration settings each time the *OPENROWSET* or *OPENDATASOURCE* functions are used, SQL Server allows you to save those configuration settings and assign them an identifier, known as a *linked server*, so they can be reused without having to retype the connection configuration settings again. A linked server is essentially a virtual server.

Another advantage of linked servers is that they can be configured using T-SQL code or SQL Server Management Studio.

Important   Using linked servers allows you to use features not available when using *OPENROWSET* or *OPENDATASOURCE*. For example, you can:

- Manage static security
- Map login names
- Query catalog information
- Configure various connection settings, such as the default connection time-out

Configuring a Linked Server Using T-SQL

To configure a linked server using T-SQL code, you need to use the *sp_addlinkedserver* stored procedure. The *sp_addlinkedserver* stored procedure accepts several parameters to configure the remote data source.

The following code shows the complete T-SQL code necessary to add a remote SQL Server as a linked server. The code in this section is included in the sample files as LinkedServer.sql in the SqlScripts folder.

```
EXEC sp_addlinkedserver @server = 'Sales',
    @srvproduct='SQL Server'
GO
```

> **Important** Previous versions of SQL Server provided a stored procedure called *sp_addserver* used to add a reference to a remote server. This stored procedure is still available in SQL Server 2005, but only for backward compatibility. Support for this stored procedure will be removed in future versions of SQL Server. You should move forward using only *sp_addlinkedserver*.

The following code shows how to create a linked server to a Microsoft Excel file.

```
-- Linked server to an Excel file
EXEC sp_addlinkedserver
    @server = 'MyEmployees',
    @srvproduct = 'Jet 4.0',
    @provider = 'Microsoft.Jet.OLEDB.4.0',
    @datasrc = 'C:\Documents and Settings\User\My Documents\
        Microsoft Press\Sql2005SBS_AppliedTechniques\
        Chapter08\EmployeeList.xls',
    @provstr = 'Excel 8.0'
GO
```

Here's how to create a linked server to an Access database.

```
-- Linked server to an Access database
EXEC sp_addlinkedserver
    @server = 'PreSales',
    @provider = 'Microsoft.Jet.OLEDB.4.0',
    @srvproduct = 'OLEDB Provider for Jet',
    @datasrc = 'C:\Documents and Settings\User\My Documents\
        Microsoft Press\Sql2005SBS_AppliedTechniques\
        Chapter08\Northwind.mdb'
GO
```

The code below shows how to create a linked server to a third-party database, such as an Oracle database.

```
-- Linked server to an Oracle database
EXEC sp_addlinkedserver
```

```
        @server = 'PostSales',
        @srvproduct = 'Oracle',
        @provider = 'msdaora',
        @datasrc = 'PostSalesDB'
GO
```

Validating Which Linked Servers Are Currently Defined

1. Open SQL Server Management Studio and connect to a SQL Server instance.

2. Retrieve the values from the *sys.servers* system view filtering by the is_linked column, as shown in this code example:

```
SELECT *
FROM sys.servers
WHERE is_linked = 1
```

3. Review the results returned by the sys.servers system view. It will return a row for each linked server defined on the current instance of SQL Server. The different columns indicate the current configurations for each of the linked servers. The following figure shows a partial result of this query:

	server_id	name	product	provider	data_source	provider_string
1	1	MyEmployees	Jet 4.0	Microsoft.Jet.OLEDB.4.0	c:\EmployeeList.xls	Excel 8.0
2	2	PreSales	OLE DB Provider for Jet	Microsoft.Jet.OLEDB.4.0	C:\Databases\Presales.mdf	NULL
3	3	PostSales	Oracle	MSDAORA	PostSalesServer	NULL

> **Important** When registering linked servers, SQL Server does not check to see if the provided parameters are valid or even if the server names exist. The *sp_addlinkedserver* stored procedure will always succeed. In the event that you provided an incorrect parameter value, you will only find out during execution time.

Removing Configured Linked Servers

If you want to remove an already registered linked server, you can use the *sp_dropserver* stored procedure as shown in the following code example:

```
EXEC sp_dropserver 'MyEmployees'
GO
```

The *sp_dropserver* stored procedure receives a single parameter, the identifier of the linked server to drop.

Configuring a Linked Server in SQL Server Management Studio

Linked servers can also be configured in SQL Server Management Studio.

1. Open SQL Server Management Studio and connect to the server you would like to configure.

2. Open Object Explorer by selecting Object Explorer from the View menu (as shown below) or by pressing the F8 key. Object Explorer allows you to easily find and manage all the services and components of an specific SQL Server instance.

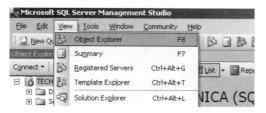

3. In the tree view shown, expand the specific SQL Server instance you want to configure, open the Server Objects folder, and then open the Linked Servers folder. The Linked Servers folder lists all the currently configured linked servers. The Providers folder lists all the installed OLE DB providers available to SQL Server in order for creating new linked servers.

4. Right-click on the Linked Servers folder and select New Linked Server from the context menu to open the wizard to configure a new linked server.

5. In the New Link Server window, shown below, configure all the parameters to access the remote data source.

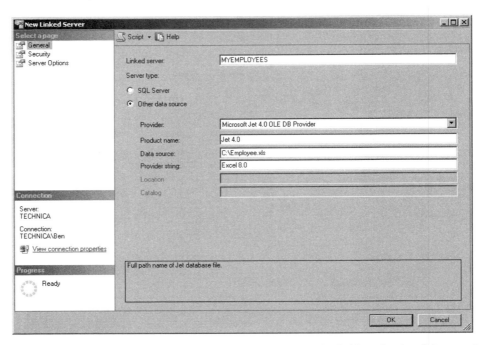

6. Click on the Security page in the Select A Page pane on the lefthand side of the window. The resulting window is shown below. If the remote data source requires authentication, you need to map the local account in the local server to local accounts in the remote server. If the authenticated login in SQL Server is a Windows account, then when calling the remote data source, SQL Server will impersonate the authenticated user. Otherwise, if the authenticated login in SQL Server is a SQL Server login, then when calling the remote data source, SQL Server will execute the remote call using the configured SQL Server service account.

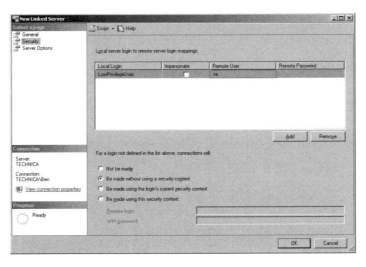

7. Click on the Server Options page in the Select A Page pane on the lefthand side of the window. The resulting window is shown below. The server options allow you to configure all the details when connecting to a remote data source. For a complete explanation of what each of these options means, see the SQL Server Books Online topic "Linked Server Properties (Server Options Page)."

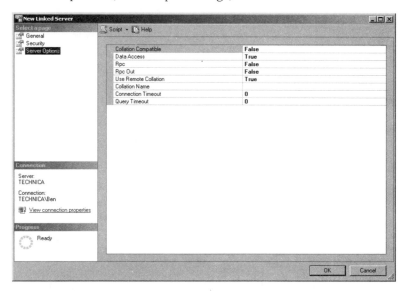

8. After configuring the linked server, press the OK button. Notice that, on the tree view in the Server Explorer panel, a new icon will be added, as shown here:

When adding a new linked server, using T-SQL or SQL Server Management Studio will yield exactly the same results.

Removing a Configured Linked Server

If you want to drop an existing linked server in SQL Server Management Studio, use the following procedure.

1. Open SQL Server Management Studio and connect to the server you would like to configure.

2. Open Object Explorer by selecting Object Explorer from the View menu or by pressing the F8 key.

3. In the tree view shown, expand the specific SQL Server instance you want to configure, open the Server Objects folder, and then open the Linked Servers folder.

4. Right-click the linked server node that you would like to delete and select Delete from the context menu, or select the node and press the DELETE key on the keyboard. The Delete Object window will open. Press the OK button to delete the linked server.

Quick Comparison Between Linked Servers and Ad Hoc Queries

- Linked servers provide more granular control over connection configuration settings.

- Linked servers are managed statically, independently of the Data Manipulation Language (DML) T-SQL code that uses them.

- Linked servers can be managed by code or using SQL Server Management Studio.

- Linked servers are easier to maintain than Ad Hoc Queries. If you want an existing linked server to point to a new remote data source, you just have to change the linked server configuration. The code need not be modified.

Reading Data Using a Linked Server

There are three ways of using a linked server in T-SQL code:

- The linked server name becomes the ServerName in a fully qualified (four-part) name to identify the object you want to retrieve from the remote data source. Thus, it can be used anywhere inside T-SQL as a reference to the remote data source.

- Use the EXECUTE...AT clause to send a query to the remote data source. The EXECUTE clause is usually used for executing DDL (data definition language) statements at the remote data source or for calling remote stored procedures.

- Use the *OPENQUERY* function to send a query to the remote data source and retrieve a rowset. *OPENQUERY* can be substituted in T-SQL code any place where a table is expected.

Specifying a Linked Server in a Fully Qualified Name

The linked server identifier becomes the ServerName in the four-part reference name of a remote data source, as shown here. The code in this section is included in the sample files as LinkedServerFullyQualifiedName.sql in the SqlScripts folder.

```
EXEC sp_addlinkedserver @server = 'SalesServer',
    @srvproduct='SQL Server'
GO


SELECT CustomerID, Date, Amount
FROM SalesServer.SalesDB.Sales.Orders
WHERE Quarter = @Quarter
```

The same syntax could be used to access an Excel file configured as a linked server called MyEmployees. In this example, Employee$ is the name of the Excel page being queried.

```
EXEC sp_addlinkedserver
    @server = 'MyEmployees',
    @srvproduct = 'Jet 4.0',
    @provider = 'Microsoft.Jet.OLEDB.4.0',
    @datasrc = 'C:\Documents and Settings\User\My Documents\
        Microsoft Press\Sql2005SBS_AppliedTechniques\
        Chapter08\EmployeeList.xls',
    @provstr = 'Excel 8.0'
GO
SELECT * FROM MyEmployees...Employees$
```

Specifying a Linked Server in the EXECUTE...AT Clause

The EXECUTE...AT clause has the following syntax:

```
EXECUTE ('query') AT LinkedServerIdentifier
```

Notice that any query written inside the apostrophes (') will be forwarded to the remote data source for execution. The remote data source could return an OLE DB rowset if needed.

The EXECUTE...AT construct is usually used for DDL statements, such as CREATE TABLE, CREATE PROCEDURE, or /DROP VIEW; for INSERT, UPDATE, or DELETE clauses; or to execute remote stored procedures as shown below. (This code is included in the sample files as LinkedServerExecuteAt.sql in the SqlScripts folder.)

```
EXEC sp_addlinkedserver @server = 'SalesServer',
    @srvproduct='SQL Server'
GO

EXECUTE ('CalculateCommissions') AT SalesServer
```

In the above code, the *CalculateCommissions* stored procedure exists in the Sales database on a remote SQL Server. This remote SQL Server has been configured as a linked server called *SalesServer*.

Using OPENQUERY to Execute Pass-Through Queries

The *OPENQUERY* function is used in a way similar to how *OPENROWSET* and *OPENDATA-SOURCE* are used. It can be used anywhere in T-SQL code where a table name is expected.

Unlike *OPENROWSET* and *OPENDATASOURCE*, however, *OPENQUERY* takes the name of the linked server to use as an input parameter, so you don't have to specify the connection configuration settings each time you make a remote call.

The syntax for the *OPENQUERY* function is:

```
SELECT columns
FROM OPENQUERY(LinkedServerIdentifier, 'query')
```

In the example shown below, the *SalesServer* linked server is a reference to the SQL Server named Sales, and it is accessed using the *OPENQUERY* function to retrieve all the Orders information. An inner join on the CustomerID keys is declared between the remote Orders table and the local OrderDetails table. This code is included in the sample files as OPENQUERY.sql in the SqlScriptExamples folder.

```
EXEC sp_addlinkedserver @server='SalesServer', @srvproduct='',
    @provider='SQLNCLI', @datasrc='SrvrName\SrvrInstance',
    @catalog='Sales'
GO

SELECT Orders.CustomerID, OrderDetails.Date, OrderDetails.Amount
FROM
    OPENQUERY(SalesServer, 'SELECT * FROM ORDERS') AS Orders
    INNER JOIN OrderDetails
        ON Orders.CustomerID = OrderDetails.CustomerID
WHERE Orders.Quarter = @Quarter
```

Inserting, Updating, or Deleting Data from Remote Sources in SQL Server

The same techniques used for reading data from remote data sources from within SQL Server can also be applied to executing INSERT, UPDATE, and DELETE statements on the remote data sources.

Using Ad Hoc Connections for Inserting, Updating, and Deleting Data

Both *OPENROWSET* and *OPENDATASOURCE* can be used on the INSERT, UPDATE, and DELETE statements to manipulate data on a remote data source.

When using *OPENROWSET*, you can specify a query to execute or you can specify a fully qualified name referencing the table you would like to update.

The code below shows how to add a new record into an Excel file. (The code in this section is included in the sample files as UsingAdHocToUpdate.sql in the SqlScripts folder.)

```
INSERT OPENROWSET(
    'Microsoft.Jet.OLEDB.4.0',
    'Excel 8.0;DATABASE=C:\Documents and Settings\User\My Documents\
        Microsoft Press\Sql2005SBS_AppliedTechniques\
        Chapter08\EmployeeList.xls',
    'SELECT FirstName, LastName, Title, Region FROM [Employees$]')
VALUES ('John',
        'Doe',
        'Consultant',
        'CA')
```

The following code shows how to insert a new record into a remote SQL Server database.

```
-- INSERT into a remote SQL Server database
INSERT OPENROWSET(
    'SQLOLEDB',
    'Server=Sales; Trusted_Connection=yes;',
    'SalesDB.Sales.Orders')
VALUES (175642, '2001-10-04', 6500.05)
GO
```

OPENDATASOURCE can be used to INSERT, UPDATE, or DELETE a fully qualified remote table. In this case, you do not need to specify a query. The code below shows this technique when working with a Microsoft Office Excel file.

```
INSERT OPENDATASOURCE(
    'Microsoft.Jet.OLEDB.4.0',
    'Excel 8.0;DATABASE=C:\Documents and Settings\User\My Documents\
        Microsoft Press\Sql2005SBS_AppliedTechniques\Chapter08\
        EmployeeList.xls')...[Employees$]
VALUES ('99',
        'Doe',
        'John',
        'Tester',
        'Mr.',
        '12/06/1964',
        '5/1/1995',
        '507 20th Ave. S.',
        'Seattle',
        'WA',
        '98122',
        'USA',
        '(206) 555-9857',
        '5467',
        'testing',
        '2')
```

Using Linked Servers for Inserting, Updating, and Deleting Data

After you create a linked server using the *sp_addlinkedserver* stored procedure, you can use that reference to execute INSERT, UPDATE, and DELETE statements on a fully qualified remote table.

The code below shows this technique when working with a remote SQL Server Database. (The code in this section is included in the sample files as UsingLinkedServerToUpdate.sql in the SqlScripts folder.)

```
EXEC sp_addlinkedserver @server = 'SalesServer',
    @srvproduct=N'SQL Server'
GO

DELETE SalesServer.SalesDB.Sales.Orders
WHERE Quarter = 3
```

To use the *OPENQUERY* function, instead of specifying a query to execute, you need to provide the name of the table to INSERT, UPDATE, or DELETE.

The following code shows this technique when working with an Excel file.

```
EXEC sp_addlinkedserver
    @server = 'MyEmployees',
    @srvproduct = 'Jet 4.0',
    @provider = 'Microsoft.Jet.OLEDB.4.0',
    @datasrc = 'C:\Documents and Settings\User\My Documents\
        Microsoft Press\Sql2005SBS_AppliedTechniques\
        Chapter08\EmployeeList.xls',
    @provstr = 'Excel 8.0'
GO
UPDATE OPENQUERY(MyEmployees, 'SELECT * FROM [Employees$]')
SET LastName = 'Newname'
WHERE Region = 'CA'
```

Conclusion

This chapter focused on how to read data from remote data sources and how to write data to remote data sources. Remote sources can be either another SQL Server instance or a different type of data source. You can do all of this using T-SQL. SQL Server Management Studio provides a user interface for managing remote sources.

Chapter 8 Quick Reference

TO	DO THIS
Execute infrequent queries against a remote resource by sending a pass-through query	Use the *OPENROWSET* function.

TO	DO THIS
Execute infrequent queries against a remote resource by referencing an object using its four-part name	Use the *OPENDATASOURCE* function.
Create a new linked server using SQL Server Management Studio	In SQL Server Management Studio's Object Explorer window, expand a SQL Server instance, open the Server Objects folder, then open the Linked Servers folder.
Create a new linked server programmatically	Use the *sp_addlinkedserver* system stored procedure.
Remove a linked server programmatically	Use the *sp_dropserver system* stored procedure.
Execute frequent queries against a remote resource by sending a pass-through query	Define a linked server and use the *OPENQUERY* function.
Execute frequent queries against a remote resource by referencing an object using its four-part name	Define a linked server and use the linked server identifier as the <ServerName> part of the fully qualified name.
Execute frequent DDL statements and stored procedures against a remote resource	Define a linked server and use the EXECUTE...AT construction.

Chapter 9

Reading SQL Server Data from the Internet

After completing this chapter, you will be able to:

- Connect securely to SQL Server from an external network by using the TCP/IP communication protocol

- Connect securely to SQL Server from an external network by using the HTTP communication protocol

- Securely access the data stored in a SQL Server database from a remote location without having to expose SQL Server to outside networks

Applications might require access to SQL Server through the Internet for a variety of reasons. For example, a client application running in a remote location outside the Local Area Network (LAN) might access SQL Server through the Internet. An application written in a different platform with no support for ODBC or OLE DB providers might use HTTP as a communication channel to SQL Server.

Depending on the network protocol used by the calling application, you can choose to expose SQL Server through the TCP/IP protocol or the HTTP protocol. Each approach is configured in a different way in SQL Server and provides different capabilities to calling applications.

If you expose SQL Server to external networks, you must be extra careful when deciding what to make available to the outside callers, and you must implement the necessary security infrastructure to avoid creating a security breach in the database system.

Another approach, instead of exposing SQL Server itself, is to provide access through a middle-tier component that listens on the required network port and forwards the calls to SQL Server, thereby minimizing the risk of compromising the database.

Direct Access to SQL Server

In order to provide direct access to SQL Server from a remote network, you first need to decide the communication protocol that client applications will use to communicate with the server. In this section we are going to focus on:

- Creating a native connection to SQL Server through TCP/IP

- Calling SQL Server through an HTTP Endpoint

With both approaches, you must take security measures into account.

Connecting through TCP/IP

SQL Server implements its own native communication protocol when using TCP/IP, called Tabular Data Stream (TDS). Client applications must use a compatible provider (ODBC, OLE DB, or SQLNCLI) in order to transform their requests into the TDS format.

Figure 9-1 shows the minimum recommended physical infrastructure required to make SQL Server available through TCP/IP over the Internet.

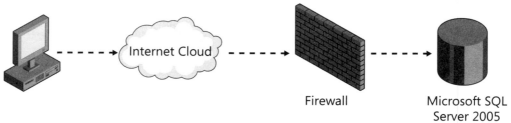

Internet Cloud

Firewall   Microsoft SQL
                      Server 2005

Figure 9-1   Physical infrastructure needed to make SQL Server available through TCP/IP over the Internet.

The firewall restricts access to the internal network by forwarding only requests targeted at specific TCP/IP addresses in the local network. This implies that:

■ The client application must know the TCP/IP address and network port where SQL Server is listening for requests.

■ The firewall must be configured to allow access to the specific TCP/IP address were SQL Server is listening for requests.

Connecting to SQL Server through TCP/IP over the Internet

1. Validate that the TCP/IP communication protocol is enabled in SQL Server.

2. Configure a SQL Server instance to listen on a specific IP address.

3. Provide client applications with the exact IP address and port where SQL Server is listening for requests, open a connection from the client application, and execute your queries.

The steps outlined above are detailed in the next sections of this chapter.

Validating that TCP/IP Is Enabled in SQL Server

SQL Server provides support for multiple communications protocols. To validate that TCP/IP is enabled, follow these steps:

1. From the Start menu, select All Programs | Microsoft SQL Server 2005 | Configuration Tools | SQL Server Configuration Manager. The SQL Server Configuration Manager is shown below:

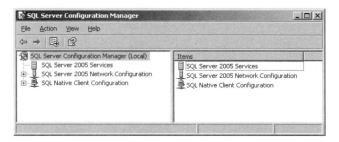

2. In the tree view control on the left pane, click the plus (+) sign next to the SQL Server Network Configuration node. Select the Protocols For <instance_name> node for the SQL Server instance you want to configure, as shown here:

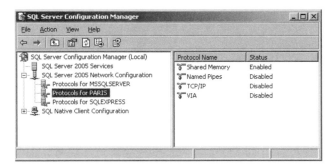

3. The righthand side pane displays a list of the available network protocols. If TCP/IP is marked as Enabled, then the server is ready to accept connections through the TCP/IP protocol. If TCP/IP is marked as Disabled, then right-click on the TCP/IP icon and choose Enable from the context menu, as shown here:

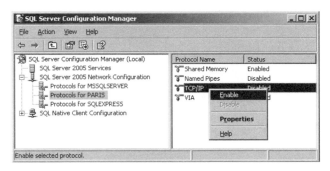

The SQL Server Surface Area Configuration Tool

The SQL Server Surface Area Configuration tool can also be used to validate whether TCP/IP is enabled. If you use the SQL Server Surface Area Configuration tool, you can further configure settings for the available communication protocols. To use this tool, do the following:

1. From the Start menu, select All Programs | Microsoft SQL Server 2005 | Configuration Tools | SQL Server Surface Area Configuration. The SQL Server Surface Area Configuration tool is shown below:

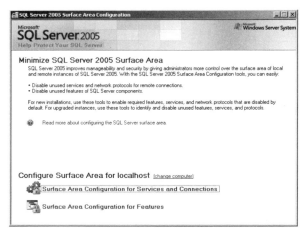

2. Click on the Surface Area Configuration For Services And Connections link at the bottom of the window.

3. In the Surface Area Configuration For Services And Connections window, in the tree view on the left side, click the plus (+) sign next to the SQL Server instance you want to configure. Similarly, open the Database Engine node and then select the Remote Connections node, as shown here:

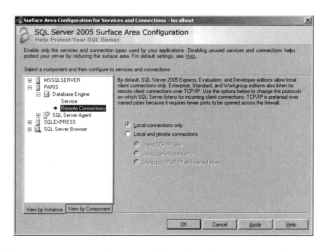

4. On the righthand side of the window, select the Local And Remote Connections option and then select the Using TCP/IP Only option, as shown here:

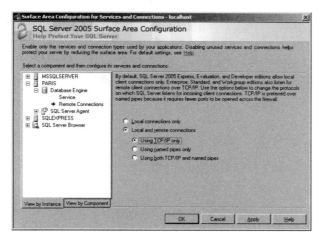

5. Click the OK button. SQL Server notifies you that the change will take effect after the SQL Server service is restarted.

Configuring SQL Server to Listen on a Specific IP Address

Default instances in SQL Server 2005 listen on TCP port 1433. Named SQL Server instances receive a dynamically assigned TCP port address when the instance is loaded. If you want to access a named SQL Server instance from the Internet, you must configure the SQL Server instance to listen on a specific port that is not assigned dynamically. To configure a named instance to listen on a specific TCP port:

1. Again open SQL Server Configuration Manager.

2. In the tree view control in the left pane, open the Server Network Configuration node by pressing the plus (+) sign. Select the Protocols For <instance_name> node for the SQL Server instances you want to configure.

3. Double-click the TCP/IP element shown on the righthand side pane.

4. In the TCP/IP Properties window, click on the IP Addresses tab, shown here:

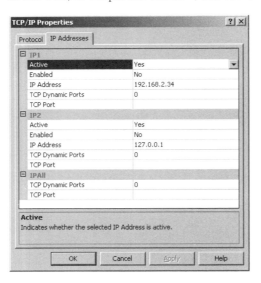

5. Notice the IPAll section at the bottom. If the TCP Dynamic Ports property contains the value 0, delete the 0, leaving the property empty. Then change the TCP Port property to the specific port number on which you want SQL Server to listen, as shown here:

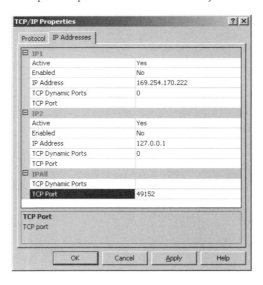

6. Click the OK button. SQL Server Configuration Manager notifies you that the change will take effect after the SQL Server service is restarted.

Important   Some ports are reserved for specific applications. SQL Server cannot listen on a port being used by another application. Check the Internet Assigned Numbers Authority listings to validate which port numbers are not in use: *http://www.iana.org/assignments/port-numbers*.

Directing the Client Application to the Correct IP Address and Executing Queries

The last step in allowing client applications to connect to SQL Server through the Internet using the TCP/IP protocol is to direct all the client application calls to the correct server, using the IP address and port number through which the server is listening for requests.

The connection string for specifying the server name must follow this format:

```
Data Source=tcp:<ip_address>/instance,<port_number>;
Initial Catalog=<database_name>; User ID=<user_id>; Password=<password>;
```

Here's an example of a connection string using the above format:

```
Data Source=tcp:190.190.200.100/Sales,1344;
Initial Catalog=AdventureWorks; User ID=sa;Password=Pa$$w0rd;
```

Note   You don't have to specify the instance if you are connecting to the default instance.

The following code sample (included in the sample files in the folder ConnectThroughTCP-port) shows how to open a connection to a SQL Server through the Internet using TCP/IP and retrieve all of the employee records from the AdventureWorks database. To use this sample, you will need to update the parts of the connection string shown in bold to match your environment. You will need a public IP address to communicate with a server across the Internet. If you are communicating within an Intranet, the server's Intranet IP address is sufficient. Use the <port_number> that you set up in the section titled "Configuring SQL Server to Listen on a Specific IP Address."

Tip   To connect to SQL Server with a user name and password, you must set SQL Server to use mixed authentication mode. See Chapter 2, "Basic Database Security Principles," for more information about mixed authentication mode. At the time of this writing, SQL Server does not recognize your Windows credentials if you use Integrated Security = true when connecting through a TCP port because TCP/IP is a non-authenticated protocol. This means that connections are not authenticated using Windows credentials. To authenticate, you must use SQL identities and specify a user name and password in the connection string.

Note   To determine your computer's IP address, select Run from the Start menu. Type *cmd* in the Run dialog box and click the OK button. A command line window will open. At the prompt, type *ipconfig* and press the Enter key. You will see your computer's IP address. Type *exit* and press the Enter key to close the command line window.

```vb
Public Sub GetEmployeeList()
    Dim connectionString As String
    connectionString = "Data Source=tcp:192.168.1.102,49152;" + _
        "Initial Catalog=AdventureWorks; User ID=Mary; password=34TY$$543"

    Dim query As String
    query = "SELECT Person.Contact.FirstName + ' ' + " + _
        "Person.Contact.LastName AS 'Employees' " + _
        "FROM Person.Contact " + _
        "INNER JOIN HumanResources.Employee " + _
        "ON Person.Contact.ContactID = HumanResources.Employee.ContactID"

    Using cn As New SqlClient.SqlConnection(connectionString)
        Using cmd As New SqlClient.SqlCommand(query, cn)
            cn.Open()
            Dim dr As SqlClient.SqlDataReader = cmd.ExecuteReader()

            While (dr.Read())
                Console.WriteLine(dr(0))
            End While

        End Using
    End Using
End Sub
```

Important   By following the steps above, you have configured SQL Server to:

1. Use TCP/IP as a network protocol.
2. Listen on a specific IP port.

You still have to configure the firewall or proxy server in your organization to allow access to SQL Server from an external application.

Connecting through HTTP Endpoints

SQL Server 2005 introduces the ability to use HTTP as a communication protocol through *HTTP Endpoints*. Here are the main benefits of using HTTP Endpoints:

- External client applications can connect to SQL Server through the Internet using the HTTP communication protocol no matter where they are located physically.

- Client applications written in programming languages or execution platforms that do not support any of the SQL Server data access providers can still execute queries in SQL Server through HTTP access.

- You don't need to open any additional ports on your firewall configuration. Communication is through port 80 just as for any other HTTP communication.

Connecting to SQL Server through HTTP

1. Create stored procedures or user-defined functions to encapsulate the operations to be exposed publicly.

2. Create and configure an HTTP Endpoint.

3. Create a reference from the client application to the HTTP Endpoint.

The steps outlined above are detailed in the next sections of this chapter.

More Info   The HTTP capabilities in SQL Server depend on the HTTP API (HTTP.sys) available on the host operating system. Currently only Windows XP SP2 and Windows Server 2003 provide support for HTTP.sys.

Creating Stored Procedures or User-Defined Functions to Encapsulate the Operations to Be Exposed Publicly

HTTP Endpoints in SQL Server 2005 provide a way to define a service-oriented interface to database operations. Service orientation means that the client applications will not be connecting or directly executing the defined stored procedures or user-defined functions, but the HTTP Endpoint will expose the stored procedures and user-defined functions as services (XML Web Services) through a pre-defined service contract, known as a Web Services Description Language (WSDL) contract.

Both client and server must adhere to the defined contract to exchange XML messages.

In the example in this section, you will create a new stored procedure that returns the list of sales order headers.

Creating a Stored Procedure

1. From the Start menu, select All Programs | Microsoft SQL Server 2005 | SQL Server Management Studio.

2. If asked to log in to a server, provide the proper authentication credentials and click the Connect button to log in to SQL Server.

3. If not already opened, click the New Query button to open a New Query window. Then enter the following text, which is included in the sample file httpEndpoints.sql.

```
USE AdventureWorks
GO
CREATE PROCEDURE GET_HEADER_LIST
AS
    SELECT * FROM Sales.SalesOrderHeader
GO
```

4. Press F5 or click the Execute button to execute the T-SQL script. Test your work so far by executing the following statement to run the stored procedure.

```
EXEC GET_HEADER_LIST
```

Creating and Configuring an HTTP Endpoint

After you have created all of the stored procedures and user-defined functions that will be exposed through the HTTP Endpoint, you must create and configure the HTTP Endpoint.

To configure an HTTP Endpoint, database administrators use a new Data Definition Language (DDL) statement, CREATE ENDPOINT.

Creating an HTTP Endpoint

1. Open a New Query window in SQL Server Management Studio.

2. Enter the following T-SQL code, which is included in the sample file httpEndpoints.sql. (The URL *tempuri.org* represents an XML namespace. You can use any string as long as it is unique to you or your organization.)

> **Note** If Internet Information Server (IIS) is running on the same machine as SQL Server, you must stop the IIS service before running the following code. Otherwise, you will receive an error stating that the specified port may be bound to another process.

```
USE MASTER
GO

EXEC sp_reserve_http_namespace N'http://localhost:80/sql/myservices'
GO

CREATE ENDPOINT [MyServices]
    STATE=STARTED
    AS HTTP (
        PATH=N'/sql/myservices',
        PORTS = (CLEAR),
        AUTHENTICATION = (INTEGRATED)
    )
    FOR SOAP (
        WEBMETHOD 'http://tempuri.org/'.'SalesHeadersList'(
            NAME=N'[AdventureWorks].[dbo].[GET_HEADER_LIST]',
```

```
                    FORMAT=ROWSETS_ONLY),
            WSDL=DEFAULT)
    GO
```

3.   Press F5 or click the Execute button to execute the T-SQL script.

The code creates an HTTP Endpoint to expose the GET_HEADER_LIST stored procedure as a service available to clients through the HTTP and Simple Object Access Protocol (SOAP) protocols.

> **Note**   To avoid name clashes between multiple HTTP endpoints, each application must reserve its namespace and register it with HTTP.sys. This can be done implicitly when creating a new Endpoint, or it can be done explicitly using the *sp_reserve_http_namespace* stored procedure. See the SQL Server Books Online topic "Reserving an HTTP Namespace" for more information.

The HTTP Endpoint defined above was given the MyServices identifier, and it is ready to start receiving requests as soon as the code above is executed because the code sets the STATE property to STARTED. Other possible values for the STATE property are STOPPED and DIS-ABLED.

The code also sets the AUTHENTICATION property to INTEGRATED. This means that SQL Server will try to authenticate the calling application based on a Windows credential using the NTLM protocol or the Kerberos protocol.

> **Note**   If you receive an HTTP 403 – Forbidden Access error when trying this example, it means that SQL Server is not able to authenticate the user identity you are using to call the Endpoint. This works differently depending on the operating system version you are using and how user security is configured. See the SQL Server Books Online topic "Specifying Non-Kerberos Authentication in Visual Studio Projects" for more information.

Other authentication protocols, such as Basic authentication, send the password in clear text during the authentication process. When using Basic authentication, SQL Server 2005 requires the communication channel to be encrypted and secured by using Secure Sockets Layers (SSL). The PORTS setting can be set to CLEAR or SSL. CLEAR indicates that the communication channel will not use SSL.

The PATH setting indicates the relative path that will be used to identify the Endpoint externally. The complete path that client applications will specify is: *http://server_name/sql/myservices*. For this example you can point Internet Explorer to *http://localhost/sql/myservices?wsdl* to examine the XML that is created.

> **Important**   When an Endpoint is created, only members of the sysadmin role and the owner of the Endpoint can connect to the Endpoint. You must grant connect permission for users to access your Endpoint. This is accomplished by executing the following statement: GRANT CONNECT ON HTTP ENDPOINT::[*EndPoint_Name*] TO [*Domain\User_Account*].

After configuring the Endpoint itself, the second part of the CREATE ENDPOINT DDL statement configures the stored procedures and user-defined functions that are going to be exposed as a service.

Database administrators can declare as many WEBMETHODs as needed. Each WEB-METHOD configures one service mapped to a single stored procedure or user-defined function.

The exposed service in this case is identified by the alias 'http://tempuri.org/'.'SalesHeader-sList'. This WEBMETHOD is mapped to the stored procedure specified in the NAME setting.

The FORMAT setting configures the type of information being returned by SQL Server. ROWSETS_ONLY indicates that only the results should be returned. A client application can then use an ADO.NET *DataSet* object to receive the data.

The WSDL setting indicates that the WSDL contract must be generated automatically by SQL Server 2005.

> **Note**   There are many important configuration options to set when creating HTTP Endpoints. See the SQL Server Books Online topic "CREATE ENDPOINT (Transact-SQL)" for more information.

Creating a Reference from the Client Application to the HTTP Endpoint

Client applications communicating through the HTTP Endpoint can only send requests that adhere to the WSDL contract. The WSDL contract is created dynamically by SQL Server by combining the metadata of all the exposed WEBMETHODs and formatting it as a valid WSDL contract.

Client applications developed using the Microsoft Visual Studio 2005 development environment can easily create a Web reference to the HTTP Endpoint.

To create a Web reference to a SQL Server HTTP Endpoint, follow the procedure below. (This project is included in the sample files in the ConsumeHTTPEndpoint folder.)

Creating a Web Reference to an HTTP Endpoint
1.   From the Start menu, select All Programs | Microsoft Visual Studio 2005 | Microsoft Visual Studio 2005.

2. From the File menu, select New | Project. Select Visual Basic in the Project Types pane, and select Windows Application in the Templates pane. Give your project a name and specify a location for it. Click the OK button to create the project.

3. If it is not shown, display the Toolbox by selecting Toolbox from the View menu. Drag and drop a DataGridView control from the Toolbox to the Form1 form in Design view.

4. Click the small arrow in the upper-right corner of the DataGridView control to display the DataGridView Tasks smart tag. On the smart tag, uncheck the Enable Adding, Enable Editing and Enable Deleting checkboxes.

5. Right-click on the project in the Solution Explorer window and choose Add Web Reference from the context menu.

6. In the Add Web Reference window, type the following URL:

   ```
   http://localhost/sql/myservices?wsdl
   ```

7. Click the Go button, and then click the Add Reference button.

8. Double-click the form in the designer and add the following code to the *Form1_Load* event handler.

   ```vb
   Private Sub Form1_Load(ByVal sender As System.Object, _
       ByVal e As System.EventArgs) Handles MyBase.Load
       Dim ws As New localhost.MyServices
       ws.Credentials = System.Net.CredentialCache.DefaultCredentials

       Dim headers As New DataSet
       headers = ws.SalesHeadersList ()
       DataGridView1.DataSource = headers.Tables(0)
       DataGridView1.AutoGenerateColumns = True
   End Sub
   ```

9. Switch to the Form1.vb[Design] tab and press F4 to open the Properties window. Select the DataGridView control in the properties window and set the Dock property to Fill by clicking the central panel in the dropdown display.

10. Press the F5 key to build and run the application.

11. The form loads and the DataGridView control shows the list of all the sales order headers retrieved from SQL Server.

> **Important**   Microsoft strongly recommends that you use SQL Server behind a firewall, even when connecting through HTTP Endpoints.

HTTP Endpoints allow you to integrate SQL Server 2005 into a service-oriented architecture.

There are some drawbacks to using HTTP Endpoints:

- Because no Web server is used, the scalability of this solution is limited.

- Not many organizations would want to expose SQL Server directly to the Internet.

You can overcome these drawbacks by providing access to SQL Server through an extra layer that keeps your SQL Server installation protected.

Interoperability with Other Systems through HTTP Endpoints

Each Relational Database Management System (RDBMS) exposes an Application Programming Interface (API) that developers can use to interoperate with the database.

OLE DB, ODBC, DB-LIB, JDBC, and SQLNCLI are all examples of data access providers. A data access provider encapsulates the complex logic implemented by the API for an RDBMS. A data access provider also exposes a common interface that allows application developers to write data access logic once and be able to interoperate with multiple RDBMSs. The fact is that, to be able to talk to a specific RDBMS, application development platforms require support from a data access provider.

With HTTP Endpoints, SQL Server 2005 provides an alternative to using a data access provider.

Since HTTP Endpoints are managed by the database administrator, he or she can carefully choose which stored procedures and user-defined functions to make available through the Endpoints, but any development platform can then connect and call those HTTP Endpoints.

The only requirement for an application to connect to an HTTP EndPoint is that the application be able to communicate through the HTTP communication protocol and that it be able to send requests conforming to the specific XML/SOAP format required by SQL Server 2005.

Programming platforms and languages with poor support for OLE DB or ODBC data access providers can take advantage of communicating with SQL Server 2005 through HTTP Endpoints.

Some examples of such platforms, languages, and new scenarios that HTTP Endpoints enable are:

- Mobile devices can connect to a corporate SQL Server through HTTP Endpoints using a wireless network.

- Applications running in Linux/Unix or any other operating system can communicate with and consume data from SQL Server 2005 without having to use JDBC.

- Scripts created in a variety of environments—such as PERL, Java, or Microsoft Office Web Services—can retrieve data directly from SQL Server or even create new data.

Access to SQL Server through an Extra Layer

So far in this chapter, we have investigated how to expose SQL Server directly to client applications on external networks.

Because SQL Server maintains valuable data, it's generally not a good idea to expose your installation to broad networks, such as the Internet, because of security issues. Additionally, exposing SQL Server directly to external networks limits scalability and performance and complicates server administration.

The benefits of implementing a middle tier between the client application and SQL Server are as follows:

- A middle tier provides an extra layer of security that filters all incoming requests.

- You can use components of the operating system infrastructure, such as Internet Information Server (IIS), to provide better scalability and performance and to allow additional configuration, administration, and security options.

- You can implement a specialized data access layer that can be reused by multiple applications.

Figure 9-2 shows an example of a possible architecture for accessing SQL Server through an extra layer.

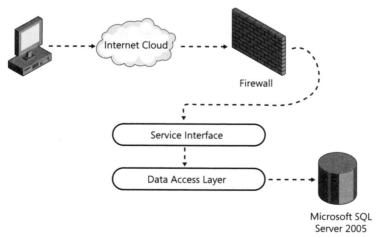

Figure 9-2   Architecture for accessing SQL Server through a middle-tier component.

A Service Interface represents a façade that is exposed to client applications. The Service Interface exposes a public interface that hides all the complexity of the internal implementation to access SQL Server. The Service Interface must also implement all necessary input validation.

The Service Interface is supported by a data access component. The data access component implements the calls to SQL Server through a data access provider, such as OLE DB or ODBC.

The Microsoft .NET Framework provides several technologies for creating a service interface. This chapter will focus on ASP.NET Web Services and Microsoft .NET Remoting.

> **Tip**   For a more complete discussion of creating data access layers, refer to the guide titled "Designing Data Tier Components and Passing Data Through Tiers" from the Microsoft Patterns & Practices Developer Center Web site, *http://msdn.microsoft.com/practices/guidetype/ Guides/default.aspx?pull=/library/en-us/dnbda/html/boagag.asp*.

ASP.NET Web Services

As an HTTP EndPoint, an ASP.NET Web Service also exposes a WSDL contract, but instead of exposing a stored procedure as a service, an ASP.NET Web Service allows you to expose application logic written in components as a Web service.

ASP.NET Web Services are deployed and hosted inside Microsoft Internet Information Services (IIS) server. To view all the code in this section, open the Solution1.sln file in the 3tiers folder in the sample files. Individual components are in subfolders as noted in the text.

In order to implement SQL Server access through the Internet but by connecting to a middle-tier ASP.NET Web Service, follow these steps:

Creating a Data Access Component and a Service Interface

1. Start by writing the data access component to connect to SQL Server. Open Visual Studio 2005 and create a new project, choosing the Class Library template in the New Project window. Name the project DepartmentDataAccess, as shown below, and click the OK button.

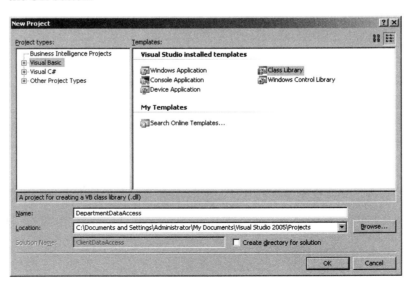

2. Replace the code in the Class1.vb file with the following code (remember to modify the connection string to match your own environment). This code is included in the sample files in the folder 3tiers\DepartmentDataAccess.

```
Imports System.Data.SqlClient

Public Class DepartmentDataAccess

    Public Function GetAllDepartments() As DataSet
        Dim result As New DataSet
        Dim connectionString As String
        Dim selectCommand As String

        connectionString = "server=(local);database=AdventureWorks;uid=sa"
        selectCommand = "SELECT * FROM HumanResources.Department"

        Dim connection As New SqlConnection(connectionString)
        Dim adapter As New SqlDataAdapter(selectCommand, connection)

        adapter.Fill(result)

        Return result
    End Function

End Class
```

The *DepartmentDataAccess* class, as an example, implements a single method called *GetAllDepartments*. It returns a *DataSet* object that contains all of the departments in the AdventureWorks company.

3. From the Build menu in Visual Studio 2005, select Build DepartmentDataAccess. Visual Studio 2005 will compile the project into an assembly. This represents our Data Access Layer.

4. Let's move on and create the service interface using an ASP.NET Web Service project. In Visual Studio 2005, select Add | New Website from the File menu. This code is included in the sample files in the 3tiers\webservice folder.

5. Choose the ASP.NET Web Service template in the New Project window, as shown below. Leave all the other options set to their default values. Click the OK button.

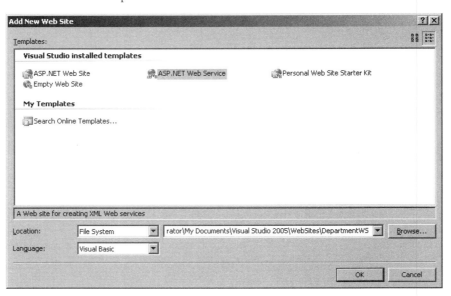

6. In the Solution Explorer window, right-click the Web Service project and select Add Reference from the context menu. (If Solution Explorer is not visible, you can select Solution Explorer from the View menu.)

7. In the Add Reference window, shown below, select the Projects tab, select the DepartmentDataAccess project, and click the OK button

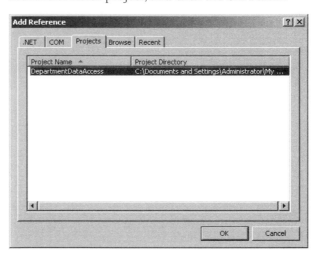

8. Under the HelloWorld function created by the Visual Studio template, enter the following code:

```
<WebMethod()> _
Public Function GetDepartments() As System.Data.DataSet
    Dim departmentsDL As New DepartmentDataAccess.DepartmentDataAccess()
    Return departmentsDL.GetAllDepartments()
End Function
```

9. Press F5 to compile the ASP.NET Web Service project and run it. If Visual Studio 2005 asks you if you would like to enable debugging, select the Run Without Debugging option, as shown here:

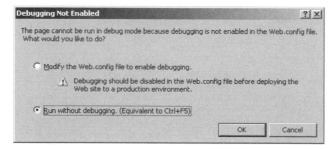

10. Internet Explorer will open a Web page where you can test your Web service, as shown below. Select the service GetDepartments.

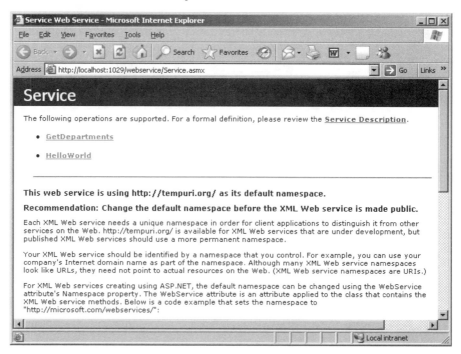

11. Internet Explorer will browse to the GetDepartments Web page, shown below. Click the Invoke button to execute the Web service.

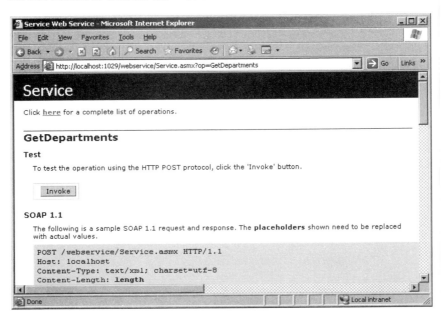

12. When the Web service is invoked, the ASP.NET code calls the data access component, retrieves the results as a dataset, and finally transforms the complete response in XML format, as shown here:

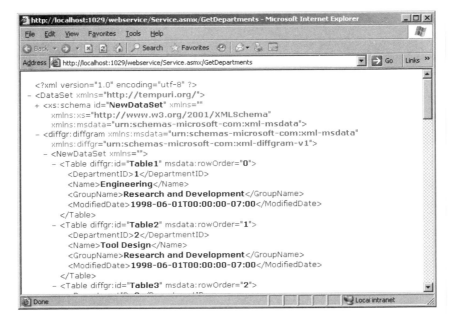

Of course, client applications will not execute your Web service using the same test page as you just did. To write a client application that consumes this Web service, you could follow the same steps as described previously in the section titled "Creating a Reference from the Client Application to the HTTP Endpoint."

Microsoft .NET Remoting

The Microsoft .NET Framework provides different technologies to allow remote clients to connect to server-side components.

If you use ASP.NET Web Services, as we did in the previous section of this chapter, your client applications will communicate using the SOAP format through a service interface.

Microsoft .NET Remoting is another technology that allows remote applications to communicate with server-side components. Microsoft .NET Remoting allows you to configure the data format you would like to use or the communication protocol you would like to use. For example, instead of XML and SOAP, you can choose Binary or any custom format, and instead of HTTP or TCP, you can choose a custom protocol.

The main difference between ASP.NET Web Services and .NET Remoting is that .NET Remoting follows an object-to-object remote procedure call (RPC) architecture instead of a service-oriented architecture.

Creating a .NET Remoting Object

We will build an example using the same code base as in the previous section. Repeat steps 1 through 4 from the previous section and then continue with the following steps:

1. After you create the DepartmentDataAccess component, you must provide a service interface component. This example creates a .NET Remoting service interface. In Visual Studio 2005, choose Add | New Project from the File menu. The code for this example is included in the sample files in the 3tiers\Remoting folder.

2. Choose the Class Library template on the New Project window and name the project DepartmentServiceInterface. Click the OK button.

3. In the Solution Explorer window, right-click the DepartmentServiceInterface project and select Add Reference from the context menu.

4. In the Add Reference window, select the Projects tab, select the DepartmentDataAccess project, and then click the OK button

5. Replace the code in the Class1.vb file with the following code:

```
Public Class DepartmentServiceInterface
    Inherits MarshalByRefObject

    Public Function GetDepartments() As System.Data.DataSet
        Dim departmentsDL As New DepartmentDataAccess.DepartmentDataAccess()
        Return departmentsDL.GetAllDepartments()
    End Function

End Class
```

6. Build the project.

The last component that you need to build is a hosting application. When we created the ASP.NET Web Service, it was configured to be hosted and executed by a Web Server, such as Microsoft Internet Information Server (IIS). In the following example, we will configure our .NET Remoting object to be hosted by IIS as well.

Configuring a .NET Remoting Object to Be Hosted by IIS

1. Create and configure a virtual directory in IIS to host the assemblies.

2. Create a web.config configuration file to configure the Remoting framework.

3. Generate a proxy to the remote object.

4. Create a client application that calls the remote object.

Creating and Configuring a Virtual Directory in IIS

By using IIS as a hosting environment, our remoting application can leverage IIS's security, communication protocols, and internal request-handling mechanisms. Install the assemblies from the DepartmentServiceInterface component in an IIS Virtual Directory:

1. Create a new directory called DepartmentRemote on the C drive.

2. Inside C:\DepartmentRemote, create a new folder called bin.

3. From the Start menu, select Settings | Control Panel. In Control Panel, double-click on Administrative Tools. In the Administrative Tools window, double-click the Internet Information Services icon.

4. In the Internet Information Services management application, click the plus (+) sign to expand the computer node, then expand the Web Sites node, then right-click the Default Web Site node, as shown below:

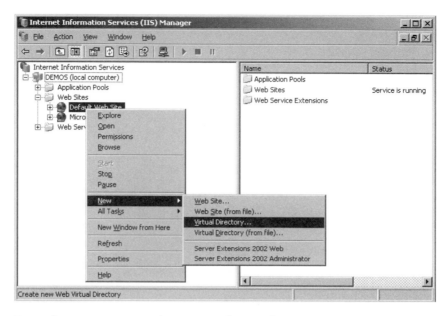

5. From the context menu, choose New | Virtual Directory.

6. Click the Next button on the Virtual Directory Creation Wizard welcome screen.

    6.1. On the Virtual Directory Alias page, type *DepartmentService* as the alias name and click the Next button.

    6.2. On the Web Site Content Directory page, type or browse to C:\DepartmentRemote in the Directory textbox and click the Next button.

    6.3. On the Access Permissions page, uncheck all the checkboxes except the Execute checkbox. Click the Next button to move to the final step.

    6.4. Click the Finish button.

7. Right-click on the newly created DepartmentRemote virtual directory and select Properties from the context menu

8. In the DepartmentService Properties window, click on the ASP.NET tab and change the ASP.NET version to 2.X.X.X as shown below. (Numbers may vary depending on your installation, but make sure it is the same version as the Visual Studio you used to compile the assemblies.) Then click the OK button to close the window.

> **Tip**   In Visual Studio, select About Microsoft Visual Studio from the Help menu to find the Visual Studio version number.

9. Using Windows Explorer, copy all the contents from the bin/debug subfolders from where you saved the DepartmentServiceInterface project (I used the Visual Studio 2005 default location: C:\Documents and Settings\Administrator\My Documents\Visual Studio 2005\Projects\DepartmentDataAccess\DepartmentServiceInterface) into the C:\DepartmentRemote\bin folder. The resulting files are shown here:

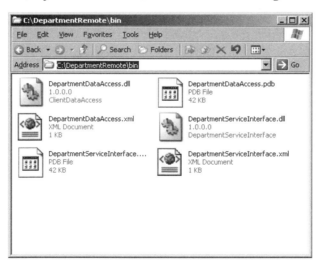

Creating a Web.Config file to Configure the Remoting Framework

1. Using Notepad, create a new file called web.config in the C:\DepartmentRemote directory.

2. Edit the web.config file with the following XML code (included in the sample files as web.config in the 3tiers folder):

```
<configuration>
    <system.runtime.remoting>
        <application>
            <service>
                <wellknown mode="SingleCall"
                type="DepartmentServiceInterface.DepartmentServiceInterface,
                DepartmentServiceInterface" objectUri="department.soap" />
            </service>
        </application>
    </system.runtime.remoting>
</configuration>
```

3. Save the web.config file

This XML file configures the remoting framework. It declares a new service called depart-ment.soap that corresponds to the *DepartmentServiceInterface.DepartmentServiceInterface* class inside the DepartmentServiceInterface assembly. The setting *Mode="SingleCall"* indicates that a new instance of this class will be created for each request.

Generating a Proxy Class for the Remote Object

To access our Service Interface component, client applications must create a proxy class. A proxy class is like a copy of the remote object; it declares the same methods and public inter-faces, but when called by a client, it routes the call to the remote object. The Microsoft .NET Framework SDK provides the SOAPSuds tool that you can use to generate a proxy class.

1. From the Start menu, select Programs | Microsoft .NET Framework 2.0 SDK | SDK Command Prompt. A DOS command prompt window opens.

2. At the command prompt, type the following commands:

   - *cd * to move to the root drive

   - *md ClientApp* to create a new directory for the client application

   - *cd ClientApp* to move to the ClientApp folder

   - *soapsuds -url:http://localhost/departmentservice/department.soap?wsdl -oa: DepartmentProxy.dll*

The SOAPSuds utility downloads a service description file automatically generated by the remoting framework that describes each of the methods exposed by the DepartmentService-Interface class. Based on this, SOAPSuds generates a new assembly called Department-Proxy.dll with a class that client applications can use to call the remote service.

Creating a Client Application that Calls the Remote Object

We can use the DepartmentProxy.dll proxy class to call into the remote service. To create a client application and use the proxy class, follow these steps:

1. Open Visual Studio 2005 and create a new project. Choose the Windows Application template on the New Project window. The code for this example is included in the sample files in the 3tiers\ClientApp folder

2. Name the project ClientApp and click on the OK button.

3. In the Solution Explorer window, right-click the ClientApp project and select Add Reference from the context menu.

4. In the Add Reference window from the .NET tab, select System.Runtime.Remoting and click the OK button.

5. Right-click the ClientApp project again to add another reference. In the Add Reference window, move to the Browse tab. Browse to the C:\ClientApp folder and select the DepartmentProxy.dll assembly, then click the OK button.

6. Add a DataGridView control from the Toolbox to the Form1 form in design view.

7. From the DataGridView Tasks smart tag, uncheck the Enable Adding, Enable Editing and Enable Deleting checkboxes.

8. Press F4 to open the Properties window. Select the DataGridView control on the form and set the Dock property to Fill.

9. Add the following code to the *Form1_Load* event handler.

    ```
    Private Sub Form1_Load(ByVal sender As System.Object, _
        ByVal e As System.EventArgs) Handles MyBase.Load
        Dim de As New DepartmentServiceInterface.DepartmentServiceInterface
        Dim departments As New DataSet

        departments = de.GetDepartments()
        DataGridView1.DataSource = departments.Tables(0)
        DataGridView1.AutoGenerateColumns = True
    End Sub
    ```

10. Press the F5 key to build and run the application.

11. The form loads and the DataGridView control displays a list of all the departments retrieved from SQL Server.

Even though it may seem complicated (it certainly is a lot of steps!), the overall architecture of our .NET Remoting example, shown in Figure 9-3, is fairly simple.

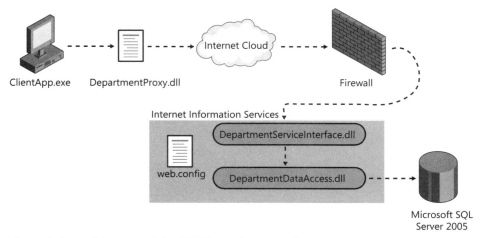

Figure 9-3   Architecture of the .NET Remoting example.

Both ASP.NET and .NET Remoting are middle-tier technologies that encapsulate a set of components and expose them as services through a Service Interface. You can use either of these solutions to deploy SQL Server in a safe environment on the backend, yet still allow remote clients to connect to your application and retrieve their data.

Conclusion

This chapter focused on how to access SQL Server data from remote client applications, either by exposing SQL Server directly to the Internet or by writing a middle-tier service interface. Using a direct connection through the Internet provides a great deal of flexibility, but also exposes your installation to security risks. Using a middle-tier architecture provides a secure interface for your SQL Server, enhances scalability and performance, and eases configuration and maintenance tasks.

Chapter 9 Quick Reference

To	Do this
Open a connection to SQL Server through TCP/IP	1. Enable the TCP/IP communication protocol.
	2. Configure a SQL Server instance to listen on a specific IP address.
	3. Provide client applications with the exact IP address and port where SQL Server is listening for requests.
	4. Configure the firewall to allow access to that port.

To	Do this
Validate that TCP/IP is enabled in SQL Server	In SQL Server Configuration Manager, expand the SQL Server Network Configuration node and select the Protocols For <instance_name> node; Or In SQL Server Surface Area Configuration, click the Surface Area Configuration For Services And Connections link, expand the instance you are configuring, expand the Database Engine node, and select the Remote Connections node.
Direct a client application to the correct IP address and port number for SQL Server	Specify the IP address and port number in the connection string using the following syntax: `Data Source = tcp:<ip_address>/instance, <port_number>;`
Access SQL Server using XML / SOAP protocols through HTTP	Configure HTTP Endpoints with the T-SQL CREATE ENDPOINT DDL statement.
Use ASP.NET Web Services in the middle tier	Use Visual Studio 2005 to create a new Web Service project. Encapsulate the data access code inside the Web service to avoid having to expose SQL Server to the Internet.
Use Microsoft .NET Remoting in the middle tier	Use Visual Studio 2005 to create a service class that encapsulates the data access code to avoid having to expose SQL Server to the Internet. Expose the service class using a hosting application, such as IIS.

Part III
How to Modify Data in SQL Server

Chapter 10

Using Transactions to Provide Safe Database Concurrency

After completing this chapter, you will be able to:

- Define Transactions in SQL Server
- Handle errors during transactions
- Choose the right transaction isolation level
- Monitor and prevent blocking and deadlock problems
- Manage transactions using ADO.NET

In the previous two chapters, you learned how to connect to remote data sources. Of particular concern to applications that involve distributed clients is the question of preventing one user from overwriting another user's input. As an application designer, you also need to make sure that a set of related changes aren't interrupted so that they end up only partially complete. These problems are so important for database applications in general that we've devoted an entire chapter to how SQL Server solves them. In this chapter, we'll explain how wrapping changes to data in a *transaction* both prevents users from stepping on each other's toes and allows application designers to ensure the integrity of the data.

Business Transactions and SQL Server Transactions

Every business process consists of one or more transactions. Imagine that you are managing an online store. When a customer orders a product, a predefined process must run to guarantee on-time delivery. The process must also include credit card processing to be sure that your company gets paid. If one of these tasks fails and cannot be corrected, the whole process must be canceled to ensure that the customer is not invoiced without getting the product or vice versa. In most cases, these processes are handled by computer systems, where all data is stored in databases. The data related to one business transaction should be changed to be reliable, consistent, and complete in order to map the business processes. This can be done by using transactions on the database level. A transaction is defined as a sequence of operations executed as a unit that follows the so called ACID properties:

- **Atomicity**   Each transaction is a unit of work. It cannot be broken into smaller parts. This property means that either all data modifications defined in the transaction are done, or none are performed at all.

- **Consistency**   A transaction cannot break any integrity checks defined in the database. To maintain consistency, all rules, constraints, checks, and triggers are applied during the transaction. Since all data modifications are applied during the transaction, the data is guaranteed to be consistent before the transaction starts and after the transaction finishes.

- **Isolation**   Transactions must be isolated from data modifications done by other transactions. This means that no other operation can change data in an intermediate (not committed) state. To keep intermediate data from being altered, the transaction must either wait until the changes from the other transactions are committed or see the data in the previously committed state.

- **Durability**   After a transaction is completed and the client application has been notified that the transaction completed successfully, the data changes are permanent regardless of any system failures.

The SQL Server database engine enforces the physical consistency of the transaction and ensures the durability of transactions by means of the transaction log. SQL Server also enforces all consistency checks against constraints, datatypes, and so on to guarantee logical consistency. This is all enforced automatically by SQL Server. However, in order to map business transactions to SQL Server transactions, the developer has to design some transactions very carefully.

1. Define the boundaries of a transaction. The developer has to define where a transaction starts and where it ends. A transaction should always be as short as possible but as long as it has to be to map to the requirements of the business process.

2. Define error management. Not all errors automatically roll back transactions. It is the developer's responsibility to implement error management.

3. Define the isolation. Isolating different transactions always has disadvantages relating to concurrency. If you fully isolate your transaction and another transaction wants to read the same data but not the previous state, it is blocked until you end your transaction. This can be a huge problem for database systems with many concurrent connections. SQL Server implements different variations of isolation levels that have to be chosen in the right way. The general rule is to choose the level that locks as little data as possible for as short a time as possible but still gives you the transaction safety you need.

In the remainder of this chapter, we will see how to design and implement transactions in SQL Server 2005.

Defining Transactions in SQL Server

Now we will have a look at how transactions can be defined and handled in SQL Server 2005. SQL Server provides different ways to handle transactions, which can be defined on a per-connection basis. Every connection can use the mode it needs to accomplish its requirements. The different modes are:

- Auto-commit transactions

- Explicit transactions
- Implicit transactions

Auto-Commit Mode

SQL Server handles everything as a transaction. It never modifies data outside of a transaction. Therefore, SQL Server has to define a transaction on its own when a transaction is not defined by the developer. Transactions defined by SQL Server are called auto-commit transactions. Auto-commit mode is the default mode in SQL Server.

Exploring Auto-Commit Transactions

1. From the Start menu, select All Programs | Microsoft SQL Server 2005 | SQL Server Management Studio. Open a New Query window by pressing the New Query button on the toolbar.

2. Enter and execute the following CREATE TABLE statement to create a small table, which you will use in the next procedure to examine transaction behavior. The code for this example is included in the sample files as ExploringAutoCommit.sql.

```
USE tempdb;
GO
CREATE TABLE table1 (
    i    int         NOT NULL PRIMARY KEY,
    col1 varchar(20) NOT NULL,
    col2 varchar(20) NULL);
```

3. Now insert three new rows into table1. To do so, enter the following statements in the query window and execute all three together.

```
USE tempdb;
GO
INSERT INTO table1 (i,col1,col2)
VALUES (1,'First row','First row');

INSERT INTO table1 (i,col1,col2)
VALUES (2,NULL,'Second row');

INSERT INTO table1 (i,col1,col2)
VALUES (3,'Third row','Third row');
```

4. You will get a message, shown below, saying that SQL Server is not allowed to insert a NULL value into col1 because it is defined as NOT NULL.

```
(1 row(s) affected)
Msg 515, Level 16, State 2, Line 4
Cannot insert the value NULL into column 'col1', table 'tempdb.dbo.table1';
column does not allow nulls. INSERT fails.
The statement has been terminated.

(1 row(s) affected)
```

5. Enter and execute the following SELECT statement to examine whether the records were successfully inserted.

```
USE tempdb;
GO
SELECT i,col1,col2
FROM table1;
```

6. As you can see, the second row was not inserted, but the first and the third rows were successfully inserted. When SQL Server uses auto-commit transactions, every statement is a transaction of its own. If one statement produces an error, its transaction is rolled back automatically. If the statement executes successfully without any errors, the transaction is automatically committed. Therefore, statements 1 and 3 were committed and statement 2, which produced an error, was rolled back. Note that this behavior occurred even though the three statements were submitted together as a batch. Batching doesn't define whether or not the statements within the batch are processed as a single transaction.

Explicit Transactions

In explicit transaction, the developer defines where a transaction starts and when it has to be committed or rolled back. This is done by using the T-SQL statements BEGIN TRANSACTION, COMMIT TRANSACTION, and ROLLBACK TRANSACTION. An explicit transaction is independent from a batch. It can span more than one batch, or there can be more than one explicit transaction in one batch.

> **Note**   You can use the abbreviation TRAN in place of the TRANSACTION keyword.

Defining Explicit Transactions

1. Start SQL Server Management Studio and open a New Query window.

2. Enter and execute the following statement to truncate table1. The code for this example is included in the sample files as DefineExplicitTransactions.sql.

```
USE tempdb;
GO
TRUNCATE TABLE table1;
```

3. Now insert the same three rows as before into table1. This time group the statements in an explicit transaction because you want to either have all the records inserted into the table or none inserted at all. Enter the following statements in the query window and execute all the statements at once.

```
USE tempdb;
GO
BEGIN TRAN

INSERT INTO table1 (i,col1,col2)
VALUES (1,'First row','First row');
```

```
INSERT INTO table1 (i,col1,col2)
VALUES (2,NULL,'Second row');

INSERT INTO table1 (i,col1,col2)
VALUES (3,'Third row','Third row');

COMMIT TRAN;
```

4. You will get the same message back as before stating that SQL Server is not allowed to insert a NULL value into col1 because it is defined as NOT NULL.

5. Enter and execute a SELECT statement to examine whether records were inserted.

```
USE tempdb;
GO
SELECT i,col1,col2
FROM table1;
```

6. You see that the result is the same as with auto-commit mode. Two of the rows are inserted and the one violating the NULL constraint is not. What happened here? As stated earlier, it is the developer's responsibility not only to define the length of a transaction, but also to determine whether it should be rolled back. So you need to add an error handler to your transaction. Without an error handler, SQL Server will simply process the next statement after the error because the batch is not aborted. In the previous batch, SQL Server simply processes each INSERT statement and afterwards processes the COMMIT TRAN statement. Therefore, you have the same result as with auto-commit mode.

7. To add an error handler, you can use the new *TRY* and *CATCH* block feature of SQL Server 2005 T-SQL. Truncate the table again and execute the transaction with an error handler as shown below.

```
--truncate
TRUNCATE TABLE table1

--transaction with error handler
BEGIN TRY
    BEGIN TRAN

    INSERT INTO table1 (i,col1,col2)
    VALUES (1,'First row','First row');
    INSERT INTO table1 (i,col1,col2)
    VALUES (2,NULL,'Second row');
    INSERT INTO table1 (i,col1,col2)
    VALUES (3,'Third row','Third row');

    COMMIT TRAN;
END TRY
BEGIN CATCH
    ROLLBACK TRAN
END CATCH;
```

In this case you don't get any error messages back, since the error was trapped by the *CATCH* block.

8. Enter and execute the following SELECT statement to examine whether the transaction was rolled back.

```
USE tempdb;
GO
SELECT i,col1,col2
FROM table1;
```

No records are returned. As you can see, then, the whole transaction was rolled back. When the violation occurred in the second INSERT statement, SQL Server jumped to the *CATCH* block and rolled back the transaction.

9. The only problem that remains with this code is that you don't get any message telling you that an error occurred. This can be managed in the *CATCH* block where you can use special functions to retrieve the error, and you can also use the *RAISERROR* function to raise a custom error. Alter the *CATCH* block as shown below.

```
BEGIN CATCH
    SELECT  ERROR_NUMBER() AS ErrorNumber,
            ERROR_SEVERITY() AS ErrorSeverity,
            ERROR_STATE() as ErrorState,
            ERROR_PROCEDURE() as ErrorProcedure,
            ERROR_LINE() as ErrorLine,
            ERROR_MESSAGE() as ErrorMessage;
    RAISERROR('Error in Transaction!',14,1)
    ROLLBACK TRAN
END CATCH;
```

10. Execute the whole transaction from step 9 again. Now you get a record back with all the information for the error and a custom error message stating that an error occurred. Of course, it is also possible to include the actual error message in the RAISERROR statement. In that case, the *CATCH* block would look like this:

```
BEGIN CATCH
    DECLARE @er nvarchar(max)
    SET @er = 'Error: '+ ERROR_MESSAGE();
    RAISERROR(@er,14,1);
    ROLLBACK TRAN
END CATCH;
```

Implicit Transactions

The third mode is called implicit transaction mode because, in this mode, SQL Server starts a transaction if no transaction exists but doesn't perform a COMMIT or ROLLBACK statement automatically the way it does in auto-commit mode. The transaction has to be ended explicitly. The following statements start a transaction implicitly when no transaction exists:

ALTER TABLE	GRANT	FETCH	DELETE
CREATE	REVOKE	INSERT	SELECT
DROP	OPEN	UPDATE	TRUNCATE TABLE

Using Implicit Transactions

1. Start SQL Server Management Studio and open a New Query window.

2. Enter and execute the following statement to set the connection to the implicit transactions mode. The code for this example is included in the sample files as UsingImplicit Transactions.sql.

```
SET IMPLICIT_TRANSACTIONS ON;
GO
```

3. Execute the following code to create a table to check if a transaction has started.

```
CREATE TABLE T1
    (i int PRIMARY KEY);
```

4. To test if a transaction is open, @@TRANCOUNT can be used; execute the SELECT statement shown below.

```
SELECT @@TRANCOUNT AS [Transaction Count];
```

5. The result is 1, which means that the connection has an open transaction. 0 would mean that no transaction is open at the moment, and a number higher than 1 would mean that there are nested transactions (which will be explained later).

6. Now insert a row into the table and check @@TRANCOUNT again by executing the following statements.

```
INSERT INTO T1 VALUES(5);
GO
SELECT @@TRANCOUNT AS [Transaction Count];
```

The value of @@TRANCOUNT is still 1. SQL Server didn't start a new transaction because there was an open transaction already.

7. Now roll back the transaction and check @@TRANCOUNT again by executing the following code. You will see that @@TRANCOUNT is 0 after the ROLLBACK TRAN statement.

```
ROLLBACK TRAN
GO
SELECT @@TRANCOUNT AS [Transaction Count];
```

8. Try to SELECT table T1.

```
SELECT * FROM T1;
```

9. You will get an error message because the table doesn't exist anymore. The implicit transaction started with the CREATE TABLE statement and the ROLLBACK TRAN statement cancelled the work done since the first statement.

10. Turn implicit transactions off by executing the following code:

```
SET IMPLICIT_TRANSACTIONS OFF;
```

> **Caution**   Be careful when using implicit transactions. Don't forget to commit or roll back your work. Because there is no explicit BEGIN TRANSACTION statement, these steps are easy to forget, leading to long-running transactions, unwanted rollbacks when the connection is closed, and blocking problems with other connections.

Nesting Transactions

Explicit transactions can be nested, which means that it is possible to start explicit transactions within other explicit transactions. One of the main reasons that this is supported is to allow transactions within stored procedures regardless of whether the procedure is itself called from within a transaction. But how are nested transactions handled in SQL Server? Let us explore nested transactions with two simple examples.

Exploring Nesting Transactions

1. Start SQL Server Management Studio and open a New Query window.

2. Use @@TRANCOUNT to figure out how SQL Server is handling nested transactions. Enter and execute the following batch. The code for this example is included in the sample files as NestingTransactions.sql.

```
PRINT 'Trancount before transaction: ' + CAST(@@trancount as char(1))
BEGIN TRAN
    PRINT 'After first BEGIN TRAN: ' + CAST(@@trancount as char(1))
    BEGIN TRAN
        PRINT 'After second BEGIN TRAN: ' + CAST(@@trancount as char(1))
    COMMIT TRAN
    PRINT 'After first COMMIT TRAN: ' + CAST(@@trancount as char(1))
COMMIT TRAN
PRINT 'After second COMMIT TRAN: ' + CAST(@@trancount as char(1))
```

3. In the result, you can see that every BEGIN TRAN statement increments @@TRANCOUNT by 1 and every COMMIT TRAN statement decrements the count by 1. As you have seen before, a @@TRANCOUNT of 0 means that there are no open transactions. Therefore, the transaction ends when @@TRANCOUNT decrements from 1 to 0, which happens when the outermost transaction is committed. Thus, every inner transaction needs to be committed. The outermost transaction determines whether the inner transactions are fully committed because the transaction starts with the first BEGIN TRAN and commits only with the last COMMIT TRAN. If this outermost transaction is not committed, the nested transactions within will not be committed either.

4. Type and execute the following batch to examine what happens when a transaction is rolled back.

```
USE Adventureworks
```

```
BEGIN TRAN
    PRINT 'After 1st BEGIN TRAN: ' + CAST(@@trancount as char(1))
    BEGIN TRAN
        PRINT 'After 2nd BEGIN TRAN: ' + CAST(@@trancount as char(1))
            BEGIN TRAN
            PRINT 'After 3rd BEGIN TRAN: ' + CAST(@@trancount as char(1))

            UPDATE Person.Contact
            SET EmailAddress = 'test@test.at'
            WHERE ContactID = 20

            COMMIT TRAN
        PRINT 'After first COMMIT TRAN: ' + CAST(@@trancount as char(1))
ROLLBACK TRAN
PRINT 'After ROLLBACK TRAN: ' + CAST(@@trancount as char(1))

SELECT EmailAddress FROM Person.Contact
WHERE ContactID = 20;
```

5. In this example, the e-mail address of a contact is updated in a nested transaction that is
    immediately committed. Then a ROLLBACK TRAN statement is issued. The ROLL-
    BACK TRAN decrements @@TRANCOUNT to 0 and rolls back the whole transaction
    with all nested transactions regardless of whether they were already committed. There-
    fore, the update made in the nested transaction is rolled back and no data is changed.

Always keep in mind that with nested transactions only the outermost transaction determines
whether the inner transactions will be committed. Each COMMIT TRAN statement always
applies to the last executed BEGIN TRAN. Therefore, a COMMIT TRAN has to be called for
every BEGIN TRAN executed to commit a transaction. The ROLLBACK TRAN statement
always belongs to the outermost transaction and therefore always rolls back the whole transaction regardless of how many nested transactions are open. Because of this, managing nested
transactions can be tricky. As stated at the beginning of this section, nested transactions
mostly happen in nested stored procedures when every procedure starts a transaction on its
own. Nesting transactions can be avoided by deciding if a transaction needs to be started or
not by checking @@TRANCOUNT at the start of the procedure. If @@TRANCOUNT is
higher than 0, it is not necessary to start a transaction because the procedure is already in a
transaction and the calling instance can roll back the transaction if an error occurs.

Managing Transaction Isolation

To comply with the ACID rules, transactions have to be isolated from each other. This means
that data that is used within a transaction has to be separated from other transactions. To
accomplish this separation, every transaction locks the data it uses to prevent other transactions from using it. A lock is defined for a locked resource, which can be an index key, a data
row, or a table. SQL Server always tries to lock resources as granularly as possible. It starts
locking on a row-level basis in most cases, but if too many rows are locked, it can decide to

escalate the lock to a table-level basis. This is done automatically. The most common lock resources that exist in SQL Server to lock data are:

- **RID**   A row identifier is used to lock a specific row in a heap, where no clustered index exists.

- **KEY**   An index key of an index is locked. When a clustered index exists for a table, this type of lock is also used to lock a row of the table because, in a clustered index, the data is part of the index. To learn more about index internals, see Chapter 6.

- **PAGE**   An 8Kb page in the database is locked, which can be an Index or a Data page.

- **TABLE**   A table lock is used to lock the whole table for an operation.

In addition, every lock has a specific lock type that defines how the lock should behave. For example, it is possible in some situations to lock data only for write access if the transaction wants to prevent other transactions from updating data, but allows other transactions to read data. In other situations, it is essential that the data is locked exclusively for the transaction, preventing any access to the data by other transactions. This behavior is implemented through lock compatibility. Each lock type by definition is compatible with certain kinds of locks from other transactions on the same resource. Because a specific lock type has to be granted for all data access operations in SQL Server, you can use lock compatibility to manage whether two or more operations can use the same data at the same time. The most common lock types used by SQL Server are:

- **Shared (S)**   Shared locks are used to lock data for read access. They prevent other transactions from changing the data, but not from reading the data. Shared locks are compatible with other shared locks, which allows more than one transaction to have a shared lock on a lock resource. Therefore, transactions can read the same data side by side.

- **Exclusive (X)**   Exclusive locks are used for every data change. They prevent other transactions from accessing the data. Therefore, an exclusive lock is not compatible with other locks.

- **Update (U)**   Update locks are a special case of shared locks. They are mainly used for supporting UPDATE statements. In an UPDATE statement, the data has to be read before it can be changed. Therefore it requires a lock type that doesn't prevent other transactions from reading the data while it reads the data on its own. Yet when SQL Server starts to change the data, it has to escalate the lock type to exclusive. For this read operation, SQL Server uses update locks which are compatible with shared locks but are not compatible with other update locks. Therefore, it is possible for other transactions to read data while the data is read for the UPDATE statement, but other UPDATE statements have to wait until the update lock is released.

- **Intent (I)**   Intent locks exist as variations of the preceding lock types, including intent shared locks, intent exclusive locks, and so on. They are used to protect locks on lower hierarchies from disallowed locks on higher hierarchies. Consider a situation when a transaction has an exclusive lock on a row in a table. In this case, it is not allowable for another transaction to get an exclusive lock on the whole table. To manage this kind of situation, intent locks are used on higher hierarchies to let other transactions know that some resources are locked on a lower hierarchy. In this case, the transaction holding the exclusive lock on the row would also lock the page and the table with an exclusive intent lock.

For a full list of lock types and lock resources in SQL Server 2005, see the SQL Server Books Online topic "Lock Modes."

Monitoring locks

To monitor which locks exists in a database, the Dynamic Management view *sys.dm_tran_locks* can be queried. This view provides a row for every single lock existing in the database at the moment.

1. Start SQL Server Management Studio and open a New Query window.

2. Enter and execute the following statements to start a transaction and query the Person.Contact table. The locking hint HOLDLOCK is used in this transaction to tell SQL Server to not release the lock after the SELECT statement. Also notice that the transaction is not committed since the locks would automatically be released with a commit. How long locks are held in a transaction will be explained later in this chapter. The code for this example is included in the sample files as MonitoringLocks.sql.

```
USE AdventureWorks;
GO
BEGIN TRAN
SELECT FirstName,LastName,EmailAddress
    FROM Person.Contact WITH (HOLDLOCK)
    WHERE ContactID = 15
```

3. To examine which locks are used by this transaction, you can use the Dynamic Management view *sys_dm_tran_locks*. To query only the locks that belong to your transaction you can join the view with another Dynamic Management view called *sys.dm_tran_current_transaction*, which retrieves information about the current transaction running in that connection. Enter and execute the following SELECT statement in the query window to get the locking information and commit the transaction.

```
SELECT resource_type, resource_associated_entity_id,
    request_mode,request_status
FROM sys.dm_tran_locks dml INNER JOIN
        sys.dm_tran_current_transaction dmt
        ON dml.request_owner_id = dmt.transaction_id;

COMMIT TRAN
```

4. Below, you can see the result of the query. It shows us that a shared lock (request_mode = S) exists on a key that represents the row in the clustered index and an intent shared lock (request_mode = IS) exists on the corresponding page and on the table Per-

son.Contact. The value GRANT in the request_status column means that all requested locks have been granted to the transaction.

	resource_type	resource_associated_entity_id	request_mode	request_status
1	OBJECT	309576141	IS	GRANT
2	KEY	72057594043236352	S	GRANT
3	PAGE	72057594043236352	IS	GRANT

5. Now check what happens when you change the WHERE clause to retrieve more rows. Change the WHERE clause as follows and execute the whole transaction.

```
BEGIN TRAN
SELECT FirstName,LastName,EmailAddress
    FROM Person.Contact WITH (HOLDLOCK)
    WHERE ContactID <7000;
```

6. Now examine the locks by executing this code:

```
SELECT resource_type, resource_associated_entity_id,request_mode,request_status
FROM sys.dm_tran_locks dml INNER JOIN
    sys.dm_tran_current_transaction dmt
    ON dml.request_owner_id = dmt.transaction_id;
COMMIT TRAN
```

You can see that the shared lock is defined on an object resource type, in this case, the table Person.Contact. SQL Server decided that holding a table-level lock for this transaction is easier and faster than holding about 7000 key locks with all the dependent intent locks. Because SQL Server used a table-level lock, it did not need to use intent locks. That's because the table is the highest level in the locking hierarchy for data. To find out which object is locked, you can use the *OBJECT_NAME* function. *OBJECT_NAME* takes the Object ID as an argument and returns the object's name. (The column resource_associated_entity_id holds the Object ID of the locked object if OBJECT is the resource_type.)

7. To see how SQL Server locks data while it is being changed, enter and execute the following transaction to UPDATE data on the Person.Contact table and query the associated locks. At the end, a ROLLBACK TRAN is issued to discard the change.

```
USE Adventureworks;
GO
BEGIN TRAN
UPDATE Person.Contact
    SET Phone ='+43 555 333 222'
    WHERE ContactID =25;

SELECT resource_type, resource_associated_entity_id,request_mode,request_status
FROM sys.dm_tran_locks dml INNER JOIN
    sys.dm_tran_current_transaction dmt
```

```
        ON dml.request_owner_id = dmt.transaction_id;
ROLLBACK TRAN
```

The result is displayed below. You can see that SQL Server locked the key with an exclusive lock (request_mode = X). Whenever data is changed, SQL Server uses an exclusive lock and holds it until the end of the transaction. As stated earlier, SQL Server also uses update locks in the first step when executing UPDATE statements. Because you queried the locks after the UPDATE statement, the lock on the row had already been escalated to an exclusive lock. What you also see is that there are two intent exclusive locks (request_mode = IX) on the page and the table again, plus a lock called Sch-S on resource type METADATA. A Sch-S lock is a schema stability lock that is issued to prevent other transactions from altering the schema of the table while the data is updated because such a change is not allowed while changing data.

	resource_ty...	resource_associated_entit...	request_mode	request_sta...
1	METADATA	0	Sch-S	GRANT
2	OBJECT	309576141	IX	GRANT
3	PAGE	72057594043236352	IX	GRANT
4	KEY	72057594043236352	X	GRANT

Transaction Isolation Levels

You have seen now that SQL Server isolates a transaction by using different lock types on lock resources. To develop safe transactions, it is crucial to not only define the contents of the transaction and the cases in which it should be rolled back, but also how—and how long—locks should be held in a transaction. This is determined through isolation levels. With different isolation levels, SQL Server gives the developer the ability to define for every single transaction how strongly it should be isolated from other transactions. Transaction isolation levels define:

- Whether locks are used when reading data
- How long read locks are held
- Which types of locks are used to read data
- What happens when a read operation wants to read data that is exclusively locked by another transaction. In that case SQL Server can:
  - Wait until the other transaction releases the lock
  - Read the uncommitted data
  - Read the last committed version of the data

ANSI 99 defines four transaction isolation levels that are all supported by SQL Server 2005:

- READ UNCOMMITTED doesn't use or check locks while reading data. Therefore, it is possible to read uncommitted data at this isolation level.

- READ COMMITTED reads only committed data and waits until the other transaction releases the exclusive lock. Shared locks used for reading data are released right after the read operation finishes. READ COMMITTED is the default isolation level of SQL Server.

- REPEATABLE READ reads data like READ COMMITTED, but holds shared locks until the end of the transaction.

- SERIALIZABLE works like REPEATABLE READ. It locks not only the data affected, but also locks the whole range. This prevents new data from being inserted into a range affected by a query, which can lead to phantom reads (see the SQL Server Books Online topic "Concurrency Effects").

In addition, SQL Server has two more transaction levels, which use row versioning to read data. (We'll examine all of these levels in detail later in this chapter.) Row versioning enables a transaction to read the last committed version of data when the data is exclusively locked. This can provide significant query performance enhancements since read operations don't have to wait until locks are released. These two levels are as follows:

- READ COMMITTED SNAPHOT is a new implementation of the READ COMMITTED level. Unlike the normal READ COMMITED level, SQL Server reads the last committed versions and therefore doesn't have to wait until locks are released when performing read operations. This level can be used as a substitute for READ COMMITTED.

- SNAPSHOT isolation uses row versioning to provide transactional read consistency. This means that within a transaction, the same data is always read as with the SERIAL-IZABLE level, but data doesn't have to be locked to prevent changes from other transactions, since the read consistency is provided through row versioning.

Regardless of which transaction isolation level is defined, data changes are always locked with exclusive locks that are held until the end of the transaction.

To define the right isolation level is not always an easy decision. As a general rule, choose the isolation level that locks as little data for as short a time as possible, but still gives the transaction the required degree of safety. In the next sections, we will see some scenarios that show how these levels works in detail and how to choose the right level.

Reading Only Committed Data

In SQL Server 2005, the READ COMMITTED isolation level is the default level when a new connection is established. This level exists in two types: the READ COMMITTED and the READ COMMITTED SNAPSHOT isolation levels. The type that is applied is defined through a database option. The READ COMMITTED level waits until blocking locks are released before reading the data, while the READ COMMITTED SNAPSHOT level uses row versioning and reads the last committed version of the data when data is blocked by other transactions.

Using the READ COMMITTED Level

1. Start SQL Server Management Studio and open a New Query window.

2. Enter and execute the following statements to read the Name and EmailAddress fields of the Person.Contact table where ContactID = 1. The code for this example is included in the sample files as ReadCommitted1.sql and ReadCommitted2.sql.

```
USE AdventureWorks;

BEGIN TRAN

SELECT FirstName, LastName, EmailAddress
FROM Person.Contact
WHERE ContactID = 1;
```

The EmailAddress gustavo0@adventure-works.com of contact Gustavo Achong is returned.

3. Now consider that another transaction changes the EmailAddress while your transaction is still open. Open a second query window and execute the following batch to UPDATE the EmailAddress without committing the transaction.

```
USE AdventureWorks;
BEGIN TRAN

UPDATE Person.Contact
SET EmailAddress = 'uncommitted@email.at'
WHERE ContactID = 1;
```

4. The UPDATE statement runs without any problems. One row was affected, even though the data was read first by the transaction in Query Window 1 and this transaction hasn't finished yet. This happens because the READ COMMITTED level doesn't hold shared locks, which are used for the SELECT statement, until the end of the transaction. The locks are released right after the data is read by SQL Server. This can be a problem when you need consistent read operation throughout your transaction. We will see how to accomplish this in the section "Getting Consistent Repeatable Read Operations" later in this chapter.

5. Now switch back to Query Window 1 and try to read the data again.

```
SELECT FirstName, LastName, EmailAddress
FROM Person.Contact
WHERE ContactID = 1;
```

The query doesn't end because the SELECT statement is blocked. SQL Server tries to get a shared lock on the key of ContactID 1, but this is not possible since the UPDATE transaction in Query Window 2 has an exclusive lock on it. Although Query Window 2 is in READ COMMITTED level (because you haven't changed the default level), the exclusive lock is still there. This lock exists because exclusive locks for data changes are always held until the end of the transaction.

6. Switch to Query Window 2, but leave the query in Query Window 1 running. Enter and execute the following SELECT statement to examine the granted and waiting locks in the database.

```
SELECT resource_type, resource_associated_entity_id,
    request_mode, request_status
FROM sys.dm_tran_locks
```

You can see that one shared lock has a request status of WAIT. This is the query running in Query Window 1. It is waiting for the query in Query Window 2, which has an exclusive lock granted on the same resource.

7. Issue a ROLLBACK TRAN in Query Window 2 to roll back the UPDATE statement and switch to Query Window 1. You can see that the query in Query Window 1 has finished and the result is the same as before. When the transaction in Query Window 2 finished, the locks were released and the query in Query Window 1 wasn't blocked anymore. Since the transaction in Query Window 2 was rolled back, you got the original data as the result in Query Window 1. If the transaction in Query Window 2 had been committed, you would have received the new data as a result in Query Window 1.

8. Execute a COMMIT TRAN statement in Query Window 1 and close all Query Windows.

You have seen now that in the (default) READ COMMITTED level SQL Server waits until exclusive locks are released to retrieve only actual and committed data. You have also seen that shared locks are only held until the data is read but exclusive locks are always held until the transaction has been committed. This behavior can be a problem when a lot of transactions are changing data almost constantly. In these situations reading data can be very slow because of blocking by the exclusive locks. But in some situations it would be adequate to use the last committed version of the data. In these situations it is possible to change the READ COMMITTED level to the READ COMMITTED SNAPSHOT level.

Using the READ COMMITTED SNAPSHOT Level

1. Start SQL Server Management Studio and open a New Query window.

2. Enter and execute the following statements to activate the READ COMMITTED SNAPSHOT level. The code for this example is included in the sample files as ReadCommittedSnapshot1.sql and ReadCommittedSnapshot2.sql.

```
USE master;
ALTER DATABASE AdventureWorks
SET READ_COMMITTED_SNAPSHOT ON
```

3. Now start a transaction and change the EmailAddress as in the procedure before (but leave the transaction open) by executing the following code:

```
USE AdventureWorks;
BEGIN TRAN

UPDATE Person.Contact
```

```
SET EmailAddress = 'uncommitted@email.at'
WHERE ContactID = 1;
```

4. Open a second query window and execute the following statements to read the Name and EmailAddress of ContactID 1.

```
USE AdventureWorks;

BEGIN TRAN

SELECT FirstName, LastName, EmailAddress
FROM Person.Contact
WHERE ContactID = 1;
```

The EmailAddress gustavo0@adventure-works.com of contact Gustavo Achong is returned since it is the last committed version of this row. Unlike the READ COMMITTED level without SNAPSHOT, the query is not blocked anymore.

5. Close Query Window 2 and switch to Query Window 1.

6. Execute the following statements to roll back the transaction and switch back to the READ COMMITED level. (This query will wait until you have closed Query Window 2.)

```
ROLLBACK TRAN
GO
USE master;
ALTER DATABASE AdventureWorks
SET READ_COMMITTED_SNAPSHOT OFF
```

> **Important** This isolation level can be used to reduce blocking, but be aware that it is a database option. When it is changed, all transactions using the READ COMMITTED level in that database change their behavior as well. Therefore, it is only advisable to use it when all of these transactions are also logically correct when they read the last committed version of data instead of the actual committed version of data.

Getting Consistent Repeatable Read Operations

One disadvantage of the READ COMMITTED level is that it is possible for data that is read by one transaction to be changed by another transaction while the first transaction runs. Therefore, with both versions of the READ COMMITTED level, you aren't guaranteed consistent reads. Getting consistent reads means that, within a transaction, the same data is always read.

- READ COMMITTED uses shared locks while reading data, but releases the locks right after the read operation. Therefore other transactions can change it.

- READ COMMITTED SNAPSHOT reads the last committed version of the data. When it reads the data a second time, the last committed version can be a newer version than before if a second transaction has committed a change to the data.

This inconsistency can lead to problems when consistent reads are needed, such as for reporting. Imagine that your transaction calculates some business values out of your data. While doing this calculation in the READ COMMITTED level, it is possible that these values are calculated incorrectly because the base data changes while your transaction is calculating. To successfully perform this calculation, the SNAPSHOT isolation level can be used. It uses row versioning to provide a committed version of the data, but unlike the READ COMMITTED SNAPSHOT level, it always provides the last committed version of the data from the beginning of the transaction. Therefore, SQL Server always reads the same data throughout the whole transaction.

Using the SNAPSHOT Isolation Level

1. Start SQL Server Management Studio and open a New Query window.

2. SNAPSHOT isolation needs to be activated for the database once. After it is activated, every connection can use it when it is needed. To allow SNAPSHOT isolation in the AdventureWorks database, execute the following statement. The code for this example is included in the sample files as SnapshotIsolation1.sql and SnapshotIsolation2.sql.

```
USE master;
ALTER DATABASE AdventureWorks
    SET ALLOW_SNAPSHOT_ISOLATION ON;
```

3. Now imagine that you want to run some reports against the Sales.SalesOrderDetail table, but you need consistent read operations. Execute the following statements to activate SNAPSHOT isolation for the transaction and start a transaction that returns the sum of line totals for an order. Remember the OrderTotal value.

```
USE AdventureWorks;

SET TRANSACTION ISOLATION LEVEL SNAPSHOT

BEGIN TRAN
SELECT SUM(LineTotal) as OrderTotal
FROM Sales.SalesOrderDetail
WHERE SalesOrderID = 43659
```

4. Open a second query window and update the SalesOrderDetail table to change the base data for the query in Query Window 1. (If you want to repeat this example, change the OrderQty from 5 to some other number so that the following code actually changes the data in the database.)

```
USE AdventureWorks;

UPDATE Sales.SalesOrderDetail
SET OrderQty = 5
WHERE SalesOrderID = 43659
AND ProductID = 777
```

5. Close Query Window 2, switch back to Query Window 1, and repeat the SELECT statement.

```
SELECT SUM(LineTotal) as OrderTotal
FROM Sales.SalesOrderDetail
WHERE SalesOrderID = 43659
```

As you can see, the result is the same as before since SNAPSHOT isolation ignores data changes while the transaction is running. It always provides the last committed values from the beginning of the transaction.

6. Commit the transaction and repeat the query again by executing the following code. Now you will see that the result has changed because the transaction has ended.

```
COMMIT TRAN

SELECT SUM(LineTotal) as OrderTotal
FROM Sales.SalesOrderDetail
WHERE SalesOrderID = 43659
```

7. Execute the following code to turn off SNAPSHOT isolation in the AdventureWorks database.

```
ALTER DATABASE Adventureworks
    SET ALLOW_SNAPSHOT_ISOLATION OFF;
```

Avoiding Simultaneous Updates to the Data

As you have seen, SNAPSHOT isolation doesn't lock the data while reading data, but provides us with a consistent view throughout the transaction. But in some situations, it is essential to lock the data for the whole transaction to avoid updates from other transactions. Suppose that you want to invoice an order. You first need to retrieve the data and check it, and then afterwards produce the invoice out of it. In such a transaction, you need to lock the data from the beginning to avoid changes made by other transactions. In this case, neither SNAPSHOT isolation nor READ COMMITTED isolation is a good choice. In such situations, the REPEATABLE READ isolation level can be used. This level works like the READ COMMITTED level without SNAPSHOT, but holds shared locks until the end of the transaction. Therefore, it prevents updates to the data.

Using the REPEATABLE READ Isolation Level

1. Start SQL Server Management Studio and open a New Query window.

2. Suppose that you want to process the order with OrderID 43659. First, the data has to be selected. To prevent other transactions from changing the data you are reading, use the REPEATABLE READ isolation. Execute the following code. (The code for this example is included in the sample files as RepeatableReadIsolation1.sql and RepeatableReadIsolation2.sql.)

```
USE Adventureworks;
```

```
SET TRANSACTION ISOLATION LEVEL REPEATABLE READ

BEGIN TRAN
SELECT SalesOrderID, SalesOrderDetailID, ProductID, OrderQty
FROM Sales.SalesOrderDetail
WHERE SalesOrderID = 43659
```

3. Open a second query window and try to update the SalesOrderDetail table to change the base data for the query in Query Window 1 by executing this code:

```
USE Adventureworks;

UPDATE Sales.SalesOrderDetail
SET OrderQty = 5
WHERE SalesOrderID = 43659
AND ProductID = 777
```

The query waits. Unlike with SNAPSHOT isolation, it is not possible to update the data since shared locks are held to prevent data changes from other transactions. The locks can be seen through the *sys.dm_tran_locks* management view you have used before.

4. Click the Cancel Executing Query button on the toolbar (shown below) to cancel the query in Query Window 2 and instead execute the following INSERT statement to add a new line item to the order:

```
INSERT INTO Sales.SalesOrderDetail
    (SalesOrderID,CarrierTrackingNumber,
    OrderQty,ProductID,SpecialOfferID,UnitPrice,UnitPriceDiscount)
VALUES(43659,'4911-403C-98',1,758,1,874,0)
```

5. Note that this statement executes successfully, even though you are in the REPEATABLE READ isolation level. This is because REPEATABLE READ locks data to prevent updates on the data, but the INSERT statement inserts new data in the database, and this is allowed. Because the new row falls into the range of the SELECT statement of the transaction in Window 1, it will be read the next time the transaction retrieves the same data. These types of rows are called phantom reads.

6. Repeat the SELECT statement and COMMIT the transaction, as shown below.

```
SELECT SalesOrderID, SalesOrderDetailID, ProductID, OrderQty
FROM Sales.SalesOrderDetail
WHERE SalesOrderID = 43659

COMMIT TRAN
```

Observe that the new row was read by the SELECT statement because it falls into the range of the statement. The REPEATABLE READ level prevents existing data from being changed, but does not prevent new data from being inserted into the range of a SELECT statement.

7. Close SQL Server Management Studio.

Blocking and Deadlocks

To ensure that your transaction doesn't read phantom data, you can *block* the data by locking the range of data you are examining. This can lead to problems with deadlocks, however.

Locking Consistent Blocks of Related Data

To prevent phantom reads, the SERIALIZABLE isolation level can be used. It is stricter than the REPEATABLE READ level and locks not only the data read by a transaction, but also the ranges the transaction reads. This is done by using special lock types, called range locks, on indexes. Range locks lock the ranges defined in the WHERE clause of the SELECT statement. These locks can be used only if a related index exists. If there is no related index, SQL Server has to use a table-level lock to prevent inserts into the range. The SERIALIZABLE isolation level should therefore be used only when absolutely necessary.

Using the SERIALIZABLE Isolation Level

1. Start SQL Server Management Studio and open a New Query window.

2. Suppose that you want to look at the same SalesOrderID as before. Now you are using the SERIALIZABLE isolation level to prevent not only changes to the data, but also phantom reads. Enter and execute the following statement. The code for this example is included in the sample files as SerializableIsolation1.sql and SerializableIsolation2.sql.

    ```
    USE AdventureWorks;

    SET TRANSACTION ISOLATION LEVEL SERIALIZABLE

    BEGIN TRAN
    SELECT SalesOrderID, SalesOrderDetailID, ProductID, OrderQty
    FROM Sales.SalesOrderDetail
    WHERE SalesOrderID = 43659
    ```

3. Open a second query window and try to insert a new line item for the order processed by Query Window 1.

    ```
    INSERT INTO Sales.SalesOrderDetail
        (SalesOrderID,CarrierTrackingNumber,
        OrderQty,ProductID,SpecialOfferID,UnitPrice,UnitPriceDiscount)
    VALUES(43659,'4911-403C-98',1,758,1,874,0)
    ```

4. Close Query Window 2 because you can see that the query is blocked. As you have now seen, SERIALIZABLE isolation also prevents the INSERT of new rows into the range of data read by the transaction.

5. Execute the COMMIT TRAN statement, and then close all query windows.

Dealing with Blocking

As you can tell from the previous example, blocking can be a big issue on multi-user database systems. Minimizing blocking should be a primary concern in transaction design. To minimize blocking, a few rules should be always followed:

- Keep the transaction as short as possible.
- Never request user input during a transaction.
- Consider using row versioning when reading data.
- Access the least amount of data possible while in a transaction.
- Use lower isolating transaction levels whenever possible.

If your application doesn't perform as expected and you think that blocking issues could be the cause, it is possible to monitor blocking through Dynamic Management Views (DMVs).

Monitoring Blocking with DMV

Let's use the same example as we used for the REPEATABLE READ isolation level to monitor blocking.

1. Start SQL Server Management Studio and open a New Query window.
2. Execute the following batch to start a transaction in REPEATABLE READ mode. The code for this example is included in the sample files as MonitoringBlocking1.sql, MonitoringBlocking2.sql, and MonitoringBlocking3.sql.

```
USE AdventureWorks;

SET TRANSACTION ISOLATION LEVEL REPEATABLE READ

BEGIN TRAN
SELECT SalesOrderID, SalesOrderDetailID, ProductID, OrderQty
FROM Sales.SalesOrderDetail
WHERE SalesOrderID = 43659
```

3. Open a second query window and execute the following UPDATE statement. It will be blocked by the transaction in Query Window 1.

```
USE AdventureWorks;

UPDATE Sales.SalesOrderDetail
SET OrderQty = 5
WHERE SalesOrderID = 43659
AND ProductID = 777
```

4. Keep the UPDATE statement running and open a third query window.

5. Enter and execute the following statement in the third query window to retrieve all user processes that have waited for more than five seconds.

```
SELECT * FROM sys.dm_os_waiting_tasks
WHERE session_id > 49
AND wait_duration_ms > 5000
```

With this statement you get information about all user processes with session id's greater than 49 that have been blocked for more than five seconds for any reason. The blocking_session_id column contains the session id of the blocking session. Note the session id in your results for use in step 7.

6. To get information about what statement the blocked process is trying to execute, the following statement can be used. This statement joins *sys.dm_os_waiting_tasks* with a view called *sys.dm_exec_requests* that gives back information about running requests. The statement also uses a function called *sys.dm_exec_sql_text()* that can retrieve the SQL statement through a handle that is provided in the *sys.dm_exec_requests* view. Execute the following code:

```
SELECT (select SUBSTRING(text,statement_start_offset/2,
    (case when statement_end_offset = -1 then
    len(convert(nvarchar(max), text)) * 2 else
    statement_end_offset end -statement_start_offset)/2)
    from sys.dm_exec_sql_text(sql_handle)) as query_text
FROM
    sys.dm_os_waiting_tasks wt
JOIN
    sys.dm_exec_requests r
ON r.session_id = wt.session_id
WHERE r.session_id > 50
AND wait_duration_ms > 5000
```

7. More information about the connections involved in the blocking scenario can be retrieved using the *sys.dm_exec_connections* view. Replace the session id in the query (51 in the code below) with the actual session id of your blocking or blocked session.

```
SELECT *
FROM sys.dm_exec_connections
WHERE session_id = 51   --Replace with your id
```

8. Execute a COMMIT TRAN statement in Query Window 1 and close all query windows.

> **More Info**   For more information about Dynamic Management Views, see the SQL Server Books Online topic "Dynamic Management Views and Functions."

Dealing with Deadlocks

Deadlocks are special blocking scenarios that lead to infinite blocking if not resolved automatically. This can happen when two or more transactions block each other. If this situation happens, every transaction waits for the others to release their locks, but this will not happen because the others are waiting as well. Such a situation is called a deadlock because the transactions will never unlock. In order to prevent this, SQL Server resolves such situations on its own by rolling back one of the transactions and returning an error to the connection in order to let the other transactions end their work.

Producing a Simple Deadlock Scenario

Let us produce a simple deadlock scenario to see how SQL Server manages deadlocks.

1. Start SQL Server Management Studio and open a New Query window.

2. Enter and execute the following code to create a small table and insert data in it without closing the transaction. The code for this example is included in the sample files as Deadlock1.sql and Deadlock2.sql.

    ```
    USE tempdb;

    CREATE TABLE t1 (i int)

    BEGIN TRAN
    INSERT INTO t1 Values(1)
    ```

3. Open a second query window and execute the following statements to create a small table, insert data into it, and try to update table t1 of Query Window 1. The transaction will be blocked because the transaction in Query Window 1 is not yet committed.

    ```
    USE tempdb;

    CREATE TABLE t2 (i int)

    BEGIN TRAN
    INSERT INTO t2 Values(1)

    UPDATE t1 SET i = 2
    ```

4. Let the query run and switch back to Query Window 1. Execute the following UPDATE statement to update table t2 and examine what is happening.

    ```
    UPDATE t2 SET i = 2
    ```

    After a few seconds, one of the transactions is canceled and an error message is returned, as shown below.

    ```
    Msg 1205, Level 13, State 45, Line 2
    Transaction (Process ID 52) was deadlocked on lock resources with another process and
    has been chosen as the deadlock victim. Rerun the transaction.
    ```

This happened because the transactions blocked each other. The transaction in Query Window 1 had a lock on table t1 and tried to update table t2 and the transaction in Query Window 2 had a lock on table t2 and tried to update table t1. Therefore, both transactions would wait forever for the other to unlock. Such situations are detected by SQL Server and solved by rolling back one of the involved transactions and firing error 1205 to the appropriate connection.

5. Close all query windows.

Some rules should be followed to prevent and handle deadlocks:

- Follow the rules to minimize blocking. With less blocking, there is less chance of deadlocking.

- Always access objects in the same order within your transactions. If both transactions in the example above had accessed the tables in the same order, there would have been no chance for a deadlock. Therefore, an access order list should be defined for all tables in the database.

- Check for error 1205 within your error handler and resubmit the transaction when the error occurs.

- Add a procedure to your error handler to log the error details.

When you follow these rules, you have a good chance of preventing deadlocks. When they happen, it is unknown to the users because the transaction is automatically reissued, but it is still possible for you to monitor deadlocking through logging.

Transactions in ADO.NET

Until now, you have used only T-SQL to manage transactions, but transactions can also be managed directly through ADO.NET. Transactions in ADO.NET are managed through the *SQLTransaction* class, which can be found in the *System.Data.SqlClient* namespace. For every transaction, an isolation level can be provided through the *IsolationLevel Enumerators* namespace.

The following example shows how a transaction can be defined through ADO.NET. The transaction is rolled back on any error and committed when no error occurs. This code is included in the sample files as Chapter10.sln. To run the sample, build and execute the solution in Visual Studio, then make sure the Output window is visible in Visual Studio while you click the two buttons on the form.

```
Private Sub TryCommand(ByVal cmd As String)
    Dim connectionString As String = _
      "Data Source=.\SQLExpress;Initial Catalog=Adventureworks;" + _
      "Integrated Security=True;"
    Using connection As New SqlConnection(connectionString)
        connection.Open()
```

```vbnet
        Dim command As SqlCommand = connection.CreateCommand()
        Dim transaction As SqlTransaction

        Dim iso As IsolationLevel = IsolationLevel.RepeatableRead

        'Start a local transaction and define the Isolation Level
        transaction = connection.BeginTransaction(iso)

        'Assign the transaction and connection object
        'to the Command object
        command.Connection = connection
        command.Transaction = transaction

        Try
            command.CommandText = cmd
            command.ExecuteNonQuery()

            ' Attempt to commit the transaction.
            transaction.Commit()
            Console.WriteLine("Transaction succeeded.")

        Catch ex As Exception
            Console.WriteLine("Commit Exception Type: {0}", ex.GetType())
            Console.WriteLine("  Message: {0}", ex.Message)

            ' Try to roll back the transaction.
            Try
                transaction.Rollback()

            Catch ex2 As Exception
                'When the connection was already closed
                'the Rollback doesn't work anymore
                Console.WriteLine("Rollback Exception Type: {0}", ex2.GetType())
                Console.WriteLine("  Message: {0}", ex2.Message)
            End Try
        End Try
    End Using

End Sub

Private Sub btnTryInvalidCmd_Click(ByVal sender As System.Object, _
    ByVal e As System.EventArgs) Handles btnSetInvalidCmd.Click
    TryCommand("This_is_an_invalid_sql_command")
End Sub

Private Sub btnTryValidCmd_Click(ByVal sender As System.Object, _
    ByVal e As System.EventArgs) Handles btnSetValidCmd.Click
    TryCommand("SELECT * FROM dbo.orders")
End Sub
```

Conclusion

In this chapter, you have learned that all data access in SQL Server is done through transactions. Every transaction conforms to the ACID rules and can be defined explicitly to correspond to business transactions. Every explicit transaction should also implement an error handler to define under which circumstances SQL Server should roll back the transaction.

You have seen how SQL Server can isolate transactions from each other through locking and row versioning and how it is possible to implement the best level of isolation for your transaction through defining isolation levels. Also, you have learned how important it is to choose the right isolation level to minimize blocking and deadlock problems in databases.

Chapter 10 Quick Reference

To	Do This
Start a transaction	BEGIN TRAN
Commit a transaction	COMMIT TRAN
Roll back a transaction	ROLLBACK TRAN
Trap for errors in a transaction	Use a TRY/CATCH statement. Use the RAISERROR statement to return an error message.
Turn on implicit transactions	`SET IMPLICIT_TRANSACTIONS ON`
Check the level of nested transactions	Use the @@TRANCOUNT function.
Monitor locks	Query the *sys.dm_tran_locks* view.
Set the isolation level	`SET TRANSACTION ISOLATION LEVEL <isolation level>`
Monitor blocking	Query the *sys.dm_os_waiting_tasks* view.
Minimize blocking	■ Keep the transaction as short as possible. ■ Never request user input during a transaction. ■ Consider using row versioning when reading data. ■ Access the least amount of data possible while in a transaction. ■ Use lower isolating transaction levels whenever possible.

To	Do This
Prevent and handle deadlocks	■ Follow the rules to minimize blocking.
	■ Always access objects in the same order within your transactions (an access order list should be defined for all tables in a database).
	■ Check for error 1205 within your error handler and resubmit the transaction when the error occurs.
	■ Add a procedure to your error handler to log the error details.

Chapter 11

Keeping History Data

After completing this chapter, you will be able to:

- Create and use database snapshots
- Design effective history tables for summarizing historical data
- Create and use indexed views to summarize your historical data
- Build audit columns and tables to track changes in your data
- Use audit tables to recover lost data

The previous chapter discussed using transactions to ensure the integrity of your data. This chapter delves into ensuring data integrity by tracking changes and storing historical versions of the data that can be restored if needed without restoring the entire database.

Historical data can take many different forms, from auditing to data warehousing for analytics. This chapter concentrates on methods for auditing and archiving your data. One of the primary goals of this chapter is to show you ways that you can recover data and track changes. As you can see from the list of objectives above, there are a number of ways to meet this goal. However, Microsoft SQL Server 2005 has methods other than these approaches, which will be highlighted throughout the chapter as alternative methods. Look for Tips as you read to learn about these alternative methods.

Taking a Snapshot of Your Database

In SQL Server 2005, you have the ability to create a snapshot of your data. A database snapshot is essentially a placeholder of the time that it is taken. At any point going forward, you can revert to the snapshot and remove the changes that you have made to your data. Here is a short list of times you may find snapshots very helpful:

- During the development cycle of the database or its related application, you can take a snapshot to create a baseline set of data to work with. Of course, this also helps developers as they will not have to recover databases as often and they can store multiple snapshots with different changes so they can go back as far as they need to without totally scrapping their work up to that point.

- You can use snapshots when doing testing. Whether you are making schema changes or testing new data-load techniques, you can use a database snapshot as a known starting point to which you can revert before rerunning a test.

- You can use snapshots to recover from a flawed bulk load on your production system.. There are many times when a bulk load can fail and not properly roll back, leaving you with your database in an unknown state. Previously, you would need to restore from a backup, but if you schedule a snapshot before you execute the bulk load, you can revert to the snapshot and quickly get up and running again.

> **Tip**   You can also use snapshots for static reporting databases. For instance, if you want to do some reporting on data from the end of last year, you can create a snapshot of the data on December 31 or January 1 and use it for your year-end reporting.

As you can see, database snapshots can be very beneficial in development, testing, and production environments.

> **Important**   Database snapshots are only available in SQL Server 2005 Enterprise Edition and SQL Server 2005 Developer Edition. Most of your development and testing personnel can use the Developer Edition, but if you would like to implement this in your production environment, you will need to use the Enterprise Edition of SQL Server 2005.

Creating a Database Snapshot

Database snapshots can only be created using Transact-SQL. They cannot be created in SQL Server Management Studio. Here is the code for creating a database snapshot using the sample database AdventureWorks. (This code is included in the sample files as Create Snapshot.sql.)

Creating a Snapshot

1. From the Start menu, select All Programs | Microsoft SQL Server 2005 | SQL Server Management Studio.

2. Open a New Query window. Enter and execute the following code to create a snapshot of AdventureWorks. Adjust the file path to suit your folder structure.

```
CREATE DATABASE AdventureWorks_SBSExample1 ON
   ( NAME = AdventureWorks_Data,
     FILENAME =
     'C:\MySnapshotData\AdventureWorks_SBSExample1.snapshot' )
AS SNAPSHOT OF AdventureWorks;
GO
```

The first thing you will notice about this CREATE statement is that it is the same statement used to create databases. This means that the user executing this statement must have the necessary permissions to create databases on the server they are working with. The next thing to note is that the snapshot must mirror all the files that are contained in the source database. In this case, AdventureWorks only has a single file – AdventureWorks_Data. However, if more than one file or file group is used in the source database, you will need to add a NAME and FILENAME clause for each file.

> **Important** You need to match the logical file name from the source database during the creation of your snapshot. If you use multiple files, those logical file names must be created with the source's logical name as well.

The last piece of the code lets SQL Server know that you are creating a snapshot of the specified database. Remember that the snapshots and their source databases need to be on the same server.

> ## Additional Considerations When Creating a Snapshot
> ### Snapshot Names
> Use names that are meaningful when you choose the name of the snapshot. In the example above, SBSExample1 refers to this book, *Step-by-Step*. However, you will find it more beneficial to use dates and times in your snapshot names so users will be able to see easily what data is in the snapshot.
>
> ### File Names
> It is generally a good practice to generate the filename from the database or logical file name. Furthermore, the extension can be whatever makes sense to you. SQL Server Books Online uses the .ss file extension, and the example used the .snapshot extension. Use the naming convention that works best for you.
>
> ### Disk Space Usage
> You will need to account for the amount of disk space required by your snapshots. Snapshots only contain changes from the source at the time of the snapshot. This means that the more changes that are made on the source database, the more space will be required to store the snapshots recording these changes. Also, think about how many snapshots you want to keep.

Reverting to a Database Snapshot

As with creating a database snapshot, you will need to use T-SQL to revert to a database snapshot. To revert to the database snapshot, you use the RESTORE DATABASE command in T-SQL.

> **Warning** When you revert to a snapshot, ALL changes made from that point forward, both schema and data changes, will be lost. If you need to track the changes made, be sure to back up your source before reverting to the snapshot.

Reverting to a Snapshot

1. You will need to choose the snapshot you want to revert to. You can view the available snapshots in SQL Server Management Studio in the Database Snapshot folder. The location of this folder is illustrated below.

2. Once you have chosen your desired snapshot, you will need to remove any snapshots that have occurred after that snapshot. Once you revert, these will no longer be usable and SQL Server will not let you revert without removing them first. See the next section, titled "Deleting a Database Snapshot," for details on deleting snapshots.

> **Troubleshooting**   You will get the following errors if you try to revert to the previous snapshot without deleting the other snapshots:
>
> ```
> Msg 3137, Level 16, State 4, Line 1
> Database cannot be reverted. Either the primary or the snapshot
>  names are improperly specified, all other snapshots have
>  not been dropped, or there are missing files.
> Msg 3013, Level 16, State 1, Line 1
> RESTORE DATABASE is terminating abnormally.
> ```

3. Enter and execute the following code, which uses the RESTORE DATABASE command to revert to your desired snapshot. (This code is included in the sample files as Restore FromSnapshot.sql.)

```
RESTORE DATABASE AdventureWorks FROM DATABASE_SNAPSHOT =
    'AdventureWorks_SBSExample1'
```

> **Tip**   If you are in development or testing, you can keep this snapshot and attempt your changes again. You will find that you can revert to this snapshot regularly and more quickly than restoring a backup, especially if your test database is rather large.

4. Now that you have finished restoring, you can use the source database as usual.

> **Tip**   You can also use table partitioning to store history data. This can be done using a sliding window technique in which you rotate out file groups and archive them. See the SQL Server Books Online topic "Index and Table Partitioning" for details on using table partitioning.

Deleting a Database Snapshot

Unlike creating and reverting to a snapshot, you can delete a snapshot using either T-SQL or SQL Server Management Studio. As you have noticed by now, snapshots use variations of the database commands in T-SQL to perform their operations. This is also the case when deleting a snapshot.

Deleting a Snapshot Using T-SQL

Use the DROP DATABASE command when deleting a snapshot using T-SQL. The same restrictions exist for dropping a snapshot as with dropping any database. You will need to have all the connections cleared and have permission to drop databases in order to perform this action. To delete the snapshot we created, enter and execute the following code in a new query window. (This code is included in the sample files as DeleteSnapshot.sql.)

```
DROP DATABASE AdventureWorks_SBSExample1;
```

Deleting a Snapshot Using SQL Server Management Studio

In SQL Server Management Studio, you can delete a database snapshot the same way you would delete a normal database.

1. Open SQL Server Management Studio.

2. Expand the Database Snapshots folder in the Object Explorer.

3. Select the snapshot you wish to delete.

4. Right-click that snapshot and select Delete from the context menu. This will open the Delete Object dialog box, shown below:

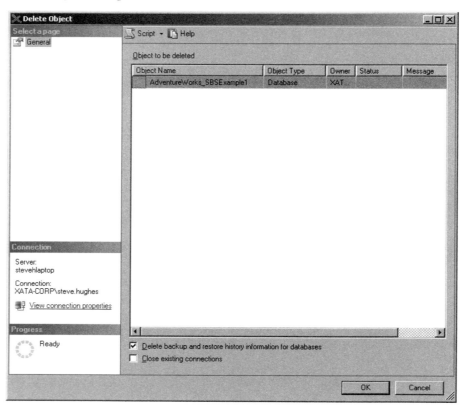

5. You can choose to have SQL Server close connections from this dialog box by selecting the Close Existing Connections checkbox. The advantage of doing this is that the delete operation will not have to wait for transactions to complete before commencing. This is the equivalent of sending KILL statements to all the connections to the database.

6. Click the OK button to delete the snapshot.

Impact on the Source Database

The source database is impacted in the following ways when database snapshots are used with it:

- Database management

  - You will not be able to drop or detach the source database while database snapshots exist. You will have to delete the snapshots first.

  - You will not be able to restore the source database while database snapshots exist.

> **Note**   Backup operations on the source database will continue to function normally. These operations are not affected when snapshots exist.

  - If you revert to a snapshot, the log chain is broken and transactional log restores will not work as expected.

  - Files cannot be dropped from the source database until the snapshots are deleted.

- Database performance

  - There will be a performance impact as the database must manage both the source and related snapshots. The database will need to copy the original value to the snapshot and then write the change to the source. This will cause additional I/O operations as long as snapshots are being used.

Summarizing Data in History Tables

By moving data to history tables, you can relieve your transactional system of the hit taken when reporting queries are run against it. History tables can be optimized for queries and maintained separately from the rest of the system. There are a number of ways to create these tables and keep them updated. We will walk through a few examples here that utilize both T-SQL and SQL Server Agent to load the tables.

In the following steps, you will create a summary table from the AdventureWorks database that will track the sales by a salesperson for given products. The goal is to be able to quickly discover how many units of a given product the salesperson has sold by querying on his or her name.

Creating and Loading a History Table

1. You will need to set up the table as shown below in your AdventureWorks database in order to use the examples verbatim. The code to create this table and its clustered index

is as follows (and is included in the sample files as CreateSalesPerson
ProductWeeklySummary.sql). Enter and execute this code in a new query window of
SQL Server Management Studio.

Column Name	Data Type	Allow Nulls
SalesPersonID	int	☑
SalesPersonFirstName	nvarchar(50)	☑
SalesPersonLastName	nvarchar(50)	☑
OrderWeekOfYear	int	☑
OrderYear	int	☑
ProductID	int	☑
ProductName	nvarchar(50)	☑
WeeklyOrderQty	int	☑
WeeklyLineTotal	money	☑
		☐

Table - Sales...tWeeklySummary / *stevehlaptop.A...te Snapsh*

```
USE AdventureWorks;
GO
CREATE TABLE Sales.SalesPersonProductWeeklySummary
    (SalesPersonID INT
    ,SalesPersonFirstName NVARCHAR(50)
    ,SalesPersonLastName NVARCHAR(50)
    ,OrderWeekOfYear INT
    ,OrderYear INT
    ,ProductID INT
    ,ProductName NVARCHAR(50)
    ,WeeklyOrderQty INT
    ,WeeklyLineTotal MONEY
    );
GO

CREATE CLUSTERED INDEX cidx_SalesPersonProductWeeklySummary
    ON Sales.SalesPersonProductWeeklySummary(OrderYear, OrderWeekOfYear,
    SalesPersonID);
GO
```

2. Next, you will need a stored procedure that can be used to select the data that will be
    loaded into the SalesPersonProductWeeklySummary table. The following code
    (included in the sample files as CreateUspGetWeeklySalesSummary.sql) creates the
    procedure. Enter and execute this code in a New Query window.

```
USE AdventureWorks
GO
CREATE PROCEDURE Sales.uspGetSalesWeeklySummary
    (@StartOfWeek DATETIME
    ,@EndOfWeek DATETIME
    )
AS
BEGIN
  SELECT hdr.SalesPersonID
```

```
        ,cntc.FirstName AS SalesPersonFirstName
        ,cntc.LastName AS SalesPersonLastName
        ,DATEPART(WEEK, hdr.OrderDate) AS OrderWeekOfYear
        ,DATEPART(YEAR, hdr.OrderDate) AS OrderYear
        ,prod.ProductID
        ,prod.Name AS ProductName
        ,SUM(dtl.OrderQty) as WeeklyOrderQty
        ,SUM(dtl.LineTotal) as WeeklyLineTotal
    FROM Sales.SalesOrderHeader hdr
        INNER JOIN Sales.SalesOrderDetail dtl
          ON hdr.SalesOrderID = dtl.SalesOrderID
        INNER JOIN HumanResources.Employee emp
          ON hdr.SalesPersonID = emp.EmployeeID
        INNER JOIN Person.Contact cntc
          ON emp.ContactID = cntc.ContactID
        INNER JOIN Production.Product prod
          ON dtl.ProductID = prod.ProductID
    WHERE hdr.OrderDate BETWEEN @StartOfWeek AND @EndOfWeek
    GROUP BY hdr.SalesPersonID
        ,cntc.FirstName
        ,cntc.LastName
        ,prod.ProductID
        ,prod.Name
        ,hdr.OrderDate
END;
GO
```

> **Tip** By using the Sales schema, you can make sure that the permissions for accessing the sales data apply to the new summary data objects as well.

3. Next, you can load the table with the *uspGetWeeklySalesSummary* stored procedure using the following code (included in the sample files as LoadSalesPersonProduct WeeklySummary.sql). Enter and execute this code in a New Query window.

```
INSERT INTO Sales.SalesPersonProductWeeklySummary
    (SalesPersonID
    ,SalesPersonFirstName
    ,SalesPersonLastName
    ,OrderWeekOfYear
    ,OrderYear
    ,ProductID
    ,ProductName
    ,WeeklyOrderQty
    ,WeeklyLineTotal
    )
EXEC Sales.uspGetSalesWeeklySummary @StartOfWeek = '1/1/2004 00:00:00',
    @EndOfWeek = '1/7/2004 11:59:59';
GO
```

4. Finally, you can use a variation of the above code in SQL Server Agent to automate the weekly loading of the data.

> **Tip** You can also use SQL Server Integration Services to load the data. If you have more than one load operation, this might be a better option for you.

5. In SQL Server Management Studio, open the New Job dialog box by expanding the SQL Server Agent node in Object Explorer and right-clicking the Jobs folder. Select New Job from the context menu.

6. On the General page of the New Job dialog box, give the job a meaningful name. You can add a description here as well.

7. On the Steps page of the New Job dialog box, click the New button to create a new job step. This will open the New Job Step dialog box, as shown here:

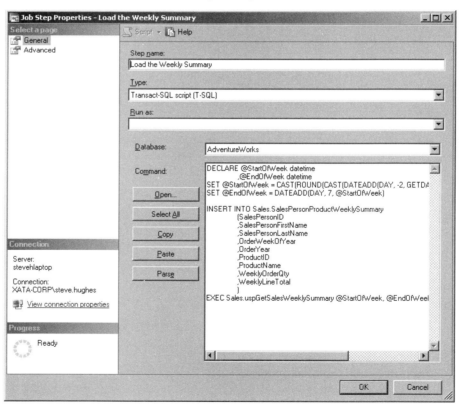

8. After giving the step a meaningful name (here we use Load The Weekly Summary), you need to select Transact-SQL Script (T-SQL) from the Type dropdown menu and AdventureWorks from the Database dropdown menu.

> **Tip** You can choose a different account to run the job by setting the Run As option. By default the SQL Server Agent account will be used to execute the command.

9. Next, set the command code. You will need to set the dates dynamically. Enter the following code to set the variables to run from Sunday to Saturday of the previous week and load the table. This step will assume that the job is scheduled to run on Tuesday. (This code is included in the sample files as ScheduledJobStep.sql.)

```
DECLARE @StartOfWeek datetime
    ,@EndOfWeek datetime
SET @StartOfWeek = CAST(ROUND(CAST(DATEADD(DAY, -2, GETDATE())
    AS FLOAT),0,1) AS DATETIME)
SET @EndOfWeek = DATEADD(DAY, 7, @StartOfWeek)

INSERT INTO Sales.SalesPersonProductWeeklySummary
    (SalesPersonID
    ,SalesPersonFirstName
    ,SalesPersonLastName
    ,OrderWeekOfYear
    ,OrderYear
    ,ProductID
    ,ProductName
    ,WeeklyOrderQty
    ,WeeklyLineTotal
    )
EXEC Sales.uspGetSalesWeeklySummary @StartOfWeek, @EndOfWeek
```

> **Tip** Because SQL Server does not have a datatype that supports date only, it is necessary to drop the time from the *DateTime* in order to set the parameters correctly. You can do this as shown above or as follows:
>
> ```
> SET @StartOfWeek = CAST(CONVERT(VARCHAR, DATEADD(DAY, -2, GETDATE()), 101)
>     AS DATETIME).
> ```
>
> You can try it either way. This method uses a string conversion, while the other code uses numeric conversion and may perform better.

10. Click the OK button to finish creating the Load the Weekly Summary job step.

11. On the Schedules page of the New Job dialog box, you can set up when the job is to execute. In this example, you will set the job up to run on a weekly recurring schedule on Tuesdays at 2:00 AM. Click the New button and enter the appropriate settings in the New Job Schedule dialog box. The screen below shows the New Job Schedule dialog box

set up to run this schedule. Click the OK button to save the new schedule and apply it to your current job.

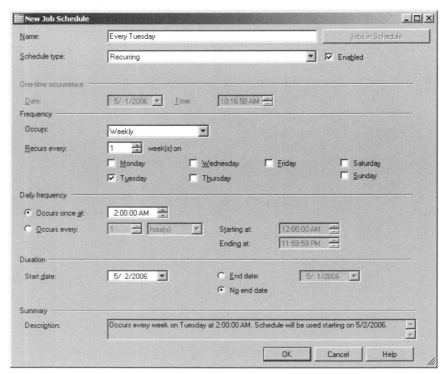

> **Tip** Many of the dialog boxes in SQL Server Management Studio contain a Script button, as shown below. Click this button to script the changes you just applied. Right before you save the job, you can use this option to generate a script for the job, job steps, and schedule.

12. Click the OK button to exit the New Job dialog box and create the new job.

Summarizing Data in Indexed Views

Another option for storing summarized history data is using indexed views. Indexed views are also known as materialized views because they will compute and store the data. What sets them apart from standard views is that they have unique clustered indexes implemented on them to improve performance of queries run against them. In general, the greatest performance gain will be realized when creating indexed views of data that has been summarized and requires many joins to get the results. If the data you want to query has few aggregations or joins or is frequently updated, indexed views will provide little, if any, performance gain.

> **Important**   Indexed views are only supported in SQL Server Enterprise Edition (2000 and 2005 versions). As with all Enterprise-only functionality, you can develop with Enterprise Edition functionality using SQL Server Developer Edition.

In the following steps, you will be creating an indexed view that will return the individual product sales by salesperson in 2004. Indexed views have many restrictions that prevent you from creating an indexed view based on varying values. In this case, you are using a date range where data most likely will not change. If you want to see this data by month, then you should create a new indexed view for each month.

> **Tip**   If you use this type of view primarily for summarized data, you could implement a set of views that would summarize the data by complete year and only use months during the current year. For example, you could have indexed views for 2004, 2005, Jan 2006, Feb 2006 and so on. At the end of each year, you could remove the monthly views for that year and create the year view.

Creating an Indexed View for Sales Summary

1. Create the view by executing the code below (included in the sample files as Create View.sql) in a New Query window in SQL Server Management Studio. Refer to the sidebar "Settings Required to Use Indexed Views" for greater explanation of the sections shown in bold. These sections are required in order to apply the index.

```
USE AdventureWorks;
GO

IF EXISTS(SELECT 1 FROM sys.objects WHERE name =
    N'v_SalesPerson2004ProductSummary')
  DROP VIEW Sales.v_SalesPerson2004ProductSummary
GO

SET ANSI_NULLS ON
SET QUOTED_IDENTIFIER ON
GO

CREATE VIEW Sales.v_SalesPerson2004ProductSummary WITH SCHEMABINDING
AS
  SELECT hdr.SalesPersonID
    ,cntc.FirstName AS SalesPersonFirstName
    ,cntc.LastName AS SalesPersonLastName
    ,prod.ProductID
    ,prod.Name AS ProductName
    ,COUNT_BIG(*) AS OrderLineCount
    ,SUM(dtl.OrderQty) as OrderQty
```

```
     ,SUM(dtl.LineTotal) as LineTotal
  FROM Sales.SalesOrderHeader hdr
    INNER JOIN Sales.SalesOrderDetail dtl
      ON hdr.SalesOrderID = dtl.SalesOrderID
    INNER JOIN HumanResources.Employee emp
      ON hdr.SalesPersonID = emp.EmployeeID
    INNER JOIN Person.Contact cntc
      ON emp.ContactID = cntc.ContactID
    INNER JOIN Production.Product prod
      ON dtl.ProductID = prod.ProductID
  WHERE hdr.OrderDate BETWEEN CONVERT(DATETIME, '1/1/2004 00:00:00',120)
    AND CONVERT(DATETIME,'12/31/2004 23:59:59',120)
  GROUP BY hdr.SalesPersonID
    ,cntc.FirstName
    ,cntc.LastName
    ,prod.ProductID
    ,prod.Name;
GO
```

2. Next, you must add the unique, clustered index to the view to make it an indexed view. In this case, you cannot use the same clustered index that was used on the table as it was not unique. In order to make the index unique, you will need to add the ProductID field to the index. Execute the following code (included in the sample files as AddIndex.sql).

```
USE AdventureWorks
GO
CREATE UNIQUE CLUSTERED INDEX cidx_v_SalesPerson2004ProductSummary
    ON Sales.v_SalesPerson2004ProductSummary
(SalesPersonID
,ProductID);
GO
```

Settings Required to Use Indexed Views

While using indexed views can increase performance when retrieving summary data from your environment, there are a number of required settings and restrictions. The view created in the section "Creating an Indexed View for Sales Summary" has been designed to handle some of those restrictions.

■ ANSI_NULLS and QUOTED_IDENTIFIER options need to be set to **on** when creating the view. The ANSI_NULLS option must have been turned on for the underlying base tables as well.

■ You must create the view using the SCHEMA_BINDING option. This will bind the schema to the schema of the underlying tables.

■ When using aggregations and the GROUP BY clause, you must include COUNT_BIG(*) in the SELECT list.

■ Only deterministic functions are permitted in the view syntax. You cannot use GET-DATE() as it is not deterministic. You also must convert the string-formatted dates to deterministic date formats. In this example, you converted the string expressions to the DATETIME datatype with the ODBC Canonical Standard style (120).

There are a number of other settings and restrictions to be aware of. See the SQL Server Books Online topic "Creating Indexed Views" for a complete list. Be sure to refer to this list before committing to using indexed views as the design might end up being overly complicated and fail to provide the desired benefit.

Tracking Changes Using Audit Columns and Audit Tables

In the previous two sections, you learned how to store and access historical summarized data. Now, you will learn techniques for tracking various changes to your data in the table itself and outside of the source table. The level of auditing you choose will depend on what you really need to know. You can choose a level of auditing as simple as recording the date of the change or as complex as holding a complete record of the change with the option to recover if necessary. This latter option utilizes audit columns, audit tables, or both.

Auditing with Columns

Auditing with columns has the benefit of having the audit information located in the same table with the data. Table 11-1 describes some of the common audit columns that are added to tables.

Table 11-1   Various Types of Audit Columns

Audited Events	Data Types	Comments
INSERT, UPDATE, or DELETE	DATETIME	Used to track the date and time the audited action occurred.
		Commonly used with GETDATE() as the default value. However, it can also be set by the calling application.
INSERT. UPDATE, or DELETE	VARCHAR	Used to track the user name or application that performed the audited action.
DELETE	BIT/TINYINT	Used to mark a record as being deleted. This can be used very efficiently in indexing and filtering.

One thing you will notice from this table is that the data change is not actually logged. The most effective use of auditing columns is tracking the fact that a change has occurred, when it occurred, and who instigated the change. You can use any combination of these columns to track changes to records within the actual table. Depending on your application and the level of auditing you desire, you will find these columns should meet most of your row-level auditing needs.

Setting Up Audit Columns

1. You need to determine the events that you wish to audit. In this example, you will learn how to add audit columns to track who made the change, when the row was created, when the row was last updated, and whether the row has been deleted in the Person.Address table in the AdventureWorks database.

2. Now that you have the table (Person.Address) and have decided what events to track, you need to decide what columns you will add to the table.

   - ModifiedDate already exists in the table. It will handle the date showing when the row was last updated or deleted.

   - The CreatedDate column will track when the record was created. It will be a column of the DATETIME datatype, using GETDATE() to provide the current date as the default value.

   - The ModifiedBy column is a VARCHAR column that will hold the username or some other means of identifying the user or application that made the modification.

   - The IsDeleted column is a BIT datatype column that will be used to record whether a record has been deleted. The date and user will be tracked via the ModifiedDate and the ModifiedBy columns. If the record has been deleted, this column will be marked and the modified columns will tell you when and by whom.

3. You can now execute the script shown below to alter the Person.Address table. (This code is included in the sample files as AlterTable.sql.)

```
USE AdventureWorks
GO
ALTER TABLE Person.Address
    ADD CreatedDate DATETIME NULL DEFAULT GETDATE()
    ,ModifiedBy VARCHAR(50) NULL
    ,IsDeleted BIT DEFAULT (0)
```

4. Next, if you are modifying a table with existing data, you should set the CreatedDate to a value far enough in the past to know that it was created before the auditing was in place. Execute the following code to set the CreatedDate value.

```
UPDATE Person.Address SET CreatedDate = '1/1/1980';
```

5. Now you will need to modify stored procedures and application code to populate these columns with the desired results. You could also use triggers to update these columns, but it is usually a better practice to control how the data can be modified and use the application code to update the audit columns.

6. The last step in this process is to add a filter to all procedures and code referencing this table to not return deleted rows. The filter to use is as follows:

```
...
WHERE IsDeleted = 0
...
```

Auditing with Tables

You have seen how to use audits to show that a change has occurred. However, the only change that can be backed out easily is the DELETE event. You can reset the IsDeleted flag and the data will be available once again. You may also be able to back out the CREATE event with enough information about the activity. However, if you need to be able to fully track the state of the data before it was modified, the best option may be to use an audit table. This is an option you want to use sparingly, as it can cause a number of maintenance and performance problems. These issues arise because rows need to be copied to the audit table and modified in the source table. For this example, you will set up table-based auditing on the Sales.Special Offer table. The goal will be to track any changes to this table and be able to back the changes out after they have been committed.

Setting Up Audit Tables

1. Open SQL Server Management Studio, and locate the Sales.SpecialOffer table in the AdventureWorks database in Object Explorer.

2. Generate the base audit script by right-clicking the Sales.SpecialOffer table and selecting Script Table As | Create To | New Query Editor Window from the context menus. This will open a New Query window with the CREATE TABLE script ready to be edited.

3. Edit the script using the following steps. For this example, the final edited version of the script is listed in step 4.

    3.1. First, remove all of the extra script. You should delete all lines of code not contained within the CREATE statement.

    3.2. Next, change the name of the table from Sales.SpecialOffer to Sales.SpecialOffer_Audit.

    3.3. Now remove any constraints on the table and allow all of the columns to accept NULL values. This will make the table more like a log table. In this case, the audit table should not prevent normal operations on the table from commencing. This should also make managing the table easier.

    3.4. Add any additional columns that will help you determine the type of change, the date of the change, and any other audit items you wish to track. In this example, you will add the columns listed in Table 11-2.

Table 11-2   Columns to Add to the Audit Table

Column Name	Datatype
AuditModifiedDate	DATETIME
AuditType	NVARCHAR(20)

4. Execute the finished script shown below on the AdventureWorks database. (This code is included in the sample files as CreateAuditTable.sql.)

```
USE AdventureWorks;
GO
CREATE TABLE Sales.SpecialOffer_Audit(
    SpecialOfferID INT NULL,
    Description NVARCHAR(255) NULL,
    DiscountPct SMALLMONEY NULL,
    [Type] NVARCHAR(50) NULL,
    Category NVARCHAR(50) NULL,
    StartDate DATETIME NULL,
    EndDate DATETIME NULL,
    MinQty INT NULL,
    MaxQty INT NULL,
    rowguid UNIQUEIDENTIFIER NULL,
    ModifiedDate DATETIME NULL,
    AuditModifiedDate DATETIME NULL,
    AuditType NVARCHAR(20) null
);
GO
```

Tip   You may want to create a new schema for audit objects.

Writing Audits to the Audit Table

Database triggers and the new OUTPUT T-SQL clause are the two primary ways to move data to the audit tables in SQL Server 2005. The use of triggers to complete this operation is pretty standard. However, the new OUTPUT clause adds some interesting capabilities. The next two sections will walk you through each of these options.

Using an UPDATE Trigger to Populate the Audit Tables

1. Create a trigger on the Sales.SpecialOffer table that writes the data's previous state to the Sales.SpecialOffer_Audit table you have created. The code below provides a sample of the syntax you can use. (This code is included in the sample files as CreateTrigger.sql.) Enter and execute this code in a New Query window in SQL Server Management Studio.

```
USE AdventureWorks
GO
CREATE TRIGGER SpecialOfferUpdateAudit ON Sales.SpecialOffer
FOR UPDATE
AS
  INSERT INTO Sales.SpecialOffer_Audit
    (SpecialOfferID
    ,Description
    ,DiscountPct
    ,[Type]
```

```
        ,Category
        ,StartDate
        ,EndDate
        ,MinQty
        ,MaxQty
        ,rowguid
        ,ModifiedDate
        ,AuditModifiedDate
        ,AuditType)
    SELECT TOP 1 d.SpecialOfferID
        ,d.Description
        ,d.DiscountPct
        ,d.[Type]
        ,d.Category
        ,d.StartDate
        ,d.EndDate
        ,d.MinQty
        ,d.MaxQty
        ,d.rowguid
        ,d.ModifiedDate
        ,GETDATE()
        ,'UPDATE'
      FROM deleted d;
GO
```

> **Note** If you have made no modifications to the Sales.SpecialOffer offer table, you most likely will need to drop the trigger that already exists on the table (uSpecialOffer). You should save the script for the trigger so you can reapply it later. If you do not remove this trigger, you will get two rows of data in the Sales.SpecialOffer_Audit table whenever you update the table.

The advantage of using a trigger is that it will capture any update that occurs on the table no matter the source. This is your "complete coverage" audit option. If you are concerned about data being changed that you are not in control of, then this is a great option. However, if you have tight control on how the data is entered into the table, especially if it is done via stored procedures, there is a new option available in SQL Server 2005 for auditing changes called the OUTPUT clause.

Using the OUTPUT Clause to Populate the Audit Tables

1. In order to use the OUTPUT clause effectively, every event you wish to audit will require work on the stored procedures and SQL statements used to UPDATE, INSERT, or DELETE data into the audited table. The OUTPUT clause gives you access to the inserted and deleted tables within these procedures and SQL statements. You are no longer required to use a trigger to access this data. The code below shows an example of using the OUTPUT clause to audit an update in the SpecialOffer table to the SpecialOffer_Audit table. (This code is included in the sample files as UsingOutputClause.sql.) Enter and execute the following code in a New Query window in SQL Server Management Studio.

> **Important**   The OUTPUT clause must insert its data into a table variable, temporary table, or—as in this case—a permanent table.

```
USE AdventureWorks
GO
UPDATE Sales.SpecialOffer
    SET description = 'Big Mountain Tire Sale'
OUTPUT deleted.SpecialOfferID
    ,deleted.Description
    ,deleted.DiscountPct
    ,deleted.[Type]
    ,deleted.Category
    ,deleted.StartDate
    ,deleted.EndDate
    ,deleted.MinQty
    ,deleted.MaxQty
    ,deleted.rowguid
    ,deleted.ModifiedDate
    ,GETDATE()
    ,'UPDATE' INTO Sales.SpecialOffer_Audit
WHERE SpecialOfferID = 10
```

2. The OUTPUT clause puts the modified data within easy access during the data modification process. The deleted prefix is available during UPDATE and DELETE operations. The inserted prefix is available during UPDATE and INSERT operations. You will notice that both are not available at the same time, unlike the deleted and inserted tables used in triggers. This mutually exclusive availability will require that you handle the various operations differently in order to collect the desired data and push it to the audit table.

> **Tip**   The OUTPUT clause can also be used to return the value from an IDENTITY column during an INSERT operation.

Recovering Data with Audit Tables

Now that you have two options for loading the audit table, you can start looking at what you want to use this data for. Because all of the changes to the table are stored in the audit table, you will be able to recover any data change by overwriting the current data with the change you want to keep. The audit table will keep multiple versions of the data, so most of the time this will be a manual operation. However, you can also create a maintenance stored procedure to back out the most recent change.

Using Audit Tables to Recover Changed Data

1. Determine which record needs to be restored. You will need to identify the record that you want to replace and the data you want to replace it with.

2. Use an UPDATE statement that will overwrite the current data with the change you need to recover to that table. In the current example, you will need to use either the rowguid or SpecialOfferID column in combination with the AuditModifiedDate as criteria for the UPDATE statement, as shown below. (This code is included in the sample files as RecoveringChangedData.sql.) Enter and execute the following code in a new query window in SQL Server Management Studio.

```
-- You will need to replace the AuditModifiedDate in this script with the
--AuditModifiedDate from your SpecialOffer_Audit table
USE AdventureWorks
GO
UPDATE Sales.SpecialOffer
    SET Description = a.Description
      ,DiscountPct = a.DiscountPct
      ,Type = a.Type
      ,Category = a.Category
      ,StartDate = a.StartDate
      ,EndDate = a.EndDate
      ,MinQty = a.MinQty
      ,MaxQty = a.MaxQty
      ,rowguid = a.rowguid
      ,ModifiedDate = a.ModifiedDate
    FROM Sales.SpecialOffer_Audit a
    WHERE SpecialOffer.SpecialOfferID = 10
      AND a.SpecialOfferID = 10
      AND a.AuditModifiedDate = '2006-04-02 22:40:27.513'
```

If you have data you need to recover regularly, you could encapsulate the above code into a maintenance stored procedure. However you choose to implement it, you now have options for recovering data entry issues. These options are good for a limited number of rows on the same table. If you are dealing with a bulk-load issue across multiple tables, you should look at using database snapshots as mentioned in the first section of this chapter.

Conclusion

You've learned how to take a snapshot of your data. Snapshots can be used effectively for different purposes in development, testing, and production. You can use historical data to summarize and analyze data from specific time frames. You've also seen how to audit changes to your data and how to restore individual records using audited data. By saving historical data and auditing changes to your database, you can ensure the integrity of your data by being able to back out individual changes without having to restore the entire database.

Chapter 11 Quick Reference

To	Do This
Create a database snapshot	Use the CREATE DATABASE statement with the AS SNAPSHOT OF option.
Revert to a database snapshot	Use the RESTORE DATABASE statement with the FROM SNAPSHOT option.
Delete a database snapshot	Use the DROP DATABASE statement or delete the database snapshot from SQL Server Management Studio.
Schedule loading a summarized history table	Create a new Job in SQL Server Agent and set the schedule to meet your needs.
Summarize data for a specific time frame	Create an indexed view for the time frame or time frames you wish to summarize.
Audit changes to your data	Add Audit columns to the table, in which to track who made the change and when it was made.
Fully track data changes and be able to recover from data entry mistakes	Create and load an audit table either with triggers or by using the OUTPUT clause.

Chapter 12

Introduction to Reporting Services

After completing this chapter, you will be able to:

- Understand reporting as a technology and business solution
- Understand Reporting Services architecture
- Create a basic report with some intermediate features
- Add summary information to a report
- Filter data in a report
- Provide interactive filtering and sorting options on a report
- Add code to a report

The primary objective of custom database applications is to manage live data by adding new data, updating data, deleting obsolete data, and so on. Therefore, it is logical that developers focus primarily on these features. However, another important aspect of applications consists of giving users the information they need for long-term consumption. These long-term goals include the ability to take data away on paper and analyze summarized or historical data.

Application developers may intend to supply this functionality by traditional methods, like using queries, business objects, and grids. However, summarized information requires complex layouts, with nesting, running totals, and conditional formatting. These layouts are by no means easy to develop or to maintain using classical development tools.

Additionally, some consumers of the application data will never access the application itself. Managers or remote employees often fall into this sort of situation. These kinds of users would prefer to receive application data in their e-mail inboxes or on their mobile devices, sent according to a predefined schedule.

Because these requirements are common, several software vendors provide packaged reporting or enterprise reporting solutions. In this chapter, we'll discuss how Reporting Services in Microsoft SQL Server 2005 meets all these requirements.

Requirements for a Reporting Solution

Some of the requirements that a reporting solution must meet are:

- Provide information to users for long-term consumption
- Allow for hard-copy versions of the information
- Allow for summary, analysis, and historical data
- Provide a simple user interface for building complex layouts, including nesting, running totals, and conditional formatting
- Provide for distribution of reports by e-mail, mobile devices, and other electronic media
- Provide for scheduling of report creation
- Provide a means for administering the reporting system
- Allow for extensions of built-in capabilities

The following sections detail these features in Reporting Services.

Creating Reports

Just as Excel or Word require a file format (.xls or .doc) that includes data and information relevant to those applications, reporting solutions need a report definition file. Microsoft Reporting Services uses Report Definition Language (RDL) files to perform this duty. RDL files are XML files that comply with a publicly available schema.

Therefore, all you need for creating reports compatible with Reporting Services is a tool that allows you to create XML (RDL) files. You might even, with perseverance, write a report definition file using Notepad. Fortunately, this is not the standard way to create reports. Microsoft SQL Server 2005 allows creating Reporting projects in Microsoft SQL Server Business Intelligence Development Studio (BIDS) through the classic designer interface.

Deploying Reports

Once a report is defined, it should be put in a place where applications and/or users can find it and request its processing. Reporting Services includes the infrastructure needed to keep reports in a central, secure repository.

Deploying can occur through three different methods: from BIDS itself, by uploading RDL files from Report Manager, or by scripting the RDL upload operation and using the rs.exe utility to execute those scripts.

Accessing Reports

Once a report is deployed, some mechanism should allow applications and/or users to find the desired report and to request its processing. Reporting Services includes a Web application, the Report Manager, tailored for administrators and interactive users. For unattended access via applications, Reporting Services includes several application programming interfaces (APIs).

Delivering Reports

The default format for report processing output is HTML 4.0. For users and/or applications that need the output in a different format, an exporting feature is provided. Reporting Services includes out-of-the-box support for the most popular formats, such as Adobe Acrobat (PDF), Microsoft Excel, and HTML.

Additionally, Reporting Services includes, by default, the ability to deliver rendered reports to file shares or to send them by e-mail.

Extending Reporting Services

You might have noticed that the expressions "by default" and "out-of-the-box" appeared in the previous feature descriptions. Reporting Services is an extensible platform that allows for adding custom code in several areas: security, data source access, rendering, and delivery. These custom code blocks are actually .NET assemblies that should be registered with Reporting Services.

Administering Reporting Services

As mentioned above, one of the enterprise reporting goals is to serve reports to any enterprise user in their preferred format and in their preferred location. Of course, not all users should, nor would, have access to all the company reports. Therefore, Reporting Services provides for administering the reporting environment.

An important enterprise reporting benefit is the ability to schedule report processing. This feature allows administrators to decide when, and how often, a report should be processed. For example, an administrator might need to schedule certain reports to be processed when some process is finished or prevent users from processing huge reports during work hours. By leveraging this Reporting Services feature, administrators can fine-tune the reporting workload according to enterprise business requirements and to the real capacity of the system.

Poor Man's Reporting

You should understand by now that enterprise reporting is a rich, somewhat complex, business solution, designed to provide solutions in demanding reporting environments. However, what if your reporting needs are far simpler or your application doesn't use a Web server at all?

Microsoft Visual Studio 2005 includes two report viewing and processing controls that allow for using the previously mentioned server infrastructure and that can be used for storing, processing, and delivering reports locally. Note that these controls are included in Visual Studio 2005 but not in Microsoft SQL Server 2005.

Design Considerations

Discussing proper report design planning is out of this book's scope; however, it is worth mentioning that a plan should be put in place before starting to create reports. The reporting plan is used to identify and analyze common report requirements in several areas, such as:

- **Report content**   Looking at the projected report catalog will give you a 10,000 foot view of the full reporting functionality that is needed. This overview will help you spot opportunities for optimization, such as consolidating two similar reports into a single report.

- **Formatting**   Consider headers, footers, versioning info, author, dates, and similar elements that should be added to every report.

- **Source code control**   Report definition files should be considered source code, and a source code control strategy is highly recommended. Additionally, because a report may produce paper or file documents that have their own life cycle, you are advised to put the report version that generates the document in a visible place on each report so you can distinguish easily which report version was used to obtain the results. Versions may have major and minor version numbers.

- **Data sources and security**   Users might request that a report show different results depending on which user actually requests the processing of the report. When planning, you must gather information about what kind of security should be applied and details about user authorization to view, process, and edit each report or batch of reports.

- **Report life cycle**   You should know certain aspects of each report's life cycle, such as how often it must be processed, how many users need the resulting information, and how long it takes to process the report. With this information, you can make the right decisions about report design.

- **Report delivery channels and formats**   Report design and previously mentioned characteristics will depend on the target delivery formats (text, RTF, PDF, Excel...) and on the delivery channel (file folder, SMTP, Web viewed, PDA viewed...). It will be to your advantage to gather these requirements and to consider them in the planning phase.

Reporting Services Architecture

Reporting Services is composed of several functional blocks. Each block performs one or more specific tasks or has different responsibilities in terms of the full solution. Reporting functionalities cover different areas, and Reporting Services' architecture has been designed to be flexible. Therefore, components are spread over different areas inside the solution server (or servers), as shown in Figure 12-1.

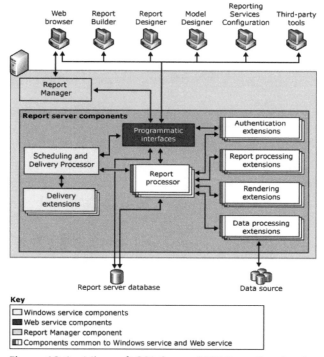

Figure 12-1   Microsoft SQL Server 2005 Reporting Services architecture.

Server Components

Reporting Services is a server product thus, the majority of its components reside on the server itself.

- **Reporting Services databases**   Reporting Services databases store solution metadata, saved reports, session-related information, and everything necessary to maintain the server state.

  Reporting Services manages two databases: ReportServer, which includes all persistent information, and ReportServerTempDB, which includes all temporary information. You will find them in the SQL Server databases catalog just like any ordinary database.

- **Report Server**   This virtual component is responsible for processing reports by requesting help from all "extension" blocks. It is implemented as two big blocks:

  - **Reporting Services Windows Service**   The Reporting Services Windows Service is responsible for initialization and server maintenance and also for scheduling processes and delivering output, assisted by the available delivery extensions.

  - **Reporting Services Web Services**   Reporting Services interacts with the outside world mainly through its Web Services interface. Indeed, Report Manager uses this interface to perform its duties. There are two available Web services: ReportingServices2005 (for management) and ReportExecutionService (for report execution).

These two blocks rely on several functional modules, including various processors and extensions:

- **The Report Server Processor**   This module does all the core work of parsing the report definition, requesting data from the data processing extensions, performing calculations, and sending the output to the rendering extension to format the output as needed.

- **The Scheduling and Delivery Processor**   This module is in charge of firing and maintaining all scheduled and expired processes and for sending the output to the appropriate delivery extension. This module is assisted by the Report Server Processor and by SQL Server Agent.

- **The Authentication Extension**   This module is responsible for authenticating and authorizing users accessing Reporting Services. You should create and register your own assemblies for using custom or unsupported authentication mechanisms.

- **The Data Processing Extension**   This module is responsible for handling interaction with data sources. Out-of-the-box supported data sources are SQL Server, Analysis Services, Oracle, OLE DB, ODBC, ADO.NET data providers, and XML. You should create and register your own assemblies for accessing unsupported databases.

- **The Rendering Extension**   Reporting Services uses this extension to generate final rendered reports in the chosen format. Reporting Services includes several rendering extensions: HTML, PDF, Excel, comma-separated values (CSV), XML, and Image. You should create and register your own assemblies for rendering reports in additional formats.

- **SQL Server Agent**   Reporting Services leverages SQL Server Agent to handle all scheduling-related tasks. Reporting Services creates and deletes SQL Server Agent jobs at its convenience. Reporting Services generates job names beginning with a GUID; you can see these in the SQL Server Agent Job list.

  These jobs do something very simple: they insert a "schedule fired" row in the Reporting Services database. This row insertion initiates the activities bound to that schedule on the Report Server.

- **Configuration files**   Although Reporting Services and SQL Server configuration tools will do the job in the majority of cases, you should be aware that several configuration files exist (*.config .NET files) and that certain settings can be changed only by editing those configuration files directly.

- **Complementary components**   Some reporting-related tasks, like authentication or delivery, depend on third-party applications or servers to perform their duties. For instance, e-mail delivery will need the assistance of an SMTP Server, and authentication will require some kind of authentication authority to be available. Therefore, a reporting installation might be affected if communication with those elements malfunctions.

Client Components

Reporting Services provides interfaces to allow external applications to communicate with the server. Available interfaces include direct URL Access and a Web services API. Therefore, there's no limit to the number of possible client components. The out-of-the-box SQL Server and Reporting Services installation includes the following client tools:

- **Report Manager**   Although this module actually runs on the server because it is an ASP.NET application, it is included here because it acts as a client. Report Manager allows end users to access and manage reports according to their authorization permissions. Report Manager is the managing web application for Reporting Services administrators.

- **Reporting Services Configuration Manager**   As mentioned, configuration is a critical aspect of Reporting Services. Apart from editing configuration files directly, you can leverage Reporting Services Configuration Manager to edit most of the configuration settings from a centralized place.

- **SQL Server Configuration Manager**   Using this tool, you will be able to start and stop the Reporting Services' Windows Service and to access Reporting Services Configuration Manager.

- **SQL Server Management Studio**   SQL Server Management Studio allows for handling some aspects of Reporting Services, such as maintaining which users are authorized for accessing Reporting Services, roles, Shared Schedules, Reporting Services folders, and objects, as well as generating SMDL (Semantic Model Definition Language) report models. SQL Server Management Studio should be considered an administrator's alternative to Report Manager.

> **More Info**   See the SQL Server Books Online topic "Reporting Services Component Overview" for further information about each component.

Scalability

Although details about how to scale a Reporting Services installation from one server to its full strength is out of the scope of this book, mentioning scalability options is worthwhile.

Reporting Services is built on standard Microsoft technologies like SQL Server databases, ASP.NET, and Internet Information Server (IIS), as you have learned in the previous paragraphs. Thus, Reporting Services can leverage the scalability options provided by these technologies.

Without delving into details, think of Reporting Services as being able to expand over a Web farm, just as any IIS installation can, and to stand over a SQL Server cluster, just as any enterprise setup can.

> **More Info**   See the SQL Server Books Online topics "Planning a Reporting Services Deployment," "How to: Install a Local Report Server and Remote Report Server Database," and "Configuring a Report Server Scale-Out Deployment" for further information about how to scale out Reporting Services.

Creating a Basic Report

Now that you understand the business and architectural concepts behind enterprise reporting in general and Reporting Services in particular, let's start creating a report.

Setting Up a Report

Creating a report involves some common sense steps: you first create a SQL Server Business Intelligence Development Studio (BIDS) project to contain the report-related files, then you instruct BIDS about what data will be shown in the report. After that, you define which data is actually needed in the report and, last but not least, you layout, test, and deploy your report.

> **More Info**   You can deploy reports through Report Manager. For more information, see the SQL Server Books Online topic "Deploying Reports Through Report Manager."

Creating a Report Project

1. From the Start Menu, select All Programs | Microsoft SQL Server 2005 | SQL Server Business Intelligence Development Studio. From the File menu, select New | Project.

2. The New Project dialog box appears. In the Project Types pane, select Business Intelligence Projects. In the Templates pane, select Report Server Project. Choose a name for the project and the destination directory. I have chosen BasicReport and SQL2005StepByStep_Reports, respectively. Your dialog box should look like this:

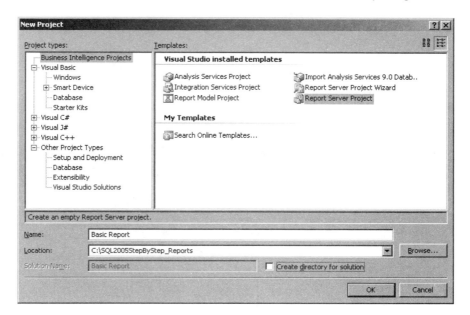

Caution   In this procedure, we will not use the other type of report project: the Report Server Project Wizard. Be sure not to choose this type of project. In case you do, the Report Wizard will appear when you click the OK button. If this happens, cancel the process and start again. The Report Wizard compresses the report creation process and partially hides it from you. This is fine for simple reports, but for this example, we will show you the usual way that experienced professionals proceed. That's why the non-wizard option is presented here.

3. Click the OK button to create the project.

4. Because the report project is quite simple, the Solution Explorer pane will show almost nothing. Don't worry, this is the expected result. You can see the Solution Explorer by selecting Solution Explorer from the View menu.

5. Now, you will add your first empty report by right-clicking on the Reports folder within Solution Explorer and selecting Add | New Item from the context menus.

> **Note** You can also start by creating a report using the Add New Report context menu option; however, this choice will fire the Report Wizard instead of adding a blank report to the project.

6. The Add New Item dialog box appears, as shown below. Here you will need to select Report in the Templates pane and enter *BasicReport v1* as the name for your report.

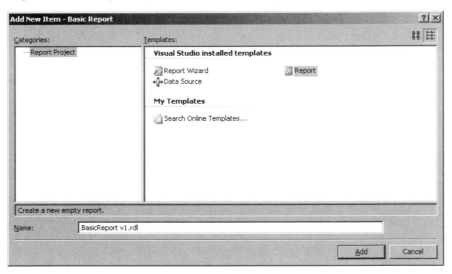

7. Click the Add button to confirm the process. BIDS displays a blank, freshly created report in the Report Designer, shown below:

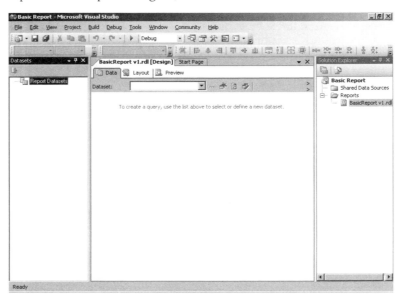

Creating a Shared Data Source

1. In order to design a report, we need to tell BIDS which data source to use. Right-click on the Shared Data Sources folder in Solution Explorer and choose Add New Data Source from the context menu. The Shared Data Source dialog box will appear.

> **Note**   You can create a report without using a shared data source by defining a data source tied to the report datasets. In this case, the data source is not shared but is private to the report. Although this option is valid in some cases, you should use shared data sources whenever you can to make reporting solution management easier in both the short run and the long run.

2. Enter *dsAdventureWorks* as the name for the data source.

> **Note**   If you need to access a data source other than Microsoft SQL Server, you can choose supported data sources from the Type dropdown list.

3. You could type the connection string, but clicking the Edit button will bring you to the familiar Connection Properties dialog box, shown below. Fill in the boxes in the manner appropriate to your system. For this example, set up a connection string to the AdventureWorks sample database.

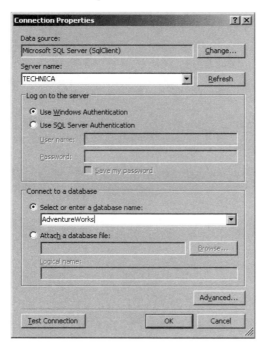

4. By clicking the respective buttons, set advanced options if you feel they are necessary to your system. Test the connection, too. After clicking the OK button, you can check the connection string generated in the Shared Data Source dialog box, shown here:

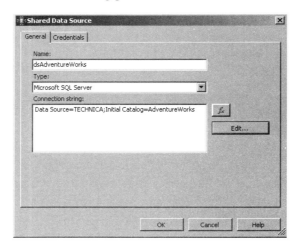

5. You will notice that authentication information is not shown on the connection string. Click on the Credentials tab to look at the available options.

6. Click the OK button to create the data source. The data source appears in the Shared Data Sources folder. Note the file extension is .rds.

Defining a Dataset

1. Now you must let BIDS know what data you want to display on the report. To do this you need to create at least one dataset, sometimes more than one. Check that the Data tab is visible in the central area of BIDS. Open the Dataset dropdown list and choose <New Dataset...>.

2. The Dataset dialog box appears, as shown below.

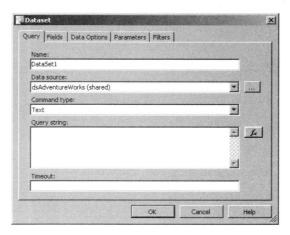

3. Enter *dsEmployeeSales* as the name for the dataset (this dataset will end up gathering and containing employee sales data).

4. Double-check that the shared data source is selected in the Data Source dropdown list and that Text is the command type. Notice the alternative of using a stored procedure instead of text.

5. You can use a more advanced query designer to assist in creating your dataset expression. For now, type this simple query into the Query String field:

```
SELECT SalesPersonID, FirstName, MiddleName, LastName, JobTitle, SalesYTD
FROM Sales.vSalesPerson
```

6. Click the OK button to accept the query. The dataset query appears on the Data tab, as shown below.

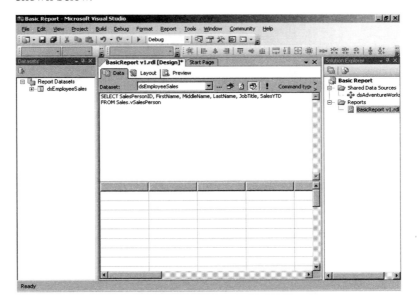

7. You can test and check the query results by clicking the Execute button (the button with the red exclamation point).

8. Do not be confused by the barebones screen you are looking at. This is the Generic Query Designer. You can switch this on and off by clicking the Generic Query Designer toolbar button, shown here:

By toggling this button, you can work with a full-blown query designer, shown on the following page, or with the initial simpler one.

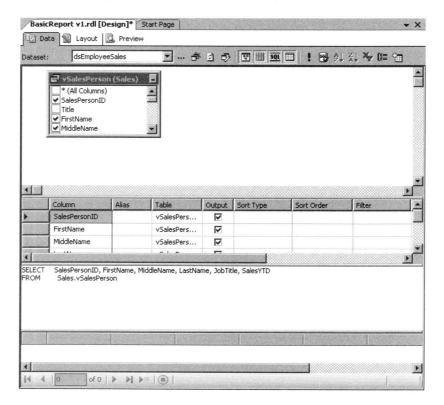

> **Note**   You may wonder why it takes so many steps to reach the typical query designer. The main reason is that Reporting Services could use many different query types, such as stored procedures or VB.NET expressions, and many of them are not well suited for the typical relational table-oriented designer. Therefore, the classical query designer is not the default option.

9. Note the asterisk symbol that appears next to the report name on the BasicReport v1.rdl[Design] tab. This asterisk means that the file has unsaved changes. Save your report by clicking the Save toolbar button. The asterisk will disappear once your work has been saved.

Laying Out, Testing, and Refining a Report

Now that you have a project and some data defined, it's time to lay out, test, and refine your report.

Laying Out a Report

1. With your report still open, switch to the Layout tab. You will see a short rectangle dotted with gridmarks.

2. Hide the Solution Explorer pane by unpinning it so you will have more room to work with in the report design area.

> **Caution**   Notice the ruler on the top and the size of the initial design area. You might wonder why this area is not the size of your preferred paper size (Letter, A4, etc.). Reporting Services is not tailored to producing paper reports, therefore the layout tools don't automatically relate to paper sizes.

3. From the View menu, select Toolbox.

4. Drag and drop a Textbox control from the Toolbox onto the grid surface. Type *Employee Sales* inside, resize the textbox to contain a bigger text, and adjust format (font size 16 points and bold) to look like the image below. The font can be adjusted by right-clicking the text, selecting Properties, and then selecting the Font tab.

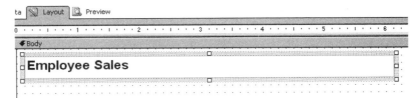

> **Caution**   If you widen the textbox too far to the right, you will notice that the design area widens to accommodate your control size. Be careful, because Reporting Services does not constrain you from overflowing the expected page size. Thus you may end up with a report spanning more than one page in width. To correct this, you can narrow your control, deselect it, and then drag the right grid border back to its original size.

5. Now create a place for hosting the report data. Drag a Table control from the Toolbox and drop it onto the design surface, as shown below. Do not worry about the specific place where you drop it, because it will expand end to end width-wise. The table will show three rows and nine cells. Note the grey top and left table borders. They will disappear when deselecting the control, and will reappear when you reselect it. The grey areas will help you to perform specific operations like selecting a full column, a full row, or the entire table.

> **Tip**   Selecting an entire table can be tricky. If you click on the control, only a cell is selected; if you click outside the control, you deselect it, as expected. How do you select the full table? You can use the orthodox method of selecting a cell to make grey borders appear and then clicking on the border in the top-left corner box, or, if no control is in the middle, by clicking outside the table on the design surface and dragging a selection box that only touches the table control.

6. Show the Datasets pane by selecting Datasets from the View menu. Then expand the dsEmployeeSales node tree.

7. Drag the SalesPersonID field and drop it into the left-most table cell of the middle row (in the Detail row). Note that an expression is shown in that cell. We will come back to that in a later step.

8. Repeat the drag-and-drop operation with LastName and JobTitle fields, filling the center and right Detail area cells, respectively. Do not worry about the FirstName and Middle-Name columns; you will use them later when building an expression to return the full employee name.

9. You will need an additional column and more space to host the SalesYTD field. To do so, narrow the SalesPersonID column by clicking and dragging the line between the Sales-PersonID and the LastName column headers. Notice the double-headed arrow icon appears when the cursor is over the mentioned line. Observe, too, that the table narrows accordingly.

10. Right-click on the JobTitle column header and choose Insert Column To The Right from the context menu to add a column to the right of the JobTitle column. Drag and drop the SalesYTD field to the newly created Detail cell.

11. Now, the design area will have expanded to the right. If you want to print the report on paper, you will need to keep the area width under control. Resize the SalesYTD column to be narrower and drag the design area border to the correct width. Which is the correct width? Check the sidebar titled "Finding the Right Design Area Width."

12. Save your work by clicking the Save button.

Finding the Right Design Area Width

Undesired empty pages are one of the confusing side effects that report designers find when printing reports or exporting to paper-like formats. What is the reason for these empty pages? Often there is a simple mathematical explanation.

Reporting Services uses three elements to determine where to place page breaks: page width, page left and right margins, and surface design width. Note that I have said surface design width and not surface design *used* width. The top ruler is your guide for seeing the width of the surface design.

You see report page layout information by selecting Report Properties from the Report menu. In the Report Properties dialog box, select the Layout tab. Here you have the page and margin dimensions.

With these values at hand, you can calculate the maximum design area width that will print the report within the width of one page.

Maximum Area Width = Page Width - Left margin - Right margin

In case you like to use the classical landscape orientation for reports instead of the document-oriented portrait one, simply switch the Page Width and Page Height values on the Layout tab. Of course, your design surface area width should use this new page width value.

Previewing a Report

1. Having our basic layout in place, let's preview what the report will look like. Click on the Preview tab in the design view. A message that the report is being generated will appear briefly before the report processing results are displayed.

Caution   Do not click on the Start Debugging green arrow toolbar button or press the F5 key. Either of these actions will trigger the Build and Deploy operation. Right now, we are just interested in seeing a preview of our report.

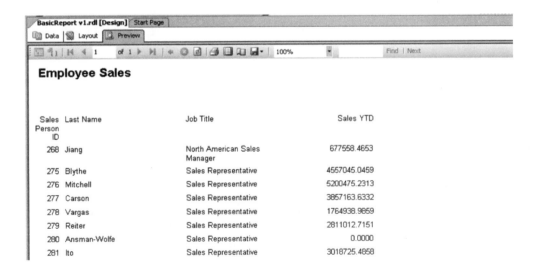

You will notice some editing is needed, like number formatting or adjusting the Sales Person ID column title. We will do that in the following sections. From the Preview tab, you can print, print preview, and export the report results.

2. To preview the report in the printing form, you can click on the Print Layout toolbar button. The Print Layout button is a toggle button; therefore, it will stay "on," although you switch tabs, until you switch it to "off" again.

> **Warning**   The Reporting Services preview tab is rendered by the Preview renderer, which is different from other renderers, like the HTML renderer or the PDF renderer. The difference shows dramatically when looking at paging behavior. If you need to deliver the report in any specific format, check the page breaks directly in that format; do not pay any attention to the page breaks you see on the Preview tab. Do not be fooled by those page breaks, as the Preview renderer does not use your page breaking settings.

3. Return to the Layout tab to continue editing the report.

Editing Text in Table Cells

1. You want to show each employee's full name instead of their last name only. You will do that in a following step by editing the expression. In the meantime, you will edit the column title. Double-click on the cell that includes the "Last Name" text to enter into edit mode. Delete the word "Last" to leave the word "Name" only.

2. Trying to repeat the operation with the "Sales Person ID" cell might be confusing because the reduced space allotted to it leaves most of the text hidden. However, you can edit the text exactly the same way. Edit the text to leave only "ID" as the column title. Alternatively you might change the value through a number of different methods:

    ■ By right-clicking on the cell and selecting Properties to display the Properties dialog box shown below. There you can edit the Value dropdown list.

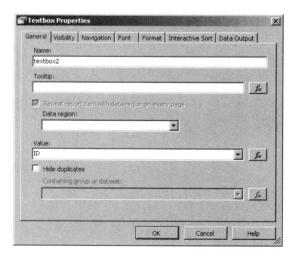

- By right-clicking on the cell and choosing Expression to bring up the Edit Expression dialog box, as shown below. There you can edit the expression.

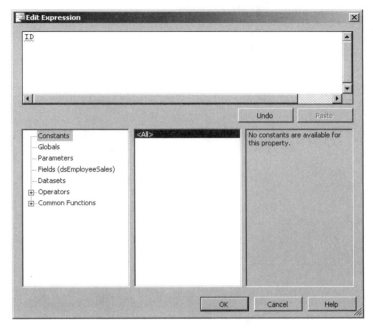

- By pressing the F4 key or clicking the Properties Window toolbar button to show the Properties window (or by clicking on the Properties window itself if it is already visible). In the Properties window, you can edit the Value dropdown list.

3. Save the report

> **Caution**   Report item properties can be edited through both the Properties dialog box and the Properties window. Some properties are easier to edit in one place than the other. Usually the Properties dialog box is the best choice because it offers more assistance in setting properties the right way. Some elements, like Groups, the Body, or the Report itself, have properties that show on the Properties window only; they have no Properties dialog box.

Formatting Items

1. Click on the cell that contains the Sales YTD field value (the right-most cell of the middle row).

2. Edit the format of the expression to make it more readable. In this case, choosing the Properties dialog box rather than the Properties window makes an important difference because the dialog box provides far more options to assist you, so right-click the cell and select Properties.

3. Navigate to the Format tab, shown below. Note the Format Code textbox and the adjacent buttons.

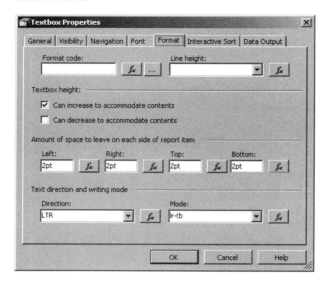

4. Click on the ellipsis (...) button to bring up the Choose Format dialog box. If you click on the Function button, the Edit Expression dialog box appears. This is the same result you will obtain if you edit the Format property on the Properties window. You can set the format from the Properties window as well, but you would need to know exactly what to write for them.

5. Choose Currency, and click the OK button. Note that the value in the Format Code textbox is "C." Format codes used by Reporting Services are the .NET Framework formatting types.

> **More Info**   You can find more details about the .NET Framework formatting types in the .NET documentation or online at
> *http://msdn2.microsoft.com/en-us/library/fbxft59x.aspx*.

6. Click the OK button to accept the edit to the textbox properties and preview the report to check the changes you have made so far.

7. Save the report.

> **Caution**   Note that if you try to save the report while on the Preview tab, the Report Designer asks you to save the report results, not the report layout. To save the report layout, you must leave the Preview tab and show the Layout tab or the Data tab.

Editing an Expression

1. Select the Last Name field value (the second-to-left cell of the middle row). You will change the expression in it to show the employee's full name instead of just the last name.

2. Right-click the cell and select Expression. The Edit Expression dialog box will open. Expressions in Reporting Services should be written in Visual Basic .NET syntax. Alternatively, you can edit the expression directly in the cell, without bringing up any dialog box at all. The latter way is perfectly suitable for minor edits, like adding a single space or something similar; however, when a more advanced edit is necessary, the Edit Expression dialog box is more practical.

3. The current expression value is:

   ```
   =Fields!LastName.Value
   ```

   You should note several elements of this expression:

   - **Equal sign (=)**   The equal sign indicates that the text following this sign is an expression and not plain text (or a *string* in programming terms).

   - **Fields!**   The *Fields!* part of the expression indicates that *LastName* is an element in the *Fields* collection. Check the sidebar titled "The Reporting Services Collections" for more information about collections in RDL.

   - **The Value property**   Every RDL object has a set of properties you can access when editing expressions. When editing the expression in the Edit Expression dialog box, Intellisense gives you a list of properties for each item type.

4. Because you want to show some additional fields, edit the expression to look like this:

   ```
   =Fields!FirstName.Value & " " & Fields!MiddleName.Value &
       ". " & Fields!LastName.Value
   ```

5. Save the expression by clicking the OK button, and preview the report to check the expression's results. You will notice that your edited expression works in most cases, but not in all of them. Look at the employees with IDs 277 and 279, for example. The former has no middle name; thus, the abbreviation dot and the separation space should be omitted. The latter has a fully spelled middle name; thus, the abbreviation dot should be omitted, but the separation space should remain.

6. You will need to edit the expression, making it a bit more complex for the sake of accuracy. Edit the expression to match the following one, and click the OK button.

   ```
   =Fields!FirstName.Value & " " &
       IIf(Len(Fields!MiddleName.Value) = 1, Fields!MiddleName.Value & ". ", "")&
       IIf(Len(Fields!MiddleName.Value) > 1, Fields!MiddleName.Value & " ", "")&
       Fields!LastName.Value
   ```

7. To enter this expression, you can follow (and mix) two paths: writing directly in the expression text-editing box or picking elements from the assisting lists at the bottom side of the dialog box. In the following figure, notice the IIf function. Play a bit with the options in order to get used to the function's behavior. Notice that Intellisense and syntax coloring help you build a valid expression.

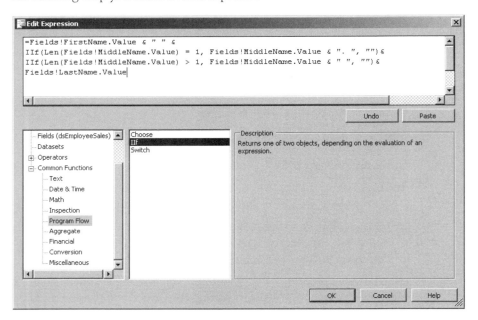

8. Preview your report and note that the issues with the middle name have now been resolved.

9. Save the report.

Adding a Total

1. You want to add a grand total showing the total sales (SalesYTD) made by the salespeople as a whole. First show the Datasets pane to view the fields. Expand the dsEmployeeSales node.

2. Drag the SalesYTD node and drop it in the right-most cell in the bottom row of the table, just under the SalesYTD details cell.

3. Note that the resulting expression is:

```
=Sum(Fields!SalesYTD.Value)
```

Report Designer has understood that you want to add a summary because the drop operation is to the Table Footer row, not the Detail row.

4. Because this item is brand new, the Format property is empty. This means that the summary will show a different numeric format than the column above it. To correct this, open the Properties window and simply type a *C* as the value for the format property.

5. Save the report.

Adding Visual Appeal

Add some visual formatting features to make the report easier to read and to practice some formatting in the Report Designer.

1. Select all the column titles by clicking on the ID cell and dragging across the top row.

2. Bring up the Properties window, and locate the Font property group.

3. Notice the plus sign (+) on the grey border on the left. It denotes you are dealing with a property group. Click on it to expand the actual Font properties.

4. Choose Bold for the FontWeight property. You can do that by typing *Bold* in the box or by selecting Bold from the dropdown list.

   Note the text on the Font property group summary entry: "Normal; Arial; 10pt; Bold." You can edit property values without expanding the nodes by simply entering values in the right positions in this string.

5. Locate the BorderStyle property group and expand it.

6. Set the Bottom property to Solid.

7. In the design surface, select the whole Details row by clicking on the grey Details row header button located on the lefthand side of the table.

8. In the Properties window, set the BorderColor property group to silver by typing *Silver* in the value box. Expand the BorderColor node to see that silver is actually the default color, as shown below.

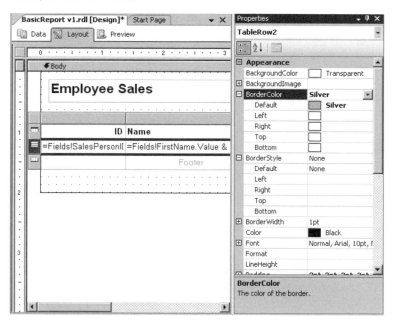

9.   Select the whole Table Footer row and set the BorderStyle.Top property to Solid.

10.   Select the Grand Total cell and set the FontWeight to Bold.

11.   Preview the report to check the changes.

12.   Switch to the Layout tab and save the report.

Conditionally Setting a Property Value

RDL relies heavily on expressions to offer a powerful set of features. Almost anywhere you can set a property, you can set the property value through an expression instead of using an explicit value. You can use this feature to highlight sales representatives who are not reaching their target.

1.   Select the SalesYTD cell in the Details row.

2.   Find the Color property in the Properties window.

3.   View the available property values by clicking on the dropdown list arrow. Notice the <Expression...> entry at the top of the dropdown list. Click on it to bring up the Edit Expression dialog box, shown below.

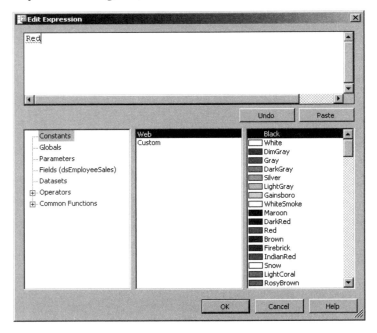

4.   Notice the color options, available as constants. Change the expression to match the following one.

```
=IIf(Fields!SalesYTD.Value<3500000, "Red", "OliveDrab")
```

Do not forget to put the equal sign at the beginning or else your entry will be considered a string not an expression.

5. Accept the expression by clicking the OK button. Check the results on the Preview tab.

6. Combine a couple of IIF functions to provide additional flexibility, for example:

```
=IIf(Fields!SalesYTD.Value<3500000, "Red",
    IIf(Fields!SalesYTD.Value>5000000, "OliveDrab", "Black"))
```

7. Preview your results, then switch to the Layout tab and save the report.

Sorting Results

The report you have built so far displays records in no particular order. Because sales info is relevant in this report, sorting data accordingly is a natural option.

1. Click anywhere in the table to display the table's grey borders.

2. Right-click the upper-left corner of the table's border and select Properties.

3. In the Table Properties dialog box, navigate to the Sorting tab.

4. In the Sort On grid, select the Fields!SalesYTD field from the dropdown list in the Expression column. Note the equal sign (=) added in front of the expression.

> **Caution**   Be aware that there are many places in dialog boxes where an expression is expected instead of an object or property name. If you specify an object or property name in these cases, you will not obtain the expected results.

5. Select Descending from the dropdown list in the Direction column.

6. Accept the changes by clicking the OK button. Save the report and check the results on the Preview tab. When finished, switch to the Layout tab again.

Letting Users Sort Results

Although having a default sort order is a good idea, letting the users change the sort expression and direction is even better.

1. Right-click the SalesYTD text cell in the Header row and select Properties from the context menu.

2. Navigate to the Interactive Sort tab.

3. Select the Add An Interactive Sort Action To This Textbox checkbox. Choose the rest of the values according to the figure on the following page.

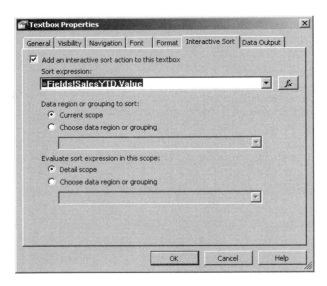

4. Accept the changes by clicking the OK button. Save the report and check the results on the Preview tab.

5. Notice the double-headed arrow next to the SalesYTD label. When you click it, the table contents sort accordingly.

6. Repeat steps 1 through 5 on the rest of the column headers in order to allow interactive sorting on any of these columns. Notice that when you apply the procedure to the Name expression column, the expression itself is not available. If you want to sort by the expression, you will need to copy the expression, actually duplicating it. To handle this issue you will learn, in a later section, how to add code that can be shared inside the report.

7. Save the report and check the results on the Preview tab, then switch to the Layout tab when finished.

Filtering Data

Most reports require the user to provide some kind of filter to be applied to the data. There-fore, you need to give the user a way to indicate what data filters should be applied. The tool to accomplish this is a report parameter. In this section, you will create a parameter to filter employees according to their territories.

1. Go to the Data tab.

2. Edit the query to add a WHERE clause that uses a parameter as shown below. You can name the parameter prmTerritory.

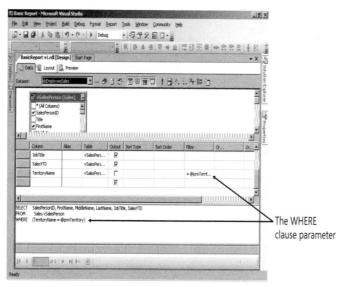

The WHERE
clause parameter

3. From the Report menu, select Report Parameters.

4. You will see that Report Designer has added a parameter by parsing the dataset query.

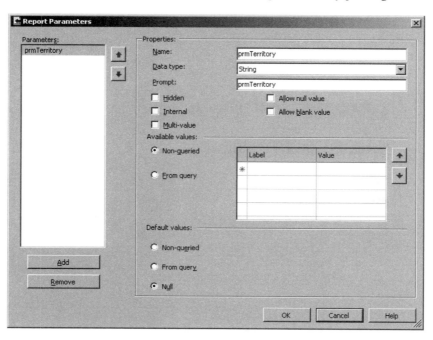

5. You will edit the parameter to make it more user friendly later, but for the moment, let's use it as it is. Click the OK button to close the Report Parameters dialog box, and preview the report.

6. Type *Central* in the textbox labeled prmTerritory and click the View Report button. The
    report will process and show the following results.

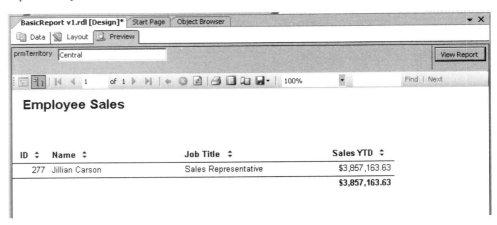

Of course, asking the user to memorize and type flawlessly all territory names is not the
best solution. You should offer some assistance to the users by letting them choose from
a list of available territories. To achieve this objective, you need to create a new dataset
and fill the parameter values with its output.

7. Go to the Data tab and save the report.

8. Open the Dataset dropdown list and select <New Dataset...>.

9. Edit the Name and Query String fields to match the ones shown below, clicking the OK
    button when you are done:

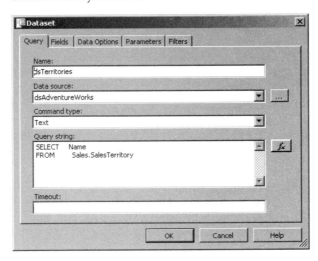

10. To use this query (or dataset) as the source for the parameter values, you will need to
    edit the parameter properties. From the Report menu, select Report Parameters.

11. Edit the parameter properties to match the following ones (note that the Prompt and Default Values have been edited too):

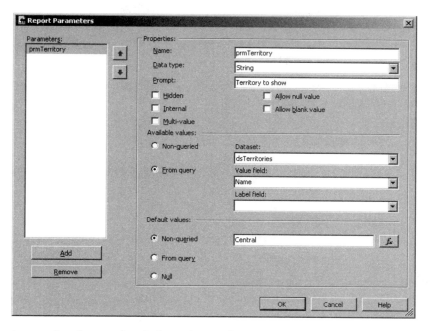

12. Accept the changes by clicking the OK button.

13. Save the report and preview it. Notice that the report is processed without waiting for the user to choose a value from the dropdown list. This is due to having a default value declared in the parameter properties. Leave the parameter default value blank to change this behavior.

14. Select a different territory from the Territory To Show dropdown list and click the View Report button to reprocess the report with the new filter value.

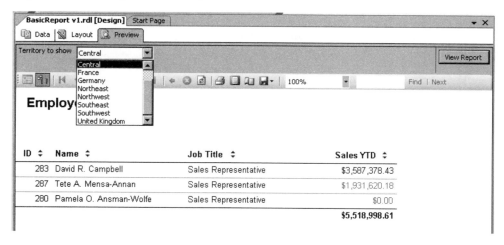

Adding Code to a Report

If you want to set several properties using the same expression, like the sales target expression you used in the previous section, you might choose to copy and paste the code in each expression. However, this approach is inefficient and hard to maintain. For example, you will have to update each occurrence if you ever need to edit the report to change the sales target.

To resolve this issue, you should put the code in a centralized place, be it the report itself or an external assembly referenced by the report. In this chapter, we will show you the first case only.

> **More Info**   To learn more about using external assemblies in reports, see the SQL Server Books Online topic "Using Custom Assemblies with Reports."

You will develop a report function to centralize the employee's full name calculation. Therefore, you will leverage the expression you entered previously in the cell under the Name column title.

Adding Code Using the Code Tab

1. Switch to the Layout tab. From the Report menu, select Report Properties.

2. Navigate to the Code tab. You will see an empty textbox where you can enter the code. This textbox offers no assistance at all in typing (no colored syntax, no Intellisense). Therefore, use it only in special cases or when you are confident in the accuracy of your entry. It's a good idea to type the code into a more powerful editor, test it, and then just paste the resulting code in this textbox.

3. Paste or type the following code into the Custom Code window (this code is wordy, but the variable names are short for the sake of code readability):

```
function FullName (fn as String, mn as String, ln as String) as String
    Dim res as string
    res = fn & " "
    res &=  IIf(Len(mn) = 1, mn & ". ", "")
    res &=  IIf(Len(mn) > 1, mn & " ", "")
    res &= ln
    return res
end function
```

4. Click the OK button to accept your changes.

5. On the Layout tab, right-click the Details row of the Name column and select Expression from the dropdown menu. Edit the content to match the following one:

```
=Code.FullName(Fields!FirstName.Value, Fields!MiddleName.Value,
    Fields!LastName.Value)
```

6. Save the report and check the results on the Preview tab. If you made a mistake when typing the code or the expression in the cell, you will receive an error on the Preview tab.

7. Now, you can leverage this code in other places, like the interactive sorting option for the Name column. Although it would make more sense to sort by last name, change the sorting field just for learning purposes as follows. Select the Name column title cell on the Layout tab.

8. Right-click the cell, select Properties, and navigate to the Interactive Sort tab.

9. Replace the current expression with the following one, clicking the OK button when you are finished:

```
=Code.FullName(Fields!FirstName.Value, Fields!MiddleName.Value,
    Fields!LastName.Value)
```

10. Save the report and check the results on the Preview tab. Notice that the Name column is sorted by the full name instead of the last name, as expected.

The Name Property and the Dataset Property

Some interesting properties are set automatically by Report Designer as we design the report layout. You need to know these properties and their meaning in order to fully understand report editing.

- All items in the report are identified by name. The Name property is set as usual, adding an ordinal after the item type, for example *textbox1, textbox2...* or *table1, table2...* Although these names are perfectly legal and usable, they are not well suited to clean programming. In the programming world, the recommendation is to give each item a user-friendly name that facilitates identifying items when coding, with no exception. In Report Designer, however, many objects exist without you noticing them until you need them for some reason. Therefore, although we hesitate recommending that you edit each item name, this is not a bad procedure at all. In any case, you should at least edit the names of items used in expressions. To see all named items that exist in your report, you can open the object drop-down list at the top of the Properties window. Alternatively, you can look directly at the RDL XML and search for the Name attribute in the elements.

- The Dataset binding property is also important. Some report items, such as those that are containers or data regions, know "magically" from where they should extract data. If you check the Dataset property value on a Table report item that contains some fields, you will notice that this property is set to a dataset name. In our example, it is set to dsEmployeeSales. This binding sets the data source for all data-dependent elements inside this container item. If you check the property in a freshly created table, you will find it to be empty until you drop a field inside or you bind it manually.

The Reporting Services Collections

In addition to the Fields collection you have used in our sample report, Reporting Services provides other collections for use in report expressions: *Globals*, *Parameters*, *ReportItems*, and *User*. Each of these collections groups a different kind of item:

- **Fields**   Refers to the fields contained in a specific dataset. Using the *Fields* collection inside a data region, such as a table, assumes the dataset it belongs to through the data region binding (data region binding is specified through the data region's Dataset property). When used outside of a data region, the *Fields* collection requires you to specify the scope (by explicitly naming the dataset).

- **Globals**   Contains items like PageNumber, TotalPages, ReportFolder, and ReportName. You will need to use the elements of this collection quite often.

- **Parameters**   Contains any parameters declared in the report. If the report declares any parameters, their properties can be accessed through this collection.

- **ReportItems**   Includes all the textboxes in the report. Keep in mind that table cells are textboxes too. Therefore, you can access an interesting set of objects through this collection.

- **User**   Includes only two objects: *User* and *Language*; however, you can access these objects only through the *User* collection.

More Info   For more information, see the SQL Server Books Online topic "Using Global Collections in Expressions (Reporting Services)."

Conclusion

In this chapter, you have learned what enterprise reporting is and been introduced to planning for reporting. You have also learned about the Reporting Services architecture, its main components, and the tasks performed by each one.

You've experimented with basic report authoring procedures: Creating a report, setting a data source and a data query, creating and editing the report layout, adding code to perform shared operations, and adding some interactivity.

SQL Server Books Online includes further detail about each of these topics. Other features you will want to explore are list and matrix data regions, grouping, expression scopes, cascading parameters, working with the visibility features, charts, subreports, language-culture usage, and reporting from Analysis Services.

Chapter 12 Quick Reference

To	Do This
Create a report	In BIDS, select New | Project from the File menu. Select the Report Server Project template and click the OK button. Right-click the Reports folder in Solution Explorer and choose Add | New Item.
Start the Report Wizard	In BIDS, select New | Project from the File menu. Select the Report Server Project Wizard template and click the OK button.
Create a shared data source	Right-click the Shared Data Sources folder in Solution Explorer and choose Add New Data Source.
Define a dataset	On the Data tab in BIDS, choose <New Dataset...> from the Dataset dropdown list.
Add a table to a report	Drag and drop a Table control from the toolbox onto your report designer surface.
Bind data to a table on a report	Drag a field from the Dataset pane and drop it onto a cell in the table.
Preview a report	Click on the Preview tab in BIDS.
Format a report control	Right-click the control and choose Properties to show the Properties dialog box or select the item, display the Properties window, and edit the properties there.
Save a report	Click the Save toolbar button.
Add a total to a table in a report	Drag the field you want to total from the Dataset pane and drop it onto a footer field in a table.
Conditionally set a property in a report	Click the <Expression...> entry in the property's dropdown list. Enter an IIf statement in the Edit Expression dialog box.
Sort the contents of a table based on values in a column	On the table's Properties dialog box, set the sorting fields on the Sorting tab.
Let users sort data interactively	On the table cell's Properties dialog box, select the Add An Interactive Sort Action To This Textbox checkbox.
Filter data on a report	Edit the report's query to add a WHERE clause that uses a parameter. From the Report menu, select Report Parameters.
Let users filter data interactively	Add a filter and define a new dataset to be used as the source for the parameter values. From the Report menu, select Report Parameters. In the Available Values frame, select the From Query option and enter the new dataset in the Dataset textbox.

Chapter 13

Introduction to Notification Services

After completing this chapter, you will be able to:

- Understand notification applications as a technology
- Understand notification applications as a business solution
- Understand Notification Services architecture
- Create and deploy a basic notification application

In the previous chapter, you learned how to use SQL Server's Reporting Services. This chapter will explain SQL Server's Notification Services. Notification Services is a powerful SQL Server component that allows developers to quickly design, implement, and deploy scalable notification applications. This objective is achieved through significant automation of two core elements: automation of all processes involved in running the solution and automation of necessary application and database object creation and management.

This automation provides productivity gains, but it does require that the design process adhere to the Notification Services way of seeing the notification world. This means that you must understand the terminology, the platform architecture, and the platform mechanics. The initial learning curve may seem a bit overwhelming, so in this chapter we will demonstrate how to apply Notification Services principles to a real-world scenario.

A Notification Services Scenario

Birdinia is an imaginary country with a long tradition of birding. Birding consists of observing bird life in the wild, noting when birds come and go, when they breed, how many birds can be found at a given location, and so on. Birders usually enjoy sharing information about which birds they have observed and when and where they observed them.

You are requested to write a notification application for a client. Your client is the National Ornithological Society of Birdinia, and it needs to alert its associates about bird sightings all around the country. Interested people should be able to choose to be alerted about sightings in their preferred area or areas.

Gathering Requirements

Given that scenario, you begin to design a draft of the database schema. Of course, in the real world, you will begin by creating a list of requirements, some UML (Unified Modeling Language) schemas, and other items before designing the database, but let's compress that process for the sake of simplicity.

Preliminary Requirements

Most likely, the schema includes the items shown in Table 13-1. It makes sense to try to design the application to be reusable for other notification scenarios not related to birding. Therefore, you will name the common elements with generic names, allowing for their reuse without having to rewrite shared items.

Table 13-1   Birding Application Schema Elements

Item	Name
List of regions	Regions
List of sightings	Events
List of interested people	Subscribers
List of which region each person is interested in	Subscriptions

It happens that the last three names coincide with Notifications Services terminology. The first item, Regions, however, contains application-specific information and has no corresponding Notifications Services term.

Additional Requirements

Bird sightings come in three categories:

- Sightings of common resident birds in a region, easy to spot all year round

- Sightings of migrant bird arrivals to a region

- Sightings of rare birds. These rare birds might stay in the region for a short time and might not be seen again in that region for several years. Thus, some birders would be very interested in knowing about those occurrences.

Therefore, your application must fulfill the following requirements:

- Subscribers should be able to sign up for immediate notifications for rare bird sightings and/or regularly scheduled notifications for non-urgent alerts.

- Subscribers should be able to be notified at their preferred device. Advanced birders would like to receive special alerts as SMS (Short Message Service) messages on their mobile phones. Other subscribers might prefer to be notified once a day or once per week through e-mail.

These two requirements lead to some changes in the application schema. We will need to keep track of:

- **Each subscriber's device info**   Device info includes e-mail address, mobile phone number, etc.

- **Which subscription corresponds to which device**   For instance, urgent alerts should be sent to a mobile phone, while regular alerts should be sent by e-mail.

- **The frequency for alerts**   Frequency might be immediate, daily, or weekly.

- **The sighting category**   Categories for this example are regular, migrant, or rare.

- **Which alerts have been sent to which subscriptions**   You will need to store actual date and time of an event occurrence as well as the date and time the application is notified. With that data at hand, the notification application should be able to identify which events, for example, have been sent to daily subscriptions and which of them have not yet been sent to weekly subscriptions.

How will you meet these new requirements?

- Device info for subscribers should be stored in its own table.

- The device preference for each subscription should be stored along with the subscription information.

- Timing information should be stored along with the subscription itself.

- The category will be stored with the event itself, and the observer will provide that value. Thus, when someone enters a sighting in the notification solution, he or she is responsible for categorizing it as regular, migrant, or rare.

Historical Information

Historical information is somewhat more complicated to manage. We need to compare the date and time the event was entered with the date and time for the last notification-sending operation. Our database schema does not include any information about when the alerts were sent. Therefore, we need to keep track of notification processing.

To keep track of notification processing, you can choose between two models:

- Recording the subscription-type processing date and time. You will record the type of subscription, daily or weekly, along with the date and time you start the sending process. When starting the sending process, the system stores the current date and time. This option results in only two records: one for weekly subscriptions and one for daily subscriptions.

- Recording each subscription processing date and time. You will record the specific subscription's identifier, along with the date and time you start the processing, or the last event identifier included in the notification.

Which one should you choose? Recording the date by type is simpler than recording it for each subscription. The former requires keeping only one record for each subscription type. The latter approach requires one record for each subscription and some logic to keep both tables (subscriptions and processes) in sync. However, in the event that a notification is not delivered, the type approach will not allow the affected subscribers to ever receive the notification. This drawback might be acceptable in some non-critical notification applications, but it is not acceptable in other kinds of applications, like those involving expected actions on the subscriber's part (a phone call to return, a contract change to act on, a customer claim, etc.). Indeed, even non-critical notification subscribers will prefer not missing any events. Therefore, for the sake of reusability and ensuring completeness, the second approach should be your choice.

> **Tip**   In Notification Services terminology, historical data is stored in *chronicle* tables.

Device Diversity

Some additional requirements arise from having different devices and media to which our application must send notifications. E-mail messages should be delivered by means of an SMTP server and SMS messages by means of a text-message server. Additionally, the e-mail format, usually HTML, is not suitable for sending SMS text messages and vice versa. Therefore, the solution should be able to send different bytes to different server types. This is a configuration issue, but also something to consider in the application architecture.

Again, several options exist to implement this functionality, from hardcoding the message-building process in the application to using third-party software that handles the conversion process. Notification Services solves this issue with openness in mind: you must supply an XSLT (eXtensible Stylesheet Language Transformation) file for each device type (to be comprehensive, you will need an XSLT file for each device and locale combination). An XSLT engine can use an XSLT template to transform an XML input to some other type of output (HTML, XML, or text). Therefore, this is a very suitable way for meeting most requirements.

Notification Information

The application's internal processes will manage information in a format that is not user friendly. For instance, the application refers to every item by ID number instead of by Name. However, when preparing the data for actual end-user delivery, translating IDs into textual information is mandatory.

In order to accelerate the final notification generation and its delivery, you should prepare the information that this process needs. For instance, instead of storing the Region ID, you would store the Region Name. You would also store the Event Description instead of the Event ID. Thus, when the engine decides to send the notification, it will not need to look in several tables and perform joins to get the information it needs. It will simply read a record from a table where all data is prepared according to its needs, ready to be sent out.

Considerations for Performance and Scalability

Although your customer might not mention it, you should consider performance issues. E-mails and text messages should be delivered to subscribers individually. It is common knowledge that writing a record in a table is much faster than sending an e-mail, mainly because of the network latency involved. In the event of notifying a large number of subscribers with a short time between events, a bottleneck might arise that could reduce the application's usefulness. You should think about possible ways of minimizing the delivery process workload. To accelerate delivery times, you have two options:

- Reduce the time needed to send an individual message
- Reduce the number of messages to be sent

Reducing the time needed to send an individual message can be achieved in multiple ways:

- Using faster hardware
- Using faster network devices
- Reducing the message size

Whatever you do, the time required to send an e-mail or text message will always depend on a network over which you have no control. Therefore, reducing the number of messages to be sent is a preferable option. By analyzing the notification nature, you might notice that many subscribers share an interest in a given region and that some subscribers have scheduled multiple regions about which to be notified. If so, you can reduce the number of e-mails to be sent by:

- Sending a single e-mail to all subscribers with identical preferences. For example, all subscribers interested in Birdinia North can receive the same message.

- Merging all scheduled notifications to a specific subscriber into a single notification so that, for example, a subscriber interested in three adjacent regions receives one message instead of three.

Note   The latter requirements will not be implemented in the scenario you are developing. They are mentioned here for the sake of completeness.

Building the Application

At this point, we have merely gathered the requirements and started to envision how those requirements should be implemented. We are just at the beginning.

You decided to use Notification Services for developing this application. Notification Services will help in accelerating development of the application, and it will offer a platform for evolving the application if this is eventually needed. Therefore, you need to understand how the requirements map onto Notification Services elements, as well as the process of building, deploying, and testing a Notification Services application.

The next sections of this chapter will provide information on:

- Understanding the components of a Notification Services application
- Understanding how the requirements for our Birding example can be converted to Notification Services elements
- Creating the development infrastructure, which consists of the application database and the development project
- Creating the Notification Services application foundation
- Performing the initial deployment
- Progressively adding functionality to the application to complete the expected requirements

Components of a Notification Application

Now that you have some initial knowledge of the data the application will manage, you need to think about how the data processing should work. In addition to having a schema, every application needs an engine that keeps everything running and does the real work with the data. The following are expected to be implemented as part of the notification solution engine:

- **A SQL Server 2005 server**   Hosts our database (both the schema and the data) and the Notification Services components.
- **A subscribing application**   Provides the interface for end users to enter and edit their subscriptions and device information. In our example, we will not build that application. Instead, you will use a couple of scripts to enter subscribers, subscriber devices, and subscription data into the application. Sometimes this interface is not actually an interface but a trigger from other applications, such as a customer management or human resources application.
- **A mechanism to receive events generated in the outside world**   Notification Services reacts to events, but how does it become aware of an event? Notification Services includes some event providers that allow events to be sent to Notification Services. The included event providers are an *Event* object API (object model), the XML Loader, and

the SQL Server API for loading events by means of stored procedures. You will find more information about these providers in the Notification Services documentation. In the Birdinia scenario, we will use another script to enter events directly in the appropriate places. Those events will trigger the notification generation and delivery process.

- **An engine to match events with subscriptions**   The engine itself is provided by Notification Services. However, you will need to inform Notification Services what the relation is between the events and the subscription through something known as a *matching rule*. A matching rule is a simple SQL statement that selects those subscriptions that should receive a specific event. In our scenario, the matching rule matches events in a specific region to subscribers holding subscriptions to that region. Thus, if an event is produced for a particular region, all subscribers holding subscriptions to that region should receive a notification. The SQL statement we need should return the list of subscriptions that correspond to a particular region.

- **A physical notification generation engine**   Once the application knows which notifications it should send to which subscriber devices, it is necessary to build the notification content with all textual information and formatting. Notification Services uses XSLT templates to generate the final notification. Notification Services functionality includes options for sending notifications in different languages (known as *cultures* in Notification Services terminology). If you decide not to use the multi-language functionality, Notification Services still requires passing a culture to be used during the process. This engine will need XSLT templates for HTML e-mails and for SMS text messages. You need to instruct Notification Services when to use which template.

- **A delivery engine for actually sending the notifications to the individual target devices**   Once the notification information is in place and the XSLT templates are ready, Notification Services sends the notification to the delivery server or servers that will perform the final delivery to the subscriber device. Notification Services supplies you with this engine, too. It is optimized for performance and scalability. The configuration data necessary for Notification Services to connect to the delivery servers, such as server names, IP addresses, and authentication information, must be provided by you.

> **Note**   In our scenario, in order to make the setup process easier, you will use the File delivery channel instead of the SMTP or SMS server. The Notification Services documentation includes information about how to set up the SMTP delivery channel. For SMS, you will need to write the code yourself or use third-party software. Although this may look overwhelming at first, remember the possibility of using Web Services-based third-party services and how easy it is to write a Web Service client with .NET.

How Notification Services Expects Its Instructions

How do you give Notification Services the information listed in the previous section?

Notification Services uses two XML files as configuration files: the Instance Configuration File (ICF) and the Application Definition File (ADF). The ADF includes most of the application-related configuration settings, but what is the ICF?

Notification Services instances   Notification Services is a component designed to serve several notification applications on the same server hardware and software. This means that you can deploy several notification applications on the same server. Notification Services knows that it is quite possible that, in such a case, you will reuse Subscriber and Subscriber Device data in more than one solution or application; therefore, it stores that information independently of specific notification solution data. The Subscriber data is stored in the instance database, while the Subscriber Device data resides in the application database. Both databases receive their names according to some internal rules, as you will see shortly.

Additionally, Notification Services will create a Windows service to keep track of all events related to the applications the instance is serving. Each instance is backed by a unique Windows service. Thus, you may think of the instance as a Windows service instance that controls several Notification Services applications.

Notification Services application   The database for the application you are trying to build will store some specific information and, although reuse is on our minds, it is clear that a stock exchange notification application, a football match result notification application, and a bird-sighting notification application will all store different sorts of data. Therefore, the schema associated with each one of those applications will differ in major or minor ways.

The purpose of Notification Services is to manage the application data on your behalf, adding tables, views, stored procedures, triggers, and any tool Notification Services needs to perform its job. As a result, Notification Services requests to receive the schema information in a way it can understand and manage by itself. That "understandable way" is actually an XML file that adheres to a specific XML schema (XSD). This file will look like a database script for creating tables, although it is written in XML.

Notification Services internal databases   Unless instructed otherwise, when deploying the configuration files to a server, the deployment process creates at least two databases: one for the instance data, and one for each application the instance is serving. The name of those databases will follow this pattern:

- The instance database is named *<instance name>NSMain*. In our scenario, this name is *SQL2005StepByStepNSMain*.

- The application database is named *<instance name><application name>*. In our scenario, this name should be *SQL2005StepByStepBirding*.

Note   In SQL Server 2005, you may use any database you like to store Notification Services element items, both instance and application related. Notification Services generates and manages many SQL Server elements; thus, you should state the schema name where these items will be grouped.

> Because the number of items generated is significant, you should use common databases only in specific circumstances. In our scenario, a common database is suitable because the additional information you are using may not warrant having a database of its own. Hence, you may create the application database and instruct Notification Services to expand it with its own objects instead of creating a new database.

Requirements Mapped to Notification Services Elements

Our requirements checklist contains the following items:

- Database schema, including:
    - Application-specific information: The list of available regions
    - Events: A list of actual sightings with a categorization
    - Subscribers: The list of interested people
    - Subscriptions: The list of which region each person is interested in, the desired periodicity for receiving notifications, and the target device
    - Subscriber devices: E-mail addresses and mobile phone numbers
    - Chronicles: Historic data about notifications
    - Notification-ready detailed data
- Scripts for:
    - Entering subscriber, subscriber device, and subscription data into the application
    - Entering events
    - The matching rule SQL statement
- Delivery-related items:
    - XSLT templates for HTML e-mails and SMS text messages
    - configuration information for connecting to the delivery servers

Mapping the Elements to Notification Services Elements

By now, you know that a Notification Services application should include the following items:

- The application-specific database, including all data not strictly related to Notification Services:
    - Region schema
    - Subscription types schema
    - Subscriber data schema

- The ICF, or instance configuration files
  - ❑ System configuration information
  - ❑ Instance configuration information
- The ADF, or application definition file, including:
  - ❑ Event schema
  - ❑ Subscription schema
  - ❑ Notification schema
  - ❑ Chronicles schema
  - ❑ The matching rule
- For our convenience, the development (SQL Server Management Studio) project, including:
  - ❑ The test data generation SQL scripts
  - ❑ The XSLT files
  - ❑ The ICF
  - ❑ The ADF

You will notice that nothing is mentioned about Subscriber and Subscriber device schemas. Notification Services will manage them and dictates their schema. The schema provided will meet our needs. However, if this were not the case, you would have to add the additional data to the application-specific database and use the SubscriberID field in the Notification Services schema as a logical join between both sources.

The Development Infrastructure

Now let's start building our sample application. SQL Server Management Studio does not include a template for Notification Services projects, although you can create a project to host the Notification Services-related files.

Instead of starting from scratch, we will use the Tutorial project to build our Birding notification application. This application will give us the scripts we need to populate the databases and to enter some events.

Installing the SQL Server 2005 Samples   The rest of this chapter uses the Tutorial sample included as one of the Notification Services samples. Although you don't have to install the samples to follow along with the chapter content, the Notification Services samples packaged with SQL Server 2005 will help you better understand Notification Services as a whole by comparing several business scenarios and their solutions. To install the SQL Server 2005 samples, see the SQL Server Books Online topic "Installing Samples."

Additionally, you can install the samples and follow the Notification Services Tutorial topics as a complement to this chapter.

> **Tip**   The "Notification Services Samples" section in SQL Server Books Online includes a topic called "Troubleshooting the Samples" that might help you if unexpected errors occur while following the steps detailed in the rest of this chapter.

Starting a New Project for Notification Services

Although Notification Services will handle all notification-related elements, it will not manage the application-specific data. In the Birding scenario, this means that it will not maintain the information about available Regions or Observation categories.

Similarly, Notification Services will include minimal data about subscribers themselves, holding just an ID for each subscriber. If you need to keep track of additional subscriber information, you should consider developing a standard application or using a membership solution. The ID maintained by Notification Services is the link between Notification Services and your subscriber tracking solution.

In our scenario, you will build a database to store all information not specific to Notification Services. This database is very simple, but useful as an example.

Creating the Application-Specific Database

1. In the Start menu, select All Programs | Microsoft SQL Server 2005 | SQL Server Management Studio.

2. From the File menu, select Open | File. Locate the BirdingDatabaseCreation.sql script in the My Documents\Microsoft Press\SQLAppliedTechSBS\Chapter13 folder.

3. Edit the database file paths to point to the folder in which you want to create the database.

4. Execute the script to create the database, its tables, and its contents.

Creating the Project and the SQL Server 2005 Management Studio Solution

1. Open SQL Server Management Studio and connect to the database server.

2. Select New | Project from the File menu. Choose SQL Server Scripts as the project template. This template is used because SQL Server Management Studio does not include Notification Services as a project template. Name the project SQL2005StepByStep_NS. Choose the location of your preference. Unselect the Create Directory For Solution checkbox. Click the OK button to create the project.

3. Using Windows Explorer, copy the following files from the My Documents\MicrosoftPress\ SQLAppliedTechSBS\Chapter13 folder to the folder where you have stored the project:

    - EmptyADF.xml

    - SQL2005StepByStepICF.xml

    - BirdingTransform.xslt (This file will not be necessary until the final processing; you are just adding it now for convenience.)

4. In the Solution Explorer Window, right-click SQL2005StepByStep_NS and select Add | Existing Item from the context menu. In the Add Existing Item dialog box, select All Files from the Files Of Type dropdown list. Add the above two files to the project. Both of them will go to the Miscellaneous folder, as shown below.

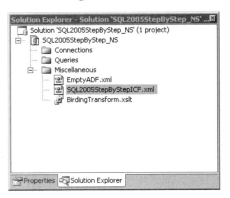

5. Right-click EmptyADF.xml and select Rename from the context menu. Rename the file as BirdingADF.xml

6. In Windows Explorer, under the project folder, create a new folder named Notifications. This folder will contain files resulting from the notification delivery process.

> **Caution**   In another part of the process, you will need to choose a user account to act on behalf of the Notification Services instance. This user account must have the necessary permissions to create and edit files in the destination folders.

The Notification Services Application Foundation

The application requires a few fundamental definitions before we can continue.

Defining the Schemas

The ADF includes several sections used to describe the schema of the tables that contain event, subscription, and notification data. As previously mentioned, the ADF is an XML file that must comply with a predefined XSD schema.

In Notification Services terminology, the distinct type of element to create is called a *class*, as in the *Events* class or the *Subscription* class. Each class will eventually include more than one table. The classes might even be split in several tables and rejoined by means of one or more views, depending on the class type.

The SQL commands that will perform matching or updating operations are called rules, as in the event rule, the event chronicle rule, or the scheduled rules.

In the following sections, you will build the ADF, including all the mentioned object schemas.

Defining the Event Class

1. Open the BirdingADF.xml file for editing by double-clicking it in the Solution Explorer window.

2. Review its content and locate the XML comments that serve as placeholders for the content to add.

3. The schema for the events must include the following fields:

    - Region

    - Date and time of observation

    - Observation description

    - Observation Category

    In place of the <!– *Replace with EventClasses XML* –> comment, write or paste the following XML fragment:

```xml
<!-- Event Classes -->
<EventClasses>
  <EventClass>
    <EventClassName>SightData</EventClassName>
    <Schema>
      <Field>
        <FieldName>RegionID</FieldName>
        <FieldType>varchar(5)</FieldType>
        <FieldTypeMods>not null</FieldTypeMods>
      </Field>
      <Field>
        <FieldName>Date</FieldName>
        <FieldType>datetime</FieldType>
        <FieldTypeMods>not null</FieldTypeMods>
      </Field>
      <Field>
        <FieldName>Observation</FieldName>
        <FieldType>nvarchar(500)</FieldType>
        <FieldTypeMods>not null</FieldTypeMods>
      </Field>
      <Field>
        <FieldName>Category</FieldName>
        <FieldType>char(1)</FieldType>
        <FieldTypeMods>not null</FieldTypeMods>
      </Field>
    </Schema>
    <IndexSqlSchema>
      <SqlStatement>
        CREATE INDEX myIndex
        ON SightData ( Date );
      </SqlStatement>
    </IndexSqlSchema>
  </EventClass>
</EventClasses>
```

Note the structure of the content. It looks like a regular database schema definition, but expressed in XML syntax. You declare the *Event* class name rather than a table name, then the fields, the datatypes, the modifiers for null acceptance, and so on.

Additionally, to declare the fields that will form the SightData event table, you can include the information about indexes you think will be useful to apply when the matching rule accesses this table. Thus, if you know that the matching rule will use the date or the RegionID as filters by itself or in a JOIN clause, you can instruct Notification Services to create the corresponding indexes. This will be useful if event data comes in big batches; this is not the case in the Bird-inia scenario and therefore indexes are not necessary. The *IndexSqlSchema* element is shown simply as a reminder. See Chapter 6, "Improving Query Performance," for more information about using indexes to enhance query performance.

> **More Info**   More options exists to define schemas in the ADF. For more information about available elements, see the SQL Server Books Online topic "Application Definition File Reference."

Defining the Subscription class   Write or paste the following XML fragment below the *<!– Subscription Classes –>* comment:

```xml
<!-- Subscription Classes -->
<SubscriptionClasses>
  <SubscriptionClass>
    <SubscriptionClassName>SightRegionSubs</SubscriptionClassName>
    <Schema>
      <Field>
        <FieldName>DeviceName</FieldName>
        <FieldType>nvarchar(255)</FieldType>
        <FieldTypeMods>not null</FieldTypeMods>
      </Field>
      <Field>
        <FieldName>SubscriberLocale</FieldName>
        <FieldType>nvarchar(10)</FieldType>
        <FieldTypeMods>not null</FieldTypeMods>
      </Field>
      <Field>
        <FieldName>RegionID</FieldName>
        <FieldType>varchar(5)</FieldType>
        <FieldTypeMods>not null</FieldTypeMods>
      </Field>
    </Schema>
    <EventRules>
      <EventRule>
        <RuleName>SightRegionEventRule</RuleName>
        <EventClassName>SightData</EventClassName>
        <Action>
          INSERT INTO SightAlerts(SubscriberId,
            DeviceName, SubscriberLocale,
            Region, Date, Observation, Category)
          SELECT s.SubscriberId, s.DeviceName, s.SubscriberLocale,
```

```
          e.RegionID, e.Date, e.Observation, e.Category
        FROM SightData e, SightRegionSubs s
        WHERE e.RegionID = s.RegionID;
      </Action>
    </EventRule>
  </EventRules>
  </SubscriptionClass>
</SubscriptionClasses>
```

The declaration of subscription schemas is similar to that of the *Event* classes in the previous section. As before, you state the *Subscription* class name rather than a table name, then the fields, and so on.

The subscription definition includes an important item: the event matching rule. The rule shows a name followed by the *Event* class to which it relates and then the T-SQL statement that constitutes the actual rule.

To understand the rule, you will need to make a small jump ahead. The purpose of the RULE statement is to insert records in the notification table, or class, that you have not yet defined. Therefore, neither the name of the destination table, nor the fields it contains are familiar to you. They will be defined in the *Notification* class definition below.

The RULE statement gathers the necessary columns from two origin classes: the *Event* and the *Subscription* class and, most importantly, includes the key to understanding how both classes relate. In the code above, the matching rule matches the Region ID from the *Event* class with that of the *Subscription* class. Thus, subscribers will receive notifications when a sighting is produced in a region stored in the subscriber's subscription record.

Defining the Notification Class   Write or paste the following XML fragment below the *<!– Notification Classes –>* comment:

```
<!-- Notification Classes  -->
<NotificationClasses>
  <NotificationClass>
    <NotificationClassName>
      SightAlerts
    </NotificationClassName>
    <Schema>
      <Fields>
        <Field>
          <FieldName>Region</FieldName>
          <FieldType>nvarchar(35)</FieldType>
        </Field>
        <Field>
          <FieldName>Date</FieldName>
          <FieldType>datetime</FieldType>
        </Field>
        <Field>
          <FieldName>Observation</FieldName>
          <FieldType>nvarchar(500)</FieldType>
        </Field>
```

```
            <Field>
              <FieldName>Category</FieldName>
              <FieldType>char(1)</FieldType>
            </Field>
          </Fields>
        </Schema>
        <ContentFormatter>
          <ClassName>XsltFormatter</ClassName>
          <Arguments>
            <Argument>
              <Name>XsltBaseDirectoryPath</Name>
              <Value>%_AppPath_%</Value>
            </Argument>
            <Argument>
              <Name>XsltFileName</Name>
              <Value>BirdingTransform.xslt</Value>
            </Argument>
          </Arguments>
        </ContentFormatter>
        <Protocols>
          <Protocol>
            <ProtocolName>File</ProtocolName>
          </Protocol>
        </Protocols>
      </NotificationClass>
    </NotificationClasses>
```

Again, the content of the *Notification* class schema is quite straightforward, but it does include something unexpected. In this case, the schema is accompanied by a *ContentFormatter* element. The *ContentFormatter* element indicates which component will be in charge of generating the notification in its final form. Details about it will be provided later in the section titled "How Do You Build the Notification Message?"

Defining the Provider Class   Write or paste the following XML fragment over the *<!–Replace with Providers –>* comment:

```
<!-- Providers XML -->
<Providers>
  <NonHostedProvider>
    <ProviderName>BirdingSPEventProvider</ProviderName>
  </NonHostedProvider>
</Providers>
```

This XML fragment indicates that the event will arrive through a route not managed by Notification Services itself. Click the Save button in the toolbar to save the BirdingADF.xml file, so the changes will not be lost.

Editing the Instance Configuration

The next step is to edit the ICF. This file is the starting point through which Notification Services will parse the configuration files and implement all necessary steps. Therefore, it contains some basic information along with data specific to the instance.

Open the SQL2005StepByStepICF.xml file by double-clicking it in the Solution Explorer window. You will need to modify its contents to suit your actual machine configuration.

- The ICF starts by defining some parameters that will be used in various places in the file. The _DBEngineInstance_ and _ServerName_ parameters will be reused when defining the database engine and the server that will support the Notification Services instance. Unless your configuration is different, leave these values as they are.

- The _InstancePath_ parameter indicates in which folder Notification Services will look for the ICFs. Edit it to point to the place where you saved the Notification Services project.

- Note the *InstanceName* element value, which in this scenario is SQL2005StepByStep.

- The *SqlServerSystem* is the server to be used. Note that it simply specifies the parameter defined above.

- The *Applications* element includes the list and details of all applications depending on the instance you are currently defining.

  ❑ Each *Application* element includes the name of the application, the directory where the corresponding ADF resides, and the name of the ADF itself. Observe that the current file is leveraging the parameters defined at the beginning of the file.

- The *DeliveryChannels* element declares the available channels and their details. In this scenario, for the sake of simplicity, only one file channel is specified. This file channel requires an argument stating the physical path to use. Edit this path to match the location of the Notifications folder you created in step 6 under "Creating the Project and the SQL Server 2005 Management Studio Solution" procedure earlier in the chapter.

> **Caution**   Do not forget to edit the _InstancePath_ parameter and Delivery channel FileName argument to match the file paths on your system. If you don't, the Notification Services instance will not run properly.

Click the Save button to save the ICF so the changes will not be lost.

> **More Info**   More options are available for defining items in the ICF. For more information about available elements, see the SQL Server Books Online topic "Instance Configuration File Reference."

Initial Deployment

You must follow a specific procedure to deploy and activate a notification application. Pay attention to these mechanics because a Notification Services instance must go through several states before it is operative. You must understand these state-steps if you want to put your solution to work. The process is summarized here:

1. Create the instance according to the settings stored in the ICF. This step will create all infrastructure items.

2. Register the instance on the operating system. This step will configure the Windows service, the processing user, and so on.

3. Enable the instance for receiving requests and events. This is equivalent to starting the application, although enabling creates a non-processing state similar to being paused.

4. Start the instance, or the Windows service associated with the instance. This allows the application to receive notice of outside world events and generate and deliver notifications.

5. Eventually, you will perform an additional step: updating the instance. This will happen each time you need to change something in the application configuration.

Creating the Instance

To create a new Notification Services instance (solution), do the following:

1. Open SQL Server Management Studio and connect to your database server.

2. In the Object Explorer window, right-click the Notification Services node and choose New Notification Services Instance from the context menu, as shown below.

3. The New Notification Services Instance dialog box appears. Specify the ICF you just created by typing the full path, by pasting it, or by clicking the Browse button to point to the file.

4. Notification Services parses the ICF to extract the parameters in it. The parameters it finds appear in the Parameters section of the dialog box. Verify that your parameters are correct. In the following figure, the parameter values reflect a particular case; your dialog box will display different folder and computer name values.

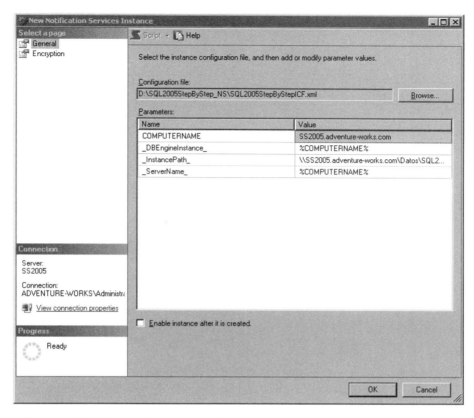

5. When you click the OK button, Notification Services processes the ICF's contents. The Creating New Notification Services Instance progress box, shown below, displays each step and will indicate whether the creation was successful.

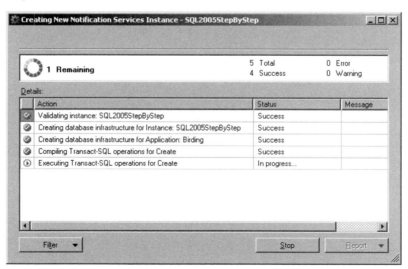

6. If the instance is created successfully, click the Close button to close the progress window. If it fails, review the error message and make necessary adjustments to correct for the given error. After resolving the error, repeat steps 2 through 5 above.

7. In SQL Server Management Studio, look at the Object Explorer window. You should notice some new elements in it, as shown below.

   ■ A new instance under the Notification Services node, with the name SQL2005StepByStep.

   ■ A couple of new databases under the Databases node called SQL2005StepByStepNSMain and SQL2005StepByStepBirding. If you browse their objects, you will see how many elements (tables, views, and stored procedures) Notification Services has created and is managing for you.

Registering the Instance

The following steps will generate the Windows service that waits for incoming events or requests for the Notification Services instance.

1. In SQL Server Management Studio, expand the Notification Services node in Object Explorer. Right-click on the SQL2005StepByStep instance and select Tasks | Register from the context menu.

2. In the Register Instance dialog box, shown below, select the Create Windows Service checkbox and provide the appropriate account credentials that will be used to run the service. If you leave the credentials blank, the service will run under the internal Network-Service account, whose privileges are low. Alternatively, you can edit the service directly and change the logon account to LocalSystem or another account. However, using a

domain account is recommended because that way you can isolate the specific permissions you grant to the account instead of changing the permissions of built-in accounts. Once you have entered your settings, click the OK button to register the instance.

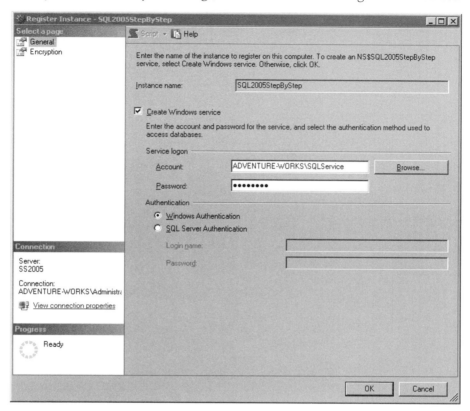

> **More Info**   To find more information about accounts and security in Notification Services, see the SQL Server Books Online topic "Configuring Windows Accounts for an Instance of Notification Services."

3. Again, a progress dialog box will confirm the success or failure of the registration process. If it fails, the most likely problem is a permissions issue. Check your settings and try registering again. Once you have succeeded in registering the instance, you can verify that the Windows service exists in the Services administration tool. You will find a service named NS$SQL2005StepByStep. The Services tool can be found by selecting Control Panel | Administrative Tools | Services from the Start menu.

Although the Notification Services instance has been created, it is not yet serving requests. To have it do so, you must enable and start the instance.

Enabling the Instance

1. In SQL Server Management Studio, locate the instance under the Notification Services node in Object Explorer. Right-click on the instance and select Enable from the context menu.

2. The Enable Instance Confirmation dialog box will ask you to double-check your command. Click the Yes button to enable the instance.

Starting the Instance

1. Right-click on the instance name in the Object Explorer window, and select Start from the context menu.

2. The Start Instance Confirmation dialog box asks you to double-check your command. Click the Yes button to start the instance.

Checking the Status of an Instance

At this point, everything should be in place to run smoothly. You can look at the instance's properties to confirm that every component is enabled and/or started. To open the Instance Properties dialog box, shown below, right-click the instance and select Properties from the context menu. (Select the Windows Services page to check whether services are started.)

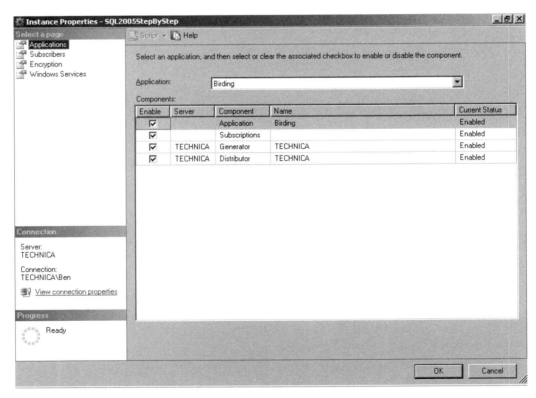

To test the application, you will need to fire an event and check that the appropriate notification is delivered.

Updating and Upgrading the Instance

Each time you change the content of an ADF, the live instance of the Notification Services application must be updated to reflect the changes you want to introduce.

Just as there is a process for setting up an instance to run, you must follow a set procedure for making updates. The update process is the inverse of the setup process.

Use the following steps to update your instance:

1. Right-click the instance within Object Explorer and select Stop from the context menu. Click the Yes button in the Stop Instance Confirmation dialog box.

2. Disable the instance by right-clicking the instance and selecting Disable from the context menu. Click the Yes button in the Disable Instance Confirmation dialog box.

3. Launch the update process by right-clicking the instance and selecting Tasks | Update from the context menu

4. The Update Instance dialog box opens. Point to the ICF, just as you did when setting the instance for the first time. Then click the OK button.

5. A new progress dialog box will appear, as shown below.

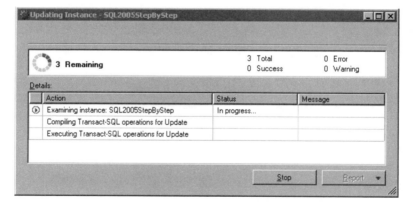

6. The first step in this process consists of comparing the updated ADF against the existing instance and application data in order to find out which changes should be performed. After examining the files, the process presents its conclusions to you in the Update Summary dialog box, shown on the following page.

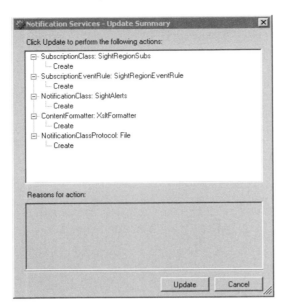

7. If correct, accept the proposed changes by clicking the Update button. The process tries to apply the changes to the databases. Eventually, the process will either succeed or stop if an error arises. In the following figure, you can see the Updating Instance dialog box showing an error. You can click on the message to see the full details or hover over it to look at a tip about the error content.

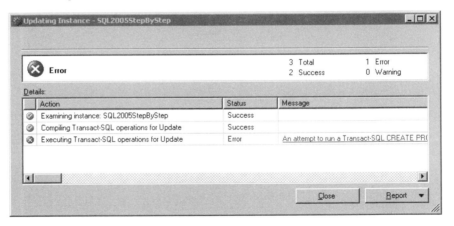

8. If the process fails due to an error, fix it and try the process again. When it succeeds, restart the instance by enabling and starting the instance again.

Running the Application

Now that you've created the application, you should verify that it runs. To do so, you will use some simple system and SQL Server scripts and use the steps detailed in the following sections.

Adding Subscribers, Devices, and Subscriptions to Your Application

In a real system, you would use an application to gather required information about subscribers, their devices, and the subscriptions they want. The nature of this subscription management application will vary. Sometimes you will write an interface devoted purely to the subscription management process. In other cases, the subscription will arise as a result of some other application. For instance, if you are writing a solution for handling customers and online book orders, checking a box titled "I'm interested in other books from this author" should generate a subscription in the background.

> **More Info**   For more information about the subscription process, see the SQL Server Books Online topic "Developing Subscription Management Interfaces."

For this example, you will use some VBScript files to add subscribers. A real system would use the Notification Services API to perform the operation exactly as these scripts do.

Adding Subscribers and Subscriptions

1. Using Windows Explorer, copy the following files from the My Documents\Microsoft Press\SQLAppliedTechSBS\Chapter13 folder to the folder where you have stored the project:

    - AddSubscribers.vbs

    - AddSubscriptions.vbs

    - ViewSubscribersAndDevices.sql

    - ViewSubscriptions.sql

2. In SQL Server Management Studio, right-click SQL2005StepByStep_NS in the Solution Explorer window. Select Add | Existing Item from the context menu. Add the four files above to the project. The .vbs files will go to the Miscellaneous folder, and the .sql files will go to the Queries folder.

3. Open the AddSubscribers.vbs file by double-clicking it in the Solution Explorer window, then browse its contents.

4. You cannot run the VBScript files from inside the Visual Studio IDE. Therefore, return to the Windows Explorer, select the AddSubscribers.vbs file, right-click it, and select Open from the context menu. The script runs. When the script is finished, the message box on the following page appears.

5. In the event that something is wrong, an error dialog box similar to the one shown below will appear. Resolve the error and re-run the script.

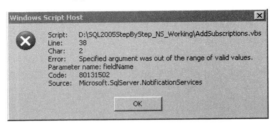

6. Repeat step 4 with the AddSubscriptions.vbs file.

7. Return to SQL Server Management Studio, open the ViewSubscribersAndDevices.sql query file, and run it. If the results window shows the subscriber's data, the script has run without problems. Notice that the query is run against a view, not a table.

8. Open the ViewSubscriptions.sql query file and run it. If the results windows show the subscription's data, the script has run without problems.

Sending Events to Your Application

Usually you will use one of the included event providers to send events to your application. You can send the events through the *Event* object model (event object API), packed in XML files (XML API), or through the provided stored procedures (SQL Server API).

> **More Info**   To find out more about events, see the SQL Server Books Online topic "Defining Event Providers."

In this example, you will use a couple of simple T-SQL scripts that will leverage the SQL Server API stored procedures.

1. Using Windows Explorer, copy the following files from the My Documents\Microsoft Press\SQLAppliedTechSBS\Chapter13 folder to the folder where you have stored the project:

    ■ AddSightEvents.sql

    ■ ViewSightEvents.sql

2. In SQL Server Management Studio, right-click SQL2005StepByStep_NS in the Solution Explorer window. Select Add | Existing Item from the context menu. Add these two files to the project. The files will go into the Queries folder.

3. Open the AddSightEvents.sql file by double-clicking it in the Solution Explorer window, then browse its contents. Note that the events are added by means of a few stored procedures named *NSEventBeginBatchSightData* and *NSEventWriteSightData*. The former starts a batch of events, while the latter adds the specific events. When the event batch is finished, the script executes the *NSEventFlushBatchSightData* stored procedure to instruct Notification Services that the batch is ready for processing. Notification Services processes the events in batches in order to improve performance. If you were not able to submit batches, Notification Services might fire when events are still being sent to the application, thus reducing the efficiency of the notification multicast and digest functionalities.

4. Execute the script. It will return the EventBatchID and the number of events received by the application. Write the EventBatchID down; you will need it in the following step. If this is the first time you have executed the script, the EventBatchID will be 1. Each time you run the script, the EventBatchID will increase.

5. To check the events in the system, open the ViewSightEvents script. Browse it and edit the @EventBatchId parameter value to match the EventBatchId returned by the previous step.

6. Execute the script. It will return both the EventBatch data and the Event details.

Specifying Which Subscribers Should Be Notified

While you are looking at the events, the system has checked the event's existence and fired the notification generation. Notification Services periodically checks for new events and executes the Event Rule in the *Subscription* class included in the ADF. The Event Rule inserts a record into the notification table. In this example, the notifications table is SightAlerts. As you see, the notification table name coincides with the *Notification* class name defined in the ADF.

You can check the expected notifications to send as follows:

Checking Notifications

1. Using Windows Explorer, copy the following file from the My Documents\Microsoft Press\SQLAppliedTechSBS\Chapter13 folder to the folder where you have stored the project:

    ■ ViewNotifications.sql

2. In SQL Server Management Studio, right-click SQL2005StepByStep_NS in the Solution Explorer window. Select Add | Existing Item from the context menu. Add this file to the project. The file will go to the Queries folder.

3. Open and run the ViewNotifications.sql script. The Results pane will show you the state of notifications.

> **Warning**   The Distributor (described in the next section) runs on its own schedule, and therefore it might take some time for the results to show up. Rerun the query every few seconds until it returns a successful or failed delivery status for each pending notification.

Building the Notification Message

Once the Event rule generates the corresponding records in the notifications table, another process called the Distributor takes over. The Distributor performs two tasks: generating the final formatted notifications, ready to send, and passing this formatted content to the actual deliverers. The Distributor will use the content formatter component for the former task, and the latter involves servers external to the solution.

The final form of the notification is stated in the ADF/ICF. As you saw when building the ADF, at the end of the *Notification* class definition, you declare the corresponding content formatter. The attributes of the content formatter designate the name of the formatter and the required arguments. The XsltFormatter is the standard one and needs no more configuration than the three arguments we will discuss in this section. Other content formatters need a fully qualified name and complementary information that enables Notification Services to locate and use it.

The standard XsltFormatter uses three arguments:

- The directory where the XSLT files are located. This corresponds to the XsltBaseDirectoryPath argument.

- The actual name of the XSLT file to apply. This corresponds to the XsltFileName argument.

- Optionally, you can instruct the content formatter that the data contained in the notification table is already in XML or HTTP format and no further content encoding is needed. You might achieve that functionality by including the DisableEscaping argument. The default value for this argument is false.

> **More Info**   To learn more about content formatters, see the SQL Server Books Online topic "Configuring Content Formatters."

In our scenario, the arguments listed above correspond to the variable *_AppPath_* for the base directory path and to the BirdingTransform.xslt file for the XSLT file name.

Note that underneath the content formatter entries, there is a *Protocol* entry. This entry points to a definition of the protocol in the ICF.

Browsing the ICF, locate the *DeliveryChannel* element at the end of the file. This element includes the *ProtocolName* element, whose argument points to an HTML file in the Notifications folder you set up at the beginning of the chapter.

In summary, the Distributor will check the notification table views. There it will find the SubscriberID, the DeliveryChannel, the SubscriberLocale, the DeviceName, and the DeviceAddress. With that information, it can call the content formatter to generate the notification "messages" and collect the output for delivery.

Delivering Notifications

When the delivery channel is a file, the process ends when the file is generated; thus, no further distribution or delivery is required.

You can check our example's results by looking in the Notifications folder you created under the project folder when setting up the infrastructure. There, you should find a file named SightNotifications.htm that should contain the formatted notifications in a row.

> **Warning**   If the SightNotifications.htm file is empty, ensure that the BirdingTransform.xslt file is in the project directory as instructed earlier in this chapter.

Real-world delivery will most likely be more complex. Delving into details of server configuration is not in the scope of this book. The scenario we have used does, however, give a good starting point for understanding how notifications work.

Conclusion

In this chapter, you have learned the basics of configuring and using a notification application through using the Notification Services component included in SQL Server 2005.

You can further develop the example presented in this chapter by adding historical data treatment, additional delivery channels, and multi-language functionality.

SQL Server is a powerful platform for your database installation, providing far more than basic data storage and retrieval. You've seen how SQL Server 2005 handles security, data protection, data transfer, and summary data. You've also seen how SQL server organizes and stores data internally, and you have some understanding of how to optimize data retrieval by modifying the internal storage structure. You've learned how to let your users create their own queries safely through your application interface, how to use remote data sources, and how to access SQL Server via the Internet. You've seen how to use transactions to protect user's data and how to store historical data so that you can back out individual transactions. And now you also know how to use SQL Server 2005's powerful reporting and event notification tools. With a little practice behind you and all this information at your ready reference, you have everything you need to begin crafting your own SQL Server 2005 installation.

Chapter 13 Quick Reference

To	Do This
Start a new project for Notification Services	Create an application-specific database, then in SQL Server Management Studio, select New	Project from the File menu and choose SQL Server Scripts as the project template. Add an ADF and an ICF.
Create a Notification Services application foundation	Define the *Event* class, the *Subscription* class, the *Notification* class, and the *Provider* class.
Deploy a Notification Services application	Create, register, enable, and start a Notification Services instance.
Create a Notification Services instance	In Object Explorer in SQL Server Management Studio, right-click the Notification Services node and choose New Notification Services Instance.
Register a Notification Services instance	In Object Explorer in SQL Server Management Studio, expand the Notification Services node, right-click the instance, and select Tasks	Register from the context menu.
Enable a Notification Services instance	In Object Explorer in SQL Server Management Studio, expand the Notification Services node, right-click the instance, and select Enable from the context menu.
Create a Notification Services instance	In Object Explorer in SQL Server Management Studio, expand the Notification Services node, right-click the instance, and select Start from the context menu.
Update a Notification Services instance	Stop and disable the instance, then in Object Explorer in SQL Server Management Studio, expand the Notification Services node, right-click the instance, and select Update from the context menu.

Index

Additional SQL Server Resources for Developers

Published and Forthcoming Titles from Microsoft Press

Microsoft® SQL Server™ 2005 Express Edition
Step by Step
Jackie Goldstein • ISBN 0-7356-2184-5

Teach yourself how to get database projects up and running
quickly with SQL Server Express
Edition—a free, easy-to-use
database product that is based
on SQL Server 2005 technology.
It's designed for building simple,
dynamic applications, with all
the rich functionality of the SQL
Server database engine and
using the same data access APIs,
such as Microsoft ADO.NET, SQL
Native Client, and T-SQL.
Whether you're new to database

programming or new to SQL Server, you'll learn how, when, and
why to use specific features of this simple but powerful database development environment. Each chapter puts you to work,
building your knowledge of core capabilities and guiding you
as you create actual components and working applications.

Microsoft SQL Server 2005 Programming
Step by Step
Fernando Guerrero • ISBN 0-7356-2207-8

SQL Server 2005 is Microsoft's
next-generation data management and analysis solution that
delivers enhanced scalability,
availability, and security features
to enterprise data and analytical
applications while making them
easier to create, deploy, and
manage. Now you can teach
yourself how to design, build, test,
deploy, and maintain SQL Server
databases—one step at a time.
Instead of merely focusing on

describing new features, this book shows new database
programmers and administrators how to use specific features
within typical business scenarios. Each chapter provides a highly
practical learning experience that demonstrates how to build
database solutions to solve common business problems.

Microsoft SQL Server 2005 Analysis Services
Step by Step
Hitachi Consulting Services • ISBN 0-7356-2199-3

One of the key features of SQL Server 2005 is SQL Server Analysis
Services—Microsoft's customizable analysis solution for business
data modeling and interpretation. Just compare SQL Server
Analysis Services to its competition to understand the great
value of its enhanced features. One of the keys to harnessing
the full functionality of SQL Server will be leveraging Analysis
Services for the powerful tool that it is—including creating a cube,
and deploying, customizing, and extending the basic calculations. This step-by-step tutorial discusses how to get started, how
to build scalable analytical applications, and how to use and ad-
minister advanced features. Interactivity (enhanced in SQL Server
2005), data translation, and security are also covered in detail.

Microsoft SQL Server 2005 Reporting Services
Step by Step
Hitachi Consulting Services • ISBN 0-7356-2250-7

SQL Server Reporting Services (SRS) is Microsoft's customizable
reporting solution for business data analysis. It is one of the key
value features of SQL Server 2005: functionality more advanced
and much less expensive than its competition. SRS is powerful,
so an understanding of how to architect a report, as well as how
to install and program SRS, is key to harnessing the full functionality of SQL Server. This procedural tutorial shows how to use the
Report Project Wizard, how to think about and access data, and
how to build queries. It also walks through the creation of charts
and visual layouts for maximum visual understanding of data
analysis. Interactivity (enhanced in SQL Server 2005) and security
are also covered in detail.

Programming Microsoft SQL Server 2005
Andrew J. Brust, Stephen Forte, and William H. Zack
ISBN 0-7356-1923-9

This thorough, hands-on reference for developers and database
administrators teaches the basics of programming custom applications with SQL Server 2005. You will learn the fundamentals
of creating database applications—including coverage of
T-SQL, Microsoft .NET Framework, and Microsoft ADO.NET. In
addition to practical guidance on database architecture and
design, application development, and reporting and data
analysis, this essential reference guide covers performance,
tuning, and availability of SQL Server 2005.

Inside Microsoft SQL Server 2005:
The Storage Engine
Kalen Delaney • ISBN 0-7356-2105-5

Inside Microsoft SQL Server 2005:
T-SQL Programming
Itzik Ben-Gan • ISBN 0-7356-2197-7

Inside Microsoft SQL Server 2005:
Query Processing and Optimization
Kalen Delaney • ISBN 0-7356-2196-9

Programming Microsoft ADO.NET 2.0 Core Reference
David Sceppa • ISBN 0-7356-2206-X

For more information about Microsoft Press® books and other learning products,
visit: **www.microsoft.com/mspress** *and* **www.microsoft.com/learning**

Additional Resources for Developers: Advanced Topics and Best Practices

Published and Forthcoming Titles from Microsoft Press

Code Complete, Second Edition
Steve McConnell • ISBN 0-7356-1967-0

For more than a decade, Steve McConnell, one of the premier authors and voices in the software community, has helped change the way developers write code—and produce better software. Now his classic book, *Code Complete*, has been fully updated and revised with best practices in the art and science of constructing software. Topics include design, applying good techniques to construction, eliminating errors, planning, managing construction activities, and relating personal character to superior software. This new edition features fully updated information on programming techniques, including the emergence of Web-style programming, and integrated coverage of object-oriented design. You'll also find new code examples—both good and bad—in C++, Microsoft® Visual Basic®, C#, and Java, although the focus is squarely on techniques and practices.

More About Software Requirements: Thorny Issues and Practical Advice
Karl E. Wiegers • ISBN 0-7356-2267-1

Have you ever delivered software that satisfied all of the project specifications, but failed to meet any of the customers expectations? Without formal, verifiable requirements—and a system for managing them—the result is often a gap between what developers think they're supposed to build and what customers think they're going to get. Too often, lessons about software requirements engineering processes are formal or academic, and not of value to real-world, professional development teams. In this follow-up guide to *Software Requirements*, Second Edition, you will discover even more practical techniques for gathering and managing software requirements that help you deliver software that meets project and customer specifications. Succinct and immediately useful, this book is a must-have for developers and architects.

Software Estimation: Demystifying the Black Art
Steve McConnell • ISBN 0-7356-0535-1

Often referred to as the "black art" because of its complexity and uncertainty, software estimation is not as hard or mysterious as people think. However, the art of how to create effective cost and schedule estimates has not been very well publicized. *Software Estimation* provides a proven set of procedures and heuristics that software developers, technical leads, and project managers can apply to their projects. Instead of arcane treatises and rigid modeling techniques, award-winning author Steve McConnell gives practical guidance to help organizations achieve basic estimation proficiency and lay the groundwork to continue improving project cost estimates. This book does not avoid the more complex mathematical estimation approaches, but the non-mathematical reader will find plenty of useful guidelines without getting bogged down in complex formulas.

Debugging, Tuning, and Testing Microsoft .NET 2.0 Applications
John Robbins • ISBN 0-7356-2202-7

Making an application the best it can be has long been a time-consuming task best accomplished with specialized and costly tools. With Microsoft Visual Studio® 2005, developers have available a new range of built-in functionality that enables them to debug their code quickly and efficiently, tune it to optimum performance, and test applications to ensure compatibility and trouble-free operation. In this accessible and hands-on book, debugging expert John Robbins shows developers how to use the tools and functions in Visual Studio to their full advantage to ensure high-quality applications.

The Security Development Lifecycle
Michael Howard and Steve Lipner • ISBN 0-7356-2214-0

Adapted from Microsoft's standard development process, the Security Development Lifecycle (SDL) is a methodology that helps reduce the number of security defects in code at every stage of the development process, from design to release. This book details each stage of the SDL methodology and discusses its implementation across a range of Microsoft software, including Microsoft Windows Server™ 2003, Microsoft SQL Server™ 2000 Service Pack 3, and Microsoft Exchange Server 2003 Service Pack 1, to help measurably improve security features. You get direct access to insights from Microsoft's security team and lessons that are applicable to software development processes worldwide, whether on a small-scale or a large-scale. This book includes a CD featuring videos of developer training classes.

Software Requirements, Second Edition
Karl E. Wiegers • ISBN 0-7356-1879-8

Writing Secure Code, Second Edition
Michael Howard and David LeBlanc • ISBN 0-7356-1722-8

CLR via C#, Second Edition
Jeffrey Richter • ISBN 0-7356-2163-2

For more information about Microsoft Press® books and other learning products,
visit: **www.microsoft.com/mspress** *and* **www.microsoft.com/learning**

Microsoft® Press

Additional Resources for C# Developers
Published and Forthcoming Titles from Microsoft Press

Microsoft® Visual C#® 2005 Express Edition: Build a Program Now!
Patrice Pelland • ISBN 0-7356-2229-9

In this lively, eye-opening, and hands-on book, all you need is a computer and the desire to learn how to program with Visual C# 2005 Express Edition. Featuring a full working edition of the software, this fun and highly visual guide walks you through a complete programming project—a desktop weather-reporting application—from start to finish. You'll get an unintimidating introduction to the Microsoft Visual Studio® development environment and learn how to put the lightweight, easy-to-use tools in Visual C# Express to work right away—creating, compiling, testing, and delivering your first, ready-to-use program. You'll get expert tips, coaching, and visual examples at each step of the way, along with pointers to additional learning resources.

Microsoft Visual C# 2005 *Step by Step*
John Sharp • ISBN 0-7356-2129-2

Visual C#, a feature of Visual Studio 2005, is a modern programming language designed to deliver a productive environment for creating business frameworks and reusable object-oriented components. Now you can teach yourself essential techniques with Visual C#—and start building components and Microsoft Windows®–based applications—one step at a time. With *Step by Step*, you work at your own pace through hands-on, learn-by-doing exercises. Whether you're a beginning programmer or new to this particular language, you'll learn how, when, and why to use specific features of Visual C# 2005. Each chapter puts you to work, building your knowledge of core capabilities and guiding you as you create your first C#-based applications for Windows, data management, and the Web.

Programming Microsoft Visual C# 2005 Framework Reference
Francesco Balena • ISBN 0-7356-2182-9

Complementing *Programming Microsoft Visual C# 2005 Core Reference*, this book covers a wide range of additional topics and information critical to Visual C# developers, including Windows Forms, working with Microsoft ADO.NET 2.0 and Microsoft ASP.NET 2.0, Web services, security, remoting, and much more. Packed with sample code and real-world examples, this book will help developers move from understanding to mastery.

Programming Microsoft Visual C# 2005 *Core Reference*
Donis Marshall • ISBN 0-7356-2181-0

Get the in-depth reference and pragmatic, real-world insights you need to exploit the enhanced language features and core capabilities in Visual C# 2005. Programming expert Donis Marshall deftly builds your proficiency with classes, structs, and other fundamentals, and advances your expertise with more advanced topics such as debugging, threading, and memory management. Combining incisive reference with hands-on coding examples and best practices, this *Core Reference* focuses on mastering the C# skills you need to build innovative solutions for smart clients and the Web.

CLR via C#, Second Edition
Jeffrey Richter • ISBN 0-7356-2163-2

In this new edition of Jeffrey Richter's popular book, you get focused, pragmatic guidance on how to exploit the common language runtime (CLR) functionality in Microsoft .NET Framework 2.0 for applications of all types—from Web Forms, Windows Forms, and Web services to solutions for Microsoft SQL Server™, Microsoft code names "Avalon" and "Indigo," consoles, Microsoft Windows NT® Service, and more. Targeted to advanced developers and software designers, this book takes you under the covers of .NET for an in-depth understanding of its structure, functions, and operational components, demonstrating the most practical ways to apply this knowledge to your own development efforts. You'll master fundamental design tenets for .NET and get hands-on insights for creating high-performance applications more easily and efficiently. The book features extensive code examples in Visual C# 2005.

Programming Microsoft Windows Forms
Charles Petzold • ISBN 0-7356-2153-5

CLR via C++
Jeffrey Richter with Stanley B. Lippman
ISBN 0-7356-2248-5

Programming Microsoft Web Forms
Douglas J. Reilly • ISBN 0-7356-2179-9

Debugging, Tuning, and Testing Microsoft .NET 2.0 Applications
John Robbins • ISBN 0-7356-2202-7

For more information about Microsoft Press® books and other learning products,
visit: **www.microsoft.com/books** *and* **www.microsoft.com/learning**

What do you think of this book? We want to hear from you!

Do you have a few minutes to participate in a brief online survey? Microsoft is interested in hearing your feedback about this publication so that we can continually improve our books and learning resources for you.

To participate in our survey, please visit:

www.microsoft.com/learning/booksurvey

And enter this book's ISBN, 0-7356-2316-3. As a thank-you to survey participants in the United States and Canada, each month we'll randomly select five respondents to win one of five $100 gift certificates from a leading online merchant.* At the conclusion of the survey, you can enter the drawing by providing your e-mail address, which will be used for prize notification *only*.

Thanks in advance for your input. Your opinion counts!

Sincerely,

Microsoft Learning

Learn More. Go Further.